The Glorious Revolution In America

DOCUMENTS ON THE COLONIAL CRISIS OF 1689

Edited by

Michael G. Hall, Lawrence H. Leder,
and Michael G. Kammen

W·W·NORTON & COMPANY·INC·

NEW YORK

This volume is published for the Institute of Early American History and Culture at Williamsburg, Virginia. The Institute of Early American History and Culture is sponsored jointly by the College of William and Mary and Colonial Williamsburg, Incorporated.

This edition first published 1972
by arrangement with The University of North Carolina Press
SBN 393 09398 0

Published simultaneously in Canada
by George J. McLeod Limited, Toronto
PRINTED IN THE UNITED STATES OF AMERICA

1 2 3 4 5 6 7 8 9 0

THE GLORIOUS REVOLUTION
IN AMERICA

DOCUMENTARY PROBLEMS IN EARLY AMERICAN HISTORY

The Great Awakening
Documents on the Revival of Religion, 1740–1745

Edited by Richard L. Bushman

The Glorious Revolution in America
Documents on the Colonial Crisis of 1689

Edited by Michael G. Hall, Lawrence H. Leder, and Michael G. Kammen

Massachusetts, Colony to Commonwealth
Documents on the Formation of Its Constitution, 1775–1780

Edited by Robert J. Taylor

Prologue to Revolution
Sources and Documents on the Stamp Act Crisis, 1764–1766

Edited by Edmund S. Morgan

PREFACE

IF the editors of this volume, the third in the *Documentary Problems in Early American History*, agreed upon any one thing at the very outset of their collaboration, it was the need to make available to their students the raw materials of one of the most exciting and crucial episodes in the first century of the nation's creation. The assignment of textbooks and monographs serves a valuable purpose by giving the student a view of either the whole scope of history or a particular phase of it. But it is a predigested view. Moreover, it is an exceptional text or monograph that can stimulate a student's intellectual inquisitiveness and appetite for historical knowledge. For this, teachers are turning more and more toward controllable collections of primary source materials. By working with the basic stuff of history, the student can formulate his own conclusions and interpretations; he can become, in at least a limited sense, his own historian.

Through study and analysis of the documents that follow, the student can participate in the events of the Glorious Revolution, reconstruct them, appreciate the subtle and often conflicting issues involved, and derive conclusions substantiated by evidence. Of particular advantage is the gathering together, from a multitude of sources, documents that would otherwise be unavailable because of their scarcity or because of the time that would be consumed. Grappling with the same range of documents that would confront the professional historian, the student acquires both substantive knowledge and an ability to exercise historical methodology with discernment and skill. Thus he can better appreciate the general complexity that faces the historian as he analyzes men and events.

The Glorious Revolution of 1688-89 is particularly suited to this approach. Its significance in English history is well known: Roman Catholicism, James II, and divine right monarchy gave way to the broadly based Protestant Church of England, William and Mary, and constitutional monarchy sharply limited by Parliament. Much less familiar, however, are the consequences of those events for the American

v

colonies. Simultaneous revolutions occurred in Massachusetts Bay, New York, and Maryland, and these molded the course of development in all the colonies for generations to come. Out of the Glorious Revolution in America emerged an altered pattern of relationships of the colonies to one another and to the mother country. Out of this turmoil developed the framework of the eighteenth-century British Empire.

The problems raised by these local upheavals are of far-reaching significance. What caused the rebellions? How were they connected to the larger movement in England? What characteristics did they share in common and what differentiated them? What changes did they effect and how were Anglo-colonial bonds reshaped for the eighteenth century? What conception did the rebels hold of their own insurrections and of the nature and uses of public authority? What is the character of a revolutionary movement? Is it a hankering after utopia, or may it also seek to retrieve the conditions of a bygone time?

These are some of the questions posed by the colonial crises of 1689, the answers to which are latent in the documents that follow. This selection of sources has been designed to suggest the many dimensions of revolution and revolutionary change: political, social, economic, and diplomatic. In illustrating the origins and outcome of ferment in seventeenth-century America the sources are balanced—wherever possible—to present the various views that prevailed among contemporaries. Moreover, public and private papers have been intermixed; for what is only alluded to in a formal dispatch may have been amply treated in a personal letter. Similarly the overblown claims of a public pronouncement may be deflated in a candid communication between political allies.

The editors hope that a collection bringing together materials on the several rebellions of 1689 will prove helpful to scholars as well as students. Many of the documents are not readily available, and several are printed here for the first time. In preparing them we have followed the "expanded method" described in the *Harvard Guide to American History* as much as possible, generally reproducing the spelling, capitalization, and punctuation of the document cited, but spelling out most abbreviations and occasionally adding punctuation for clarity. In one very illiterate document (No. 23 C), however, the spelling and punctuation have been modernized to make the text more readily understandable. In some cases, paragraphs have been broken up for readability. The new year has been treated as beginning January 1 for consistency in dating.

The unit on Massachusetts Bay has been edited by Michael G. Hall, that on New York by Lawrence H. Leder, and the Maryland section by Michael G. Kammen. The editors must acknowledge their great debt to James Morton Smith, editor of publications at the Institute of Early

American History and Culture, and Susan Lee Foard, assistant editor. They were wonderfully diligent as co-ordinators, smoothing out the many rough spots involved in a joint venture. Without their good-natured prodding, patience, and constructive efforts, this volume would not now be in the readers' hands. However, all three editors assume collective responsibility for the work in its entirety.

Michael G. Hall would also thank for their unfailing help and permission to publish material on Massachusetts: Mr. Joseph D. Ward, Secretary of the Commonwealth of Massachusetts; Dr. Richard Walden Hale, archivist, and Mr. Leo Flaherty of the Massachusetts Archives; Miss Norma Cuthbert of the Henry E. Huntington Library and Art Gallery, San Marino, California; Dr. Stephen T. Riley of the Massachusetts Historical Society; and Dr. Clifford K. Shipton of the American Antiquarian Society. For typing the documents, he wishes to thank Mrs. Beverly M. Schell and Mrs. Patricia C. Blatt.

Lawrence H. Leder wishes to express his gratitude to a number of people and their staffs who have assisted by making materials available: Mr. Herman Kahn, formerly director of the Franklin D. Roosevelt Library at Hyde Park, New York; Mr. Wilbur Leech of The New-York Historical Society; Miss Norma Cuthbert of the Henry E. Huntington Library and Art Gallery; and Dr. Lester J. Cappon of the Institute of Early American History and Culture. Personal thanks are also due Professors Wesley Frank Craven of Princeton University and Brooke Hindle of New York University. Bernice Kadish Leder has been of invaluable help in the preparation of the materials.

For their gracious help and for permission to publish documents in their custody, Michael G. Kammen wishes to thank the following persons: Dr. M. L. Radoff and Mrs. A. R. Clark of the Hall of Records, Annapolis; Mr. M. W. Waring of the Land Office, Annapolis; Mr. J. D. Kilbourne and Mr. T. S. Eader of the Maryland Historical Society, Baltimore; Dr. Elizabeth Merritt, editor of the *Archives of Maryland;* Mr. R. W. Hill of the New York Public Library; Mr. Philip F. Detweiler, managing editor of the *Journal of Southern History,* for permission to publish document No. 61, which is copyrighted by the Southern Historical Association; Mr. E. W. Beitzell, editor of the *Chronicles of St. Mary's,* and Mr. Charles Fenwick, president of the St. Mary's County Historical Society, for a wonderful journey retracing the road to revolution. Carol Koyen Kammen was endlessly helpful, particularly as paleographer in transcribing some difficult seventeenth-century scripts.

Michael G. Hall   *Austin, Texas*
Lawrence H. Leder   *New Orleans, Louisiana*
Michael G. Kammen   *Cambridge, Massachusetts*

CONTENTS

PART II
LEISLER'S REBELLION IN NEW YORK

LIST OF MAPS

THE GLORIOUS REVOLUTION
IN AMERICA

THE COLONIAL CRISIS OF 1689

THE Glorious Revolution of 1688, which forced James II from the English throne and established the reign of William and Mary, created a major crisis among the English colonies in America. Following news of England's revolution, a series of rebellions and insurrections erupted in colonial America from Massachusetts to Carolina. Although the upheavals of 1689 were sparked by local grievances in each of the rebellious colonies, there were also general causes for the repudiation of Stuart authority in the New World, fundamental motives and political aspirations which linked the colonies together and in the outcome radically altered the course of colonial development.

After the Restoration of Charles II in 1660, his government, anxious to assure the restoration of monarchy in America as well as in England, became increasingly insistent on obedience to the Crown from each of the colonial governments and eventually cracked down on colonies violating colonial trade regulations. Massachusetts, the most stubbornly independent colony of all, was penalized by having its charter withdrawn in 1684. Closely linked with the effort to ensure obedience to the Crown was a growing desire in London for some sort of uniform and centralized administration of the colonies. When James II came to the throne in 1685, he inaugurated a radical policy of imperial organization, placing Massachusetts, Plymouth, New Hampshire, Rhode Island, and Connecticut under a single government, the Dominion of New England. In this new jurisdiction, perhaps modeled on the viceroyalties of Spanish America or New France, colonial administration was centralized under a royal governor-general and an appointive council. Local representative governments were abolished. In 1688 New York and New Jersey were added to the Dominion of New England, and there is evidence that Pennsylvania and even Maryland were to be next. But before these imperial plans could mature, James II was toppled from the throne by the Glorious Revolution.

In his efforts to extend and systematize what Charles had begun, James was either inept or unfortunate. Charles had leaned heavily toward the Roman Catholic Church, but James openly avowed his Catholicism. Once on the throne he claimed that he had authority as a divine right monarch to make exceptions to acts of Parliament which had barred Catholics from office. He issued a Declaration of Indulgence, which freed many Protestant Dissenters from jail, but which also was designed to exempt Roman Catholics from political restrictions. When Church of England bishops refused to comply with James' demands, he accused them of sedition and had them tried at law. Perhaps more ominous than all the rest, he placed a standing army near London and gave army commissions to Roman Catholics. Already the Protestant world had been shocked by Louis XIV's revocation of the Edict of Nantes in 1685, an event which announced the renewal of Roman Catholic persecution of Protestants in France. Every sign indicated that James II would soon follow suit in England.

But James' Catholicism was not his only drawback. Just as he had eliminated representative institutions in the Dominion of New England, he dissolved Parliament in England and attacked the right of corporate boroughs to send members to the House of Commons, at once threatening the privileges of Englishmen and alarming everyone by his direct assault on chartered rights. Thus in both England and America, James' policies aroused bitter hostility.

Englishmen were at first willing to tolerate a Catholic king, however, because his heirs, Mary and Anne, were Protestants, and England would eventually be governed by a Protestant ruler. But even this hope disappeared in 1688, when a son was born to James' second wife. The Prince of Wales would take precedence over James' daughters and would certainly be raised a Roman Catholic. Aroused Englishmen promptly invited William of Orange and Mary, James' older Protestant daughter, to rescue England. William invaded England in November 1688, James escaped to France, and a Convention Parliament ratified the Glorious Revolution by offering the Crown to William and Mary.

Reaction to the news of James' overthrow came first in Boston, where Massachusetts rebelled against the Dominion of New England in April 1689. The conflagration quickly spread to New York, where the remnants of Dominion authority were destroyed in May and June. Farther to the south, it flared again in St. Mary's City in July and August, when Marylanders revolted against Lord Baltimore in the hope that William's anti-Catholicism would protect the Protestant majority from the domination of a Catholic proprietor. Elsewhere there were varying degrees of protest and rebellion. Connecticut and Rhode Island, for example, quickly filled the political vacuum created by the over-throw of the administration imposed by James; they quietly resumed their old forms of government. In Virginia the House of Burgesses made it so hot for the governor, Lord Howard of Effingham, that he left the colony for London.

But the revolutions were most clear-cut in Massachusetts, New York, and Maryland; in each of these colonies the disruption of society was based on local grievances, colonial cleavages, and internal disorgani-zation as well as on such external factors as the threat of imperial Catholi-cism, the fear of arbitrary rule under the Stuarts, and a rumored attack by the French and Indians. The discontented threw their support to the Dutch Protestant invader, hailed his movement as "glorious," promptly identified their own particular cause with his, and then waited anxiously to learn whether William and Mary would concur in that identification.

In the sections that follow, the major upheavals in New England, the Middle Colonies, and the Southern Colonies are discussed in the order that the revolutions occurred. The problem in each of the three colonies is divided into three chapters, the first giving the background of the upheavals, the second tracing the outbreak and course of the revo-lution, and the third assessing the consequences of the uprisings and the patterns of the revolutionary settlements.

PART I

THE OVERTHROW OF THE DOMINION OF NEW ENGLAND

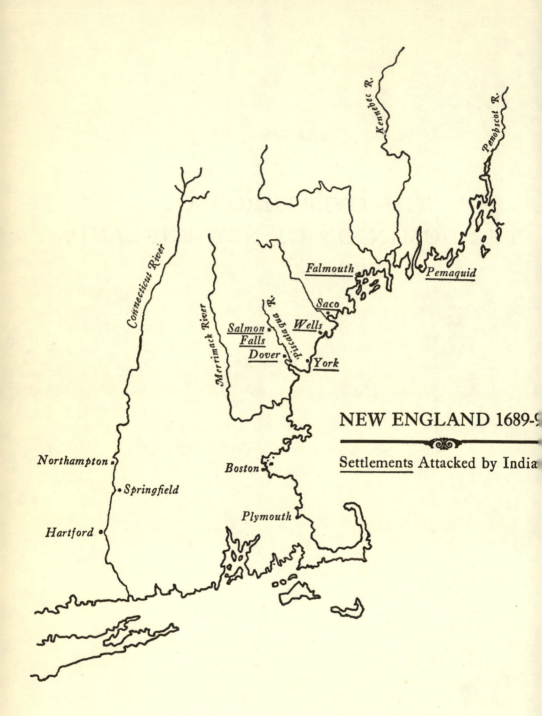

NEW ENGLAND 1689-9

Settlements Attacked by India

CHAPTER ONE

SEEDS OF DISCONTENT

THE revolution in Boston in 1689 had its origins in a contest over who should rule, the King of England or the Puritans of New England. All the deep-lying issues between the province and the metropolis came down to this. Until 1686 even religious issues—and in seventeenth-century Boston every subject was discussed with a mental attitude colored by Protestantism—were of little direct importance compared to the constitutional question of authority.

There was no issue of theology or doctrine between the Crown and the colony. It is true that the government of Charles II hounded English and Scottish Puritans who refused to conform to the ways of the Anglican Church—a brutal, bitter, and often bloody reprisal for the humiliations heaped on monarchists during the Civil War and Commonwealth periods (1642-60). But even though the Non-Conformists or Dissenters were persecuted in Great Britain, no plan was ever drafted in London, not even after James II came to power in 1685, to extend that persecution to America. First and last, royal policy was to establish religious freedom in Massachusetts. Until 1686 the religious goal of the colonists, on the other hand, was to maintain the monopoly of the New England Church—the Congregational Church. Even without interference from England, however, that monopoly was weakening more and more as the religious enthusiasm of the earlier settlers waned in later generations.

When James II took the throne in 1685, the situation changed dramatically. James was both a Roman Catholic and a bad enough politician to proclaim his faith publicly. There can be no doubt that the Glorious Revolution of England was caused, in large part, by the actions of James II in putting Roman Catholics in political and military office. The New England colonists had good reason to fear that this tendency would sooner or later be extended to their lands. Although there was no Roman Catholic plot of significance, the anxiety over such a plot crept like a specter over Boston and did much to cause the revolt.

Had the Massachusetts Puritans been able to keep their independence, however, they would have had little to fear. They could then have congratulated themselves on the wisdom of their fathers in establishing this haven of Protestantism three thousand miles from England. The Massachusetts of the first settlers had in fact become independent and entirely self-governing by 1660. The important officers of the colonial government—the governor and the bicameral legislature (the "General Court")—were elected annually by voters, who were called "freemen." Any adult male member of a Congregational church could be a freeman. It is difficult to determine exactly what proportion of the population was entitled to vote in Massachusetts under this franchise, but without a doubt it was a far larger proportion than was entitled to vote in any European country. But the important point here is that in 1660 the King of England exercised no function of government in Massachusetts at all.

This independence had developed while England was absorbed in twenty years of civil war and interregnum. Massachusetts had been allowed to go its own way. The representative democracy had evolved from a joint-stock trading company (precursor to the modern corporation) where every shareholder had a vote. That trading company had been created by a charter from Charles I, and this charter became, illogically but in fact, a constitution as precious to the Boston Puritans in 1660 as the United States Constitution was to become for its citizens after 1789. The Massachusetts Charter was considered a written guarantee of civil and political liberties and the right of self-government, just as these same Puritans thought of the Magna Carta as a general guarantee to all Englishmen, themselves included, of civil liberties and the right to representative government.

After he was restored to the throne in 1660 Charles II demanded strict acknowledgment of his sovereignty. Furthermore, the administration of government in England in the decades after the Restoration fell steadily into the hands of men whose positions were closely tied to the authority of the King. Like all bureaucrats, they considered their offices as extensions of the central authority—in this case the Crown—and they demanded an obedience to themselves as King's agents similar to the allegiance to the King himself. Bureaucracy was by no means new in England; but after 1660 it developed with great expansive force. Soon it spread to the American colonies, where it eroded the earlier de facto independence of the colonial governments.

The Revolution of 1689 began with these conflicts. In 1661 the General Court in Boston stated its own view of how far Massachusetts was self-ruling and how far subordinate to the Crown (No. 1). In the middle of the decade the King sent a commission of five men under Colonel Richard Nicolls to adjust boundary disputes in New England, capture New York from the Dutch, and persuade Massachusetts to accept fully the sovereignty of the King (No. 2). The last part of the program was a total failure. Then in 1676 Edward Randolph, who was the entering wedge of the new colonial bureaucracy, was sent to Boston, where he insisted on thorough recognition of royal authority.

Many of the richer men, especially merchants, who relied on smooth relations with England in order that they might have access to credit and that their ships would be protected on the high seas, were ready to acquiesce in the demands of the royal government. But the large majority of settlers, indifferent to the needs of the merchant group, insisted on independence. One issue was whether the laws of England were in force in New England. The majority argued that they were not. Argument centered over the Navigation Acts, not because they restricted Massachusetts trade but because it was under the authority of one of these statutes that Edward Randolph was sent as the first royal official to reside in Massachusetts (No. 3).

Thus the battle that ensued in the Massachusetts General Court was not over the substance of the Navigation Acts, which all were agreed to accept, but rather over whether Parliament in London or the General Court in Boston had the authority to legislate for Massachusetts. In the upper house of the General Court, where merchant sentiment was strong, the Magistrates drafted a bill frankly recognizing Parliament's Navigation Acts. In the lower house, however, the Deputies wrote a bill which repeated in detail the substance of those laws, but carefully omitted any reference to Parliament, just as if the Navigation Act of Massachusetts were of its own concoction and in force by its own authority (No. 4). In this struggle within the colony over the true relation to the Crown and to Parliament, the Deputies won hands down. This was more than mere face-saving. The General Court was struggling to prevent the slightest acknowledgment of a position subordinate to Parliament. The Puritans meanwhile did everything they could to break the power of Edward Randolph, for he was a servant of the King instead of one of their own appointees.

With these developments the contest over authority came to a climax. In 1683 the King asked that Massachusetts voluntarily submit its charter to him for revision. When the Puritans in Boston voted not to do so (No. 5), the King (or rather the new bureaucrats in London, who framed the charges [No. 6]), succeeded in having the charter dissolved by legal action, and Massachusetts lost its "constitution" and became a royal colony in 1684.

After this the situation worsened quickly. The King installed his own government under Sir Edmund Andros. The other New England colonies lost their charters, and all were lumped together into one province, the Dominion of New England, which extended from Maine to New Jersey (No. 7). The new royal government for this vast territory had no representative legislature. So when taxes were imposed, the colonists objected that they had lost an ancient and precious right of Englishmen: not to be taxed without consent. In several towns the colonists refused to pay the taxes and organized resistance in local town meetings, which were of a very democratic nature. Governor Andros squashed the resistance with heavy jail sentences and forbade all but one town meeting a year. An effort was made to reorganize land grants so that property would be held by a title originating with the King, as was done in England. By English legal standards, real estate titles in New England were in chaos. The reform, however, was administered in such a clumsy way as to cause considerable expense to the colonists and also to make the people fear that their lands were about to be expropriated (No. 8).

Finally, the Governor and a handful of public officials under him were members of the Church of England. They had brought from England an Anglican minister, but because they had no church building, Governor Andros commandeered one of the Congregational churches in Boston. This highhandedness could not fail to insult deeply the Puritan congregation. All these actions of Governor Andros were the fagots from which revolt flamed up (No. 9). Most of them were not basic issues but rather the result of inept administration. The fundamental complaint—that the representative assembly had been abolished—was not Andros' fault but that of James II, the last ruler of England to believe he could govern by the divine right of kings.

Who Shall Rule In New England

1. The General Court Reports on Massachusetts' Allegiance to the Crown, June 10, 1661

[Nathaniel B. Shurtleff, ed., *Records of the Governor and Company of Massachusetts Bay in New England*, 5 vols. (Boston, 1853-54), IV, Pt. 2, 24-26]

The Court mett at the time appointed.

The answers of the committee unto the matters proposed to theire consideration by the honnored Generall Court:—

1. Concerning our liberties.

1. Wee conceive the pattent (under God) to be the first and maine foundation of our civil politye here, by a Gov-

ernor and Company, according as is therein exprest.

2. The Governor and Company are, by the pattent, a body politicke, in fact and name.

3. This body politicke is vested with power to make freemen.

4. These freemen have power to choose annually a Governor, Deputy Governor, Asistants, and theire select representatives or deputies.

5. This government hath also to sett up all sortes of officers, as well superior as inferior, and point out theire power and places.

6. The Governor, Deputy Governor, Asistants, and select representatives or deputies have full power and authoritie, both legislative and execcutive, for the government of all the people heere, whither inhabitants or straingers, both concerning eclesiasticks and in civils, without appeale, excepting lawe or lawes repugnant to the lawes of England.

7. The government is priviledged by all fitting meanes (yea, and if neede be, by force of armes) to defend themselves, both by land and sea, against all such person or persons as shall at any time attempt or enterprise the destruction, invasion, dettriment, or annoyance of this plantation, or the inhabitants therein, besides other priviledges mentioned in the pattent, not heere expressed.

8. Wee conceive any imposition prejudiciall to the country contrary to any just lawe of ours, not repugnant to the lawes of England, to be an infringement of our right.

2. Concerning our duties of alleagiance to our soveraigne lord the king.

1. Wee ought to uphold and to our power mainteine this place, as of right belonging to our soveraigne lord the king, as holden of his majesties mannor of East Greenwich, and not to subject the same to any forreigne prince or potentate whatsoever.

2. Wee ought to endeavor the preservation of his majesties royall person, realmes, and dominions, and so farre as lieth in us, to dicover and prevent all plotts and conspiracies against the same.

3. Wee ought to seeke the peace and prosperitie of our king and nation, by a faith full discharge in the governing of this people committed to our care:—

1. By punishing all such crimes (being breaches of the first or second table) as are committed against the peace of our soveraigne lord the king, his royall crowne and dignity.

2. In propogating the gospell, defending and upholding the true Christian or Prottestant religion according to the faith given by our Lord Christ in his word; our dread soveraigne being stiled 'defender of the faith.'

The premisses considered, it may well stand with the loyalty and obedience of such subjects as are thus priviledged by theire rightfull soveraigne, (for himself, his heires, and successors for ever,) as cause shall require, to pleade with theire prince against all such as shall at any time endeavor the violation of theire priviledges.

Wee further judge that the warrant and letter from the kings majesty, for the apprehending of Col. Whalley and Col. Goffe, ought to be diligently and faithfully executed by the authority of this country.

And also, that the Generall Court may doe safely to declare, that in case (for the future) any legally obnoxious, and flying from the civil justice of the state of England, shall come over to these partes, they may not heere expect shelter.

Boston, 10 4 mo., 1661. By the order and consent of the committee.

THO: DANFORTH.

The Court allowes and approves of the returne of the committee.

2. Royal Commissioners Assert the Sovereignty of the King, April 23, 1664

[Edward B. O'Callaghan, ed., *Documents Relative to the Colonial History of the State of New York*, 11 vols. (Albany, 1853-61), III, 57-61]

Private Instructions to Coll. R. Nicolls etc.

Instructions to our trusty and welbeloved Coll. Richard Nicolls Sir Robert Carre Knight George Cartwright Esq. and Samuell Mavericke Esq. Commissioners employed by us to our Plantations in America in and about New England to be considered and communicated only betweene themselves.

CHARLES R.

1. Though the maine end and drift of your employment is to informe yourselves and us of the true and whole state of those severall Colonies and by insinuateing yourselves by all kind and dextrous carriage into the good opinion of the principall persons there, that soe you may (after a full observation of the humour and interest both of those in government and those of the best quality out of government and, generally, of the people themselves) lead and dispose them to desire to renew their Charters and to make such alterations as will appeare necessary for their owne benefit:—Yet you may informe all men that a great end of your designe is the possessing Long Island, and reduceing that people to an entyre submission and obedience to us and our governement, now vested by our grant and Commission in our Brother the Duke of Yorke, and by raising forts or any other way you shall judge most convenient or necessary soe to secure that whole trade to our subjects, that the Dutch may noe longer ingrosse and exercise that trade which they have wrongfully possessed themselves of; that whole territory being in our possession before they, as private persons and without any authority from their superiors and against the lawe of Nations and the good intelligence and allyance between us and their superiors, invaded and have since wrongfully obteyned the same, to the prejudice of our Crowne and Dignity, and therefore ought in justice to be resumed by us, except they will entyrely submitt to our goverment and live there as our good subjects under it; and in that case you shall lett them knowe both by private significations and treatyes or by any publicke declaration sett out by you in our name,—That wee will take them into our protection, and that they shall continue to enjoy all their possessions (Forts only excepted) and the same freedome in trade with our other good subjects in those parts. And as you will need the assistance of our other colonies towards this reduction, soe wee conceive they will all for their owne interest bee ready to engage with you herein.

2. This being the case, and the prosecution of that designe being not absolutely in your owne power in respect of wind and weather, wee leave it entirely to your discretion whether you choose to goe first upon Long Island, which seems most reasonable to designe in respect of the troops you carry, or to New England, resolveing to approve of what you doe in that perticular, lett the successe bee what it will, and if it please God you have the successe wee hope for upon Long Island, you will improve the consideration of the benefit thereof to all the Colonies, and how much happier they are by our care in the removeing such ill neighbours from them, at our owne cost and charges.

3. You are to use great dilligence to-

gether in the careful and exact perusall of the first and second Charter, granted by our Royall Father for the undertaking and settling those plantations, and any other Charters which have been granted to any perticular Colonies by our father and ourselfe, or the late usurping powers; to the end that upon the full consideration thereof, and if any difficultys arise upon doubtfull or contradictory expressions, you may eyther by resorting to our Councill at Lawe in some points, and to our Secretary of State in other, receave full and cleare information and directions, and you must bee the more conversant and fully informed of all contained in the said Charters (of which you ought to carry authentick Coppyes with you) because the ground and foundation of your employment is the exact observation of the Charters and reduceing to that rule whatsoever hath swerved from it. Besides you will thereby observe all those clauses in the severall Charters which are either too short and restrained and the enlargeing thereof would bee for the publick benefit of the plantation; or such other inconvenient ones, as for our dignity and authority should bee altered by a generall consent and desire. Amongst which it were to bee wished that the severall Governours should hold thier places three or five yeares and that before the midle of the last yeare three names should be sent over and presented to us, that one of them might be chosen by us for the next Governour which we should as well approve and would be more easily consented to, then the remitting the entyre choice to us.

4. You are with the like dilligence and care to peruse the collection of the lawes published in those Colonies during the late usurping Government, or at any tyme before or since; to the end that upon examination thereof you may discerne both the indecent expressions and materiall and important points and determinations in them, which are contrary to our dignity and to the lawes

and customes of this realme, and to the justice thereof; all which they have obliged themselves to cancell and repeale; and if the same bee not already done, you are in the first place to cause it to be done, especially and perticularly that the oaths enjoyned by the severall Charters be taken, and the administration of justice be performed in our name.

5. Since the great and principall ends of all those who first engaged themselves in those Plantations in which they have spent much tyme and money, was liberty of concience, and the same is expressely provided for in the first and subsequent Charters as they could desire to be done, and the observation and preservation thereof is our very hearty purpose and determination: You are to bee very carefull amongst yourselves and with all persons who have any relation to, or dependance upon any of you, that nothing be said or done, from or by which the people there may thinke or imagine that there is any purpose in us to make any alteration in the Church Government or to introduce any other forme of worshipp among them then what they have chosen: all our exception in that particular being that they doe in truth deny that liberty of conscience to each other, which is equally provided for and granted to every one of them by their charter: all which you will find wee have more at large taken notice of in our letter of the 28th June 1662, a coppy whereof is delivered to you, and of which you shall in due season, and when you are well acquainted with them, dexterously take notice, and presse the execution and observation of the same, according to the Charter. And that you may not give any umbrage or jealousy to them in matters of religion, as if you were at least enimyes to formes observed amongst them, you shall do well to frequent their churches and to be present at their devotion, though wee doe suppose and thinke it very fitt that you carry with you some learned

and discreet Chaplaine, orthodox in his judgement and practice, who in your owne familyes will reade the Booke of Common Prayer and performe your devotion according to the forme established in the Church of England, excepting only in wearing the surplesse which haveing never bin seen in those countryes, may conveniently be forborne att this tyme, when the principall busynesse is, by all good expedients, to unite and reconcile persons of very different judgements and practice in all things, at least which concerne the peace and prosperity of those people and their joint submission and obedience to us and our government.

6. Since it is very notorious that there are not only very great factions and animosityes in one Colony against the other, but in one and the same Colony betwene persons of different opinions in religion, so that it is very probable all discontented persons will make application to you according to their severall humours and interest; it will concerne you to be very wary in your conversation, that being sent as persons equall to determine controversyes amongst them, you may not bee thought to enclyne to a party, or to bee yourselves engaged in their passions and appetite, and you must principally guard yourselves against two sorts of people (till upon the severall informations you shall receive, and by your own observation and experience you can make some judgement of their sincerity) that is not to seeme too forward in concurring with them in whatsoever they propose. The first is, they that pretend to have a great prejudice against the forme of Religion there professed, and as great a zeale for the establishing the Booke of Common Prayer, and it may bee the Episcopacy itselfe, and the whole discipline of the Church of England.

The second is, they who will appeare soliciteous to advance our proffit and to settle a present revenue upon the Crowne; which they will suppose may bee looked upon as such an unquestionable instance of their affection to us and our service, that it will give them credit and advantages in all their pretences.

To the first of these, after you have used them with kindnesse and encouragement to bee present when they please at your private devotions, you shall let them know that you have noe order from us, (for many of those overtures may be made only for discovery of your intentions) to make the least attempt, or to encourage alteration in the way they proffesse of religion; for though nobody can doubt but that wee could looke upon it as the greatest blessing God Almighty can conferre upon us in this world that Hee would reduce all our subjects in all our dominions to one faith and one way of worship with us; yet wee could not imagine it probable that a confederate number of persons, who separated themselves from their owne countrey and the religion established, principally (if not only) that they might enjoy another way of worship, presented or declared unto them by theire owne consciences, could in soe short a tyme be willing to returne to that forme of service they had forsaken; and therefore that wee had been soe farre from giveing you any direction to promote or countenance any alteration in the religion practised there, that you have expresse order to the contrary. But if they only insisted upon the liberty granted them by their Charter, and that they would provide peaceably for the exercise of their religion in the forme they best liked, without troubling or reproaching those who dissent from them, and only desire that this libertie of conscience might produce noe prejudice to them in their civill interests or relation to the Government:—You may lett them know that it is no more than what wee have already recommended to the Governour and Councill by our former letters, and wherein you will doe them all the offices within your power.

Butt even in this point wee conceive

you should proceed very warily and not enter upon it, till you have made some progresse in your lesse difficult busynesse; and indeed you should rather advise those who seeme to bee serious and hearty in that desire that they cause it to be first proposed and sett on foot in the Generall Assembly that shall bee called, then any way touched upon, before the present Governour and Councill, and promise them your utmost assistance there, in the promoteing any thing for their ease which will not evidently disturbe the peace of the countrey.

To the second sort of people which will be active in many projects for our proffit and benifitt, you must not bee forwards too much, since most overtures of that kind are but ayrey imaginations, and cannot bee put in practise by our owne imediate power and authority, without manifest violation of their Charter which wee resolve to keep observe and maintaine.

Upon those discourses therefore you shall declare that you have no direction to make any attempt of that kind, without there appeare a good and voluntary inclination to that purpose in the Generall Assembly, which probably may find it convenient to make some newe desires and propositions to us for their benefitt, and in lieu thereof may make some grants and concessions to us: and in truth it will not be rationall for you to appeare solicitous to make any change in the matters of Religion, or to make any attempt to bring any change to that people, except both arise amongst themselves in the Generall Assembly, and then you shall give such countenance to it as you shall judge necessary for our service.

7. You shall as soon as you are arrived and have delivered our letters to the Governour and Councill presse them that a Generall Assembly may be convened as soon as may be according to our letter to them.

And because much of the good wee expected from your journey depends upon the wisdome and fidelity of that Assembly, you shall use your utmost endeavours privately, and by those means which are most proper and without offence, to gett men of the best reputation and most peaceably inclined, to be chosen into that Assembly, and then according to the interest and credit you have, give them all advice and encouragement to promote our service, and then you shall informe them of the great affection wee have for them, and that wee looke upon them with the same fatherly care as if they lived in the centre of eyther of our kingdomes.

You shall shew them the coppy of the letter and addresse made to us by the Governour and Councill after our happy returne into England, and of our answer to that Addresse, as likewise what wee have now writ to the Governour and Councill there; all which wee directed you to communicate, to the end that wee may receive their advice and information how wee may advance the happyness of that our people. And in order hereunto you are ready to conferre with them upon all perticulars relateing to your negotiation or to the end thereof, and soe you are to behave yourselves towards them as you find may most conduce to the end of your employment.

8. Besides the generall disposeing that people to an entyre submission and obedience to our government which is their owne greatest security in respect of their neighbours and leading them to a desire to renew their Charters, which in many respects ought to bee desired by them; there are two points wee could heartily wish should be gained upon them.

The first that wee may have (as wee expressed before) the nomination of the Governour, or approbation.

The other, that the Militia should bee putt under an officer nominated or recommended by us; and it may bee, if they will consider their Charter, they will not find that they have in truth, the disposall of their owne Militia as they imagine.

But how to approach to those two points wee cannot tell, butt must leave it to your skill and dexterity, after you have enough conversed with them and know the principall leading men of the severall partyes. In the meane tyme wee should looke upon it as a good omen, if they might bee soe wrought upon at the Generall Assembly as that Coll. Nicolls might bee chosen by themselves for their present Governour and Collonell Cartwright for their Major Generall.

All designes of proffit for the present seeme unseasonable and may possibly obstruct the more necessary designe upon their obedience and loyalty, if they shall apprehend that it cost them money; soe that it should not be affected farther (except the Generall Assembly appeare to have other franknesse then wee can reasonably expect) then to settle some annuall tribute of the growth of that country, as masts, corne, and fish, to bee presented to us, as was intimated, by the two messengers employed hither, to bee their purpose to doe.

9. In the last place, Wee doe enjoyne and command you, as you will answer to the contrary, to live with entyre confidence and kindnesse in and towards each other, which can only support the credit and reputation of your trust and employment. That you constantly communicate together what eyther of you hath collected upon private intercourses or information from perticuler persons, and that thereupon in all your Councills you acquiesse with the judgement of the major part (except it bee expressely contrary to our Instructions, and in which wee have not left you a latitude to doe according to your discretion) and pursue it accordingly, and that you are not transported by any private consideration of proffit or friendship to swerve from the right rule of advanceing our service. And wee shall be more sensible of any error of this kind, then of any other misfortune that may bring inconvenience to our service in your employment.

Our other Instructions for your procedings in the severall Colonies you shall communicate as you see cause, and as you enter upon the severall perticulars, as at your first audience you shall doe well to tell them, that instead of entertaining them of any discourse of your owne, you will deliver them the copy of your first Instructions, and shall deliver it them accordingly.

Given at our Court at Whitehall this 23d day of Aprill 1664 in the 16th yeare of our Reigne.

By His Majesties command

HENRY BENNETT.

3. Massachusetts Rejects the Jurisdiction of English Laws, September 20, 1676

[Robert N. Toppan and Alfred T. S. Goodrick, eds., *Edward Randolph; Including His Letters and Official Papers* (Prince Society, *Publications*, 24-28, 30-31 [1898-1909]), II, 216-21]

A Short narrative touching the delivery of your Majesties letters to the Magistrates of Boston in New England, by Edward Randolph.

May it please your Majestie,

Having receaved your Majesties letters for the governor and magistrates of your Majesties town of Boston in N.E. dated 10th of March last, with my particular instructions from the right hon. secretary Coventry, upon the 30th of the sayd month I sayled from the Downes. After a tedious passage of 10 weeks arrived at Boston on 10th June. At my landing I went immediately to the governor John Leveret, and shewed him your Majesties passe and acquainted him with the cause of my coming, and that I had brought a letter from his Majestie unto the magistrates of that colony, and did therefore desire him that, with what convenient speed might be, the magistrates might be assembled to hear your Majesties letter read. The governor answered, that the council was to meet that afternoon, upon other businesse, and that then I should be sent for; as I was, by the marshall of their court; where being come and admitted into the councill, I delivered your Majesties letters to the governor, their being six of the magistrates and their secretary assembled with him, and there being a chaire placed purposely for me, I was desired by the governor to sitt. . . .

The day after, I went to visit the governour at his house, and among other discourse I told him I tooke notice of severall ships that were arrived at Boston, some since my being there, from Spain, France, Streights, Canaries and other parts of Europe, contrary to your Majesties lawes for encouraging navigation, and regulating the trade of the plantations. He freely declared to me that the lawes made by your Majestie and your parliament obligeth them in nothing but what consists with the interest of that colony, that the legislative power is and abides in them solely to act and make lawes by virtue of a charter from your Majesties royall father, and that all matters in difference are to be concluded by their finall determination, without any appeal to your Majestie, and that your Majestie ought not to retrench their liberties, but may enlarge them if your Majestie please, and said, your Majestie had confirmed their charter and all their privileges by your Majesties letter of the 28th of June, 1662, and that your Majesty could doe no lesse in reason than let them enjoy their liberties and trade, they having upon their own charge and without any

contribution from the crown made so large plantation in the wildernesse, and that during the Dutch warrs your Majestie sent ammunition to New-Yorke for that place, but sent them word they must shift for themselves and make the best defence they could, and that notwithstanding the colony had many enemies, yet they did believe your Majestie to be their very good friend, for that your Majestie had by severall letters expressed your kindnesse to them. . . .

About the beginning of July, I went into the province of New-Hampshire, belonging to Mr. Mason, but now divided by the Bostoneers into three counties, and by them called Norfolk, Suffolk and Middlesex. And travelled through severall of the most considerable towns, acquainting the inhabitants with the occasion of my coming into the country, and read Mr. Mason's letter unto them, which gave them great satisfaction, the whole country complaining of the oppression and usurpation of the magistrates of Boston, imposing ministers upon them, not admitting them to the sacrament of the Lord's Supper, denying baptism to their children, and liberty of choosing their own magistrates and officers because they were not members of their congregations. And as a farther marke of their power and sovereignty over them they send twice a year magistrates from Boston to keep courts for trying of causes, and that they lay at pleasure what impositions, fines and taxes they thinke fit upon their estates, persons and trade, contrary to the lawes of England, and that they have been for a long time earnestly expecting to be delivered from the government of the Massachusets Bay, and doe humbly hope your Majestie will not permitt them any longer to be oppressed, but will be graciously pleased to give them relief, according to the promises made them by your Majesties commissioners in 1665, who were then in that province, and declared them not to be under the government of Boston.

4. The General Court Writes Its Own Navigation Act

A. THE MAGISTRATES DRAFT A BILL RECOGNIZING THE AUTHORITY OF PARLIAMENT, FEBRUARY 24, 1682

[Massachusetts Archives, LXI, 237-38]

For the Regulation of the navigation and trade of this Colony According to the Acts of Parliament referring thereunto; and particularly those of the 12. 15. and 25 of his majesty, and in pursuance of an order of this Jurisdiction made october 10th 1677 This Court does order and enact that the aforesaid acts of Parliament and the aforesaid orders be forthwith published in the exchainge of Boston by sound of Drumme and further that the order of this Court made in 1670 prohibiting trade with any vessell till they Come under command and Ride in our usuall harbors hereafter named upon the penalty of the forfeiture of all such goods so traded be in the like manner published. And the ports allowed for delivery shall be Boston to which is annexed Charlstowne; Salem to which is Annexed Marblehead; Newbery to which is Annexed Ipswich and no other. And It is hereby further Ordered that all shipps and vessells Arriving in any of the said Ports shall before they breake bulke make entry with the Governor or such officer as the Governor shall Appoint in the abovenamed Ports as the acts of Parliament requires, And all shipps and vessells outward bound shall in like manner attend what in the said Acts of Parliament is required of them by Giving in bond to deliver their Lading in parts and ports allowed by the said Acts of Parliament and receive thence cirtificates from the said Governor or his order. And the Governor is heereby ordered and directed in every of the said respective ports of this Jurisdiction to Appoint and Constitute under his hand and seale one able and sufficient person to dischardge and performe the said trust who may receive such fees for entering bonds cirtificates as the said Acts of Parliament doe Allow and no other person shall Assume or execute the said office but as abovesaid. And it is further ordered that the Governor or his officer in the severall ports above named shall keepe faire books of all entries cirtificates bonds etc. which shall be always liable to the review of any officer or any other that may Informe of the breach of any of the said Acts of Parliament or of our lawes in pursuance thereof or referring to the Trade of this Jurisdiction. And for the better direction of merchants and marriners that may not so fully understand those acts of trade this Court does desire Mr. Elisha Cooke and Capt. Elisha Hutchinson to make a true abstract of all the clauses relating to the plantations conteyned in those acts and the same to be forthwith printed.

The magistrates have passt this their bretheren the Duputies hereto Consenting.

EDWARD RAWSON SECRET

The Deputies Consent not hereto

WILLIAM TORREY CLERIC

B. The House of Deputies Denies Parliament's Authority, February 23, 1682

[Massachusetts Archives, LXI, 234-35]

This Court haveing Considered the Statutes of England, his Majestie's Commands and our owne Laws Refering to trade and Navigation Doe order and Inact that no Commodities Shal be Imported into or Exported out of this Collony, in any other Ship or Vessel whatsoever but such as doe truly belong only to the people of England, Ireland, Dominion of Wailes or Towne of Berwick upon Tweed, or are of the Bilt of and belonging to some of his Majestie's plantations in Asia Africa or America, and whereof the Mastor and three fourths of the Marinors at least are English, under the penalty of the forfiture and loss of all the goods and Commoditys which shal be imported into, or Exported out of this Collony in any other ship or vessel, as also of the ship or vessel with all its guns, furniture, takel, Ammunition and Apparel, one third part thereof to his Majesty his Heirs and Successors, one third part to the Governor and Company, and the other third part to him or them whoe shal Informe seize and sue for the same.

It is also ordered that no Alian or person not borne within the Allegence of our Soveraine Lord the King, or Naturalized or made a free Denison, shall Exersize the trade or occupation of a Marchant or factor in this Collony, upon paine of the forfiture and loss of all his goods and Chattels or that are in his possession, one third part to his Majesty one third part to the Governor and Company and the other third to him or them whoe shall Informe seize and sue for the same.

It is also Ordered that no Commodity of the groth production or Manifacture of Europe, shal be Imported into this Collony but what shal be bona fide and without fraude Laden and Shipped in England Wales or Towne of Berwick upon Tweede, and in English built shiping and maned as aforesaid under the penalty of the Loss of all such goods and Commoditys soe Imported, also the Loss of such ship or vessel with al its guns, furniture, takel, Ammunition and Apparel, one third to his Majesty one third to the Governor and Company, and the other third to him or them whoe shall Informe seize and sue for the same.

And for the better prevention of fraudes it is hereby Ordered that no ship or vessell Coming from any porte bey and the sease of New England into this Collony shall Lade or unlade any goods or Commoditys whatsoever until the Mastor or Commandor of such ship or vessell have made knowne to the Governor or officer thereunto Authorised, the Arrival of the said shipp or vessell with her name and burthen, the name of the Mastor or Commandor and have shewed to him that she is an English built ship or vessel, or produce sufficiant Cirtificate that she is such a ship or vessel as hath Liberty to trade here. And have delivered ane perfect Inventory or Invoyce of her Lading together with the place or places wher such goods were Laden into said ship or vessel under the paine of the loss of the shipp or vessel with all her guns Ammunition takel furniture and Apparel, and of all such goods of the groth production or Manufacture of Europe, as were not Bona fide Laden in England Wales or Towne of Berwick, to be Recovered and devided in maner aforesaid.

Provided this law nor any thing therin contained Extends not to Bulloyn salt, wines of the groth of Madera the Western Islands or Azores Nor to any sorte of victules of the groth or production of England Scotland Ireland or said Islands, Nor to any goods taken by way of Reprisal by vertue of Commission or Authority Derived from his Majesty his Heirs or Successors;

And it is heerby Ordered that this Court shall from time to time appoynt meet persons in our port Towns, viz. Boston, Salem, and Newbery, whoe shall have Commission from the Governor under the seale of the Collony, and be sworne to the faithfull discharge of his trust, And that they and only they, take Entrys of all such shipps and vessels, Receive and grant Cirtificates to all such Mastors and Commandors; which said Officers shall keepe faier books of all Entrys Cirtificates etc. which shall be always lyable to the view of any officer or other person that may Informe of the breach of any Laws Relating to trade, and that said officers once every six Months doe transcribe fare Coppys of all Entrys Cirtificates etc. and deliver the same to the governour for the time being, for which service said officers shal take to themselves such fees, from said Mastor or Commandor, boath for Entering and Transcribing, as Clarkes and Recordors are by Law alowed.

And it shal be in the liberty of any Informer or other person whatsoever by warrant from the Governor or any Majestrate or the Officer that is deputed to Receive Entrys for the time being to search seize and secure any such ship, vessel, or goods as shal be brought into this Collony Contrary to Law, the said Informer or other person first giving sufficient security to Respond all Costs and damages that shall arise, by his wrongfull seizing or detaining any such vessel or goods.

The deputyes have passed this desiring the Consent of the honored majistrates hereto. Feb. 23-[16]81

WILLIAM TORREY CLERIC

Not consented to by the magistrates

EDWARD RAWSON SECRET

5. Massachusetts Refuses to Surrender its Charter for Revision

A. SAMUEL NOWELL TO JOHN RICHARDS, MARCH 28, 1683

[Massachusetts Historical Society, *Collections*, 5th Ser., 1 (1871), 434-35]

Capt. Richards, Honored Sir,—I received yours, and am greatly indebted to you for that and all your former kindnesses to my selfe, which I know not how to requite but by my poor prayers, in which way (tho poor mine be worth little) I reckon my selfe as deeply indebted to your selfe as to any man. I am heartily sorry for that unavoidable excercise which the only wise God hath been pleased to carve out for you, it being not possible to please the country and the Court too. We have been togither since the 7th of Febr. last, this session being not much unlike the time we spent two years agoe. God is pleased to hide from us the right methods of unity and agreement, and indeed the matter is so weighty about yielding or denying appeals, that it hath taken up the most of our time, and what we shall come to in the conclusion will be sent to you. I have little exspectation that all we can or shall do will put a stop to a Quo Warranto; for ife we doe not give you power, it will go on; if we do give you the power required, and you do not make use of it to our prejudice, the Quo Warranto will still go on; but if you do make use of the power to answer demands, we do then pull downe the house ourselves, which is worse than to be passive only. By our Pattent we have full and absolute power to rule and governe, pardon and punish, etc.; by which allways hithertoo we have judged ourselves free from appeales, and either we may finally judge of and determine all things, or else appeals ly in all cases, which will make the Government here to be a meer cypher, more contemptible than any other Government in all the Plantations, in regard we are under an ill aspect; hence every pragmatick person will refuse to submit to the judgment of our courts, hoping for relief in England, or by some commissioners here, to which our Government must be subordinate; the case in 1664. For example, Robt. Orchard, being strained upon for two pewter platters, prefers a complaint against us at Whitehall, and it is taken notice of, as I suppose you will be particularly advised more about it. That, and Masons case, by which we fear the greatest part of the country will be disposed off to Mr Mason, maketh us afraid of appeals. The grant of the

wasts to him is to us a plaine demonstration that his claime is intended to be fully allowed when by his appeale from our judgment it shall be carried back to England; for our law of Title Possession was pleaded before the K. and council in my hearing, and is disallowed of by what is allready done, and our title to the soile by our Pattent is accounted of as nothing worth, by reason our former Agents did in the case between Gorge and Mason renounce the soile. The Lord fit you and us for his holy will and pleasure in such trialls as seeme comming.

Mr Willard and Mr Allen came into the Court this day to make a motion for reliefe to be sent for a release of Mr Dudly and yorselfe, but I doubt it will not be granted. So commending you and your affairs and ours to the Lord, I rest

Yor obliged friend and servt,

S:N:

B. Increase Mather's Argument, 1683

[M. G. Hall, ed., "The Autobiography of Increase Mather," in American Antiquarian Society, *Proceedings*, 71 (1962), Pt. 2, 307-8]

In the latter end of this year, that came to pass, which occasioned no small Trouble and Temptation to me. For there arrived a vessel which brought the Kings declaration, wherein hee signifieth to the Countrey that except they would make a full submission and entire Resignation to his pleasure, a Quo warranto should be prosecuted against their Charter. Some desired me to deliver my apprehensions on the Question whether the countrey could without sin against God make such a Resignation as was proposed to them. Several papers were brought to me some that came out of England or Holland others written in New England which argued for the Negative. I put those arguments into Form, and added some more of my owne, and then communicated them to some of the

Magistrates, who so well approved of them as to disperse copyes thereof, that they came into many hands, and were a meanes to keep the Countrey from complying with that proposal. The other party conjectured me to be the author of that M.ss. and were not a little displeased thereat. Nevertheless, I believe it was a good worke, and I hope acceptable to the Lord.

Also on January. 23. The freemen of Boston mett to consider what they should do. The deputies of Boston and several others requested me to be present and to give my thoughts as to the case of conscience before them. In the Townhouse I made a short speech to the Freemen in these words, "As the Question is now stated, (viz. whether you will make a full submission and entire Resignation of your Charter and priviledges of it, to his Majesties' pleasure) wee shall sin against God if wee vote an Affirmative to it. The scripture teacheth us otherwise. Wee know that Jephthah said, That which the Lord our God has given us, shall not we possess! And Naboth, tho he ran a great hazard by the refusal, yet said, God forbid that I should give away the Inheritance of my Fathers. Now would it be wisdome for us to comply. Wee know that David made a wise choice, when He chose to fall into the hands of God rather than into the hands of men. If wee make a full submission and entire Resignation to pleasure, we fall into the hands of men immediately. But if wee do it not, we keep ourselves still in the hands of God, and Trust ourselves with his providence and who knoweth what God may do for us? Moreover, there are examples before our eyes, the consideration whereof should be of weight with us.

Our brethren hard by, what have they gained by their readiness to submit and comply, who if they had abode by their liberties longer would not have bin miserable so soon. And wee hear from London, that when it came to they would not make a full submission and entire Resignation to pleasure, lest haply their posterity should curse them. And shall we do it then? I hope there is not one Freeman in Boston that will dare to be guilty of so great a sin. However, I have discharged my conscience in thus delivering my selfe to you."

Upon this speech many of the Freemen wept, and they said generally, we thank you Sir for this instruction and encouragement. The Question being put to vote was carried in the Negative Nemine Contradicente. This Act of Boston had a great Influence on the Countrey, many other Towns following this example.

6. The Grounds for Revoking the Colonial Charter, June 4, 1683

[Toppan and Goodrick, eds., *Randolph Letters*, III, 299-30]

1. They have erected a Publick mint in Boston and Coine money with their Own Impresse.

2. They impose upon the Consciencyes of his Majesties Subjects in matters of Religion by their Lawes Ecclesiasticall being repugnant to the Lawes of England.

3. They refuse appeals to his Majestie in Councill in matters relating to the Crown.

4. They impose Dutyes and Customs upon goods imported their Colony by his Majesties Subjects from England where those goods have paid all his Majesties dues.

5. They levye what Rates and taxes they please upon his Majesties Subjects inhabiting their Colony altho' not free of their Company.

6. They have in opposition to his Majesties letters Patents sett up a Navall Office altho' no such power is granted them in their Charter.

7. They assume a power of Making freemen not allowed and otherwise then their Charter directs.

8. They have erected Courts of Admiralty.

9. They have refused a legall tryall in their Courts in a Cause relating to his Majestie.

10. They have imprisoned his Majesties Officers for doing their Dutyes and refused the Plea of Generall issue when Offred in their Defence.

11. They have forced his Majesties Officer to pay money in their Courts before he Could be admitted to prosecute on his Majesties behalfe no Law or Or-

der of Generall Court warranting the Same.

12. They have putt Severall persons to Death for Breach of their Lawes. No power granted by Charter for so Doing.

13. They have imposed illegall oaths upon his Majesties Subjects Inhabiting the Colony.

14. They have Caused some of the Inhabitants to signe a Mutinous addresse to his Majestie altho' the best persons of estates in the Colony have refused.

15. They have raised great Sums of money upon the Nonfreemen to purchase for themselves the Province of Maine.

16. They have not yet suffered his Majesties letters Patents to be publickly read in their Courts at tyme of tryall of Causes relating to his Majesties Customs.

17. They have not owned the Act for preventing frauds made in the 14th. of the King nor the Act for better securing the Plantation trade made in the 25th. of the King to be the Lawes of their Colony.

[Endorsed] Articles against the Government of Boston. Recd. 4 June 1683.
MR. RANDOLPH.

Establishment of the Dominion of New England

7. Sir Edmund Andros' Commission as Governor, April 7, 1688

[Francis N. Thorpe, ed., Federal and State Constitutions, Colonial Charters, and Other Organic Laws, 7 vols. (Washington, 1909), III, 1863-67]

James the Second by the Grace of God King of England, Scotland France and Ireland Defender of the Faith etc. To our trusty and welbeloved Sir Edmund Andros Knight Greeting: Whereas by our Commission under our Great Seal of England, bearing date the third day of June in the second year of our reign wee have constituted and appointed you to be our Captain Generall and Governor in Chief in and over all that part of our territory and dominion of New England in America known by the names of our Colony of the Massachusetts Bay, our Colony of New Plymouth, our Provinces of New Hampshire and Main and the Narraganset Country or King's Province. And whereas since that time Wee have thought it necessary for our service and for the better protection and security of our subjects in those parts to join and annex to our said Government the neighboring Colonies of Road Island and Connecticutt, our Province of New York and East and West Jersey, with the territories thereunto belonging, as wee do hereby join annex and unite the same to our said government and dominion of New England. Wee therefore reposing especiall trust and confidence in the prudence courage and loyalty of you the said Sir Edmund Andros, out of our especiall grace certain knowledge and meer motion, have thought fit to constitute and appoint as wee do by these presents constitute and appoint you the said Sir Edmund Andros to be our Captain Generall and Governor in Cheif in and over our Colonies of the Massachusetts Bay and New Plymouth, our Provinces of New Hampshire and Main, the Narraganset country or King's Province, our Colonys of Road Island and Connecticutt, our Province of New York and East and West Jersey, and of that tract of land circuit continent precincts and limits in America lying and being in breadth from forty degrees of Northern latitude from the Equinoctiall Line to the River of St. Croix Eastward, and from thence directly Northward to the river of Canada, and in length and longitude by all the breadth aforesaid and throughout the main land from the Atlantick or Western Sea or Ocean on the East part, to the South Sea on the West part, with all the Islands, Seas, Rivers, waters, rights, members, and appurtenances, thereunto belonging (our province of Pensilvania and country of Delaware only excepted), to be called and known as formerly by the name and title of our territory and dominion of New England in America. . . .

And Wee do hereby give and grant unto you full power and authority to suspend any member of our Councill from sitting voting and assisting therein, as you shall find just cause for so doing. . . .

And Wee do hereby give and grant unto you full power and authority, by and with the advise and consent of our said Councill or the major part of them, to make constitute and ordain lawes statutes and ordinances for the public peace welfare and good government of our said territory and dominion and of the people and inhabitants thereof, and such others as shall resort thereto, and for the benefit of us, our heires and successors. Which said lawes statutes and ordinances, are to be, as near as conveniently may be, aggreeable to the lawes and statutes of this our kingdom of England: Provided that all such lawes statutes and ordinances of what nature or duration soever, be within three months, or sooner, after the making of the same, transmitted unto Us, under our Seal of New England, for our allowance or disapprobation of them, as also duplicates thereof by the next conveyance.

And Wee do by these presents give and grant unto you full power and authority by and with the advise and consent of our said Councill, or the major part of them, to impose assess and raise and levy rates and taxes as you shall find necessary for the support of the government within our territory and dominion of New England, to be collected and leveyed and to be imployed to the uses aforesaid in such manner as to you and our said Councill or the major part of them shall seem most equall and reasonable.

And for the better supporting the charge of the government of our said Territory and Dominion, our will and pleasure is and wee do by these presents authorize and impower you the said Sir Admund Andros and our Councill, to continue such taxes and impositions as are now laid and imposed upon the Inhabitants thereof; and to levy and distribute or cause the same to be levyed and distributed to those ends in the best and most equall manner, untill you shall by and with the advise and consent of our Councill agree on and settle such other taxes as shall be sufficient for the support of our government there, which are to be applied to that use and no other. . . .

And Wee do further hereby give and grant unto you full power and authority with the advise and consent of our said Councill to erect constitute and establish such and so many Courts of Judicature and public Justice within our said Territory and Dominion as you and they shall think fitt and necessary for the determining of all causes as well Criminall as Civill according to law and equity, and for awarding of execution thereupon, with all reasonable and necessary powers authorities fees and privileges belonging unto them.

And Wee do hereby give and grant unto you full power and authority to constitute and appoint Judges and in cases requisite Commissioners of Oyer and Terminer, Justices of the Peace, Sheriffs, and all other necessary Officers and Ministers within our said Territory, for the better administration of Justice and putting the lawes in execution, and to administer such oath and oaths as are usually given for the due execution and performance of offices and places and for the cleering of truth in judiciall causes. . . .

And Wee do hereby give and graunt unto you full power where you shall see cause and shall judge any offender or offenders in capitall and criminall matters, or for any fines or forfeitures due unto us, fit objects of our mercy, to pardon such offenders and to remit such fines and forfeitures, treason and wilfull murder only excepted, in which case you shall likewise have power upon extraordinary occasions to grant reprieves to the offenders therein untill and to the intent our pleasure may be further known.

And Wee do hereby give and grant unto you the said Sir Edmund Andros by your self your Captains and Commanders, by you to be authorized, full power and authority to levy arme muster command or employ, all persons whatsoever residing within our said Territory and Dominion of New England, and, as occasion shall serve, them to transferr from one place to another for the resisting and withstanding all enemies pyrats and rebells, both at land and sea, and to transferr such forces to any of our Plantations in America or the Territories thereunto belonging, as occasion shall require for the defence of the same against the invasion or attempt of any of our enemies, and then, if occasion shall require to pursue and prosecute in or out of the limits of our said Territories and Plantations or any of them, And if it shall so please God, them to vanquish; and, being taken, according to the law of arms to put to death or keep and preserve alive, at your discretion. And also to execute martiall law in time of invasion insurrection or warr, and during the continuance of the same, and upon soldiers in pay, and to do and execute all and every other thing which to a Captain Generall doth or ought of right to belong, as fully and amply as any our Captain Generall doth or hath usually don. . . .

And Wee do hereby give and grant unto you the said Sir Edmund Andros full power and authority to erect one or more Court or Courts Admirall within our said Territory and Dominion, for the hearing and determining of all marine and other causes and matters proper therein to be heard and determined, with all reasonable and necessary powers, authorities fees and priviledges.

8. The Uncertainty of Land Tenure

A. SAMUEL SEWALL'S DIFFICULTIES, 1687-88

1. The Dominion Questions Sewall's Title to Hogg Island

[*Diary of Samuel Sewall* (Mass. Hist. Soc., Collections, 5th Ser., 5[1878]), I, 172, 176, 181, 195, 212, 219, 220]

April 8. [1687] I goe to Hog-Iland with Cous. Savage, to view the place.

May 2. I go to Hog-Iland. Mr. Moodey, Oakes, Capt. Townsend and Seth Perry in one Column; Capt. Hill, Mr Parson and Mr. Addington in the other, witness my taking Livery and seised of the Iland by Turf and Twigg and the House.

July 1, 1687. Went to Hog-Iland; . . . As went, saw a Surveyor with two redcoats, and another measuring and surveying Noddles-Iland.

Tuesday, Nov. 15th. Began to lay

down the Wharf at Hog-Iland, went thether with Mr. Newgate.

Wednesday, May 2. [1688] Went to Hog-Island with Mr. Newgate, where by appointment we meet with Cousin Savage trying to adjust the difference between them as [to] said Newgate's claim of Marsh.

Thursday, July 12. Mr. Jno. Hubbard tells me there is a Writt out against me for Hog-Island, and against several other persons for Land, as being violent intruders into the Kings Possession.

Satterday, July 14. Jeremiah Belcher comes and brings me the Information Mr Sherlock left with him on Thorsday last in the Afternoon, when he served on him a Writt of Intrusion.

2. Sewall's Petition to Governor Andros

[Diary of Samuel Sewall, I, 220-21]

To Sir Edmund Andros Knight, Capt. General and Governour in Chief of His Majesties Territory and Dominion of New-England in America, the humble Petition of Samuel Sewall of Boston, Sheweth.

That whereas your Petitioner stands seized and possessed of a certain Island or Islands, commonly called and known by the name of Hogg-Island, lying scituat near Boston aforesaid, in the present tenure and occupation of one Jer. Belcher, having been peacably and quietly possessed by your Petitioner and his Predecessors for the space of fourty years or upwards by past: And whereas the said Belcher hath been lately served with a Writt of Intrusion at His Majesties Suit, And your Petitioner not being willing to stand Suit, but being desirous of His Majesties Confirmation for the said Island or Islands:

He therefore humbly prays your Excellencies favour that he may obtain His Majesties Grant and Confirmation of the said Hogg-Island, with the members and Appurtenances thereof, unto your Petitioner his Heirs and Assigns forever under the Seal of this His Majesties Territory. To be holden of His Majesty, His Heirs and Successors, upon such moderat Quit-Rent as your Excellency shall please to order.

And your Petitioner shall ever pray.

SAM. SEWALL

3. Sewall Complains to Increase Mather in London

[Boston, New Engl. July 24, 1688, Diary of Samuel Sewall, I, 231-32]

Reverend Sir,—I writt to London of the 16th inst. by Belcher, giving an account of the serving of several Writts of Intrusion, on Colonel Shrimpton for Dear-Island, on Mr. Lynde of Charlestown, for land of his there; and on Mr. Russell of the same place, for land of his near old Abraham's. Mr. Lynde quickly made his peace with Mr. James Graham, the Attorney-General. Mr. Russell followed not long after, prevaild with by Mr. Stoughton's advice. I was urged by my friends two contrary wayes; but at last have this day petitioned for a Patent for Hogg-Island. Mr. Dudley, Stoughton and several principal men having taken Patents, and intend to doe it; some of which were formerly most averse. I had resolved once to have come to you by Bilbao, in Mr. Curtis, by whom I send this, but when it came to, my friends would by no means part with me, my wife being very near her time. Twere good if you could come to know whether persons are thus to be compelled to take Patents. The Judges did as good as tell us we should be cast; and Appeal-ing to England does not hinder the Ex-ecution going forth. The generality of People are very averse from complying with any thing that may alter the Tenure of their Lands, and look upon me very sorrowfully that I have given way. . . .

I am, Sir, Your obliged friend and servant.

SAM. SEWALL.

B. EDWARD RANDOLPH TRIES TO GRAB LAND IN CAMBRIDGE, 1688

1. The Council Cooperates

["Att a Councill held . . . in Boston . . . the 29th of febr. 1687 [1688]," Toppan and Good-rick, eds., Randolph Letters, IV, 207]

His Excellency Sir Edm. Andros, Knight, etc.; Joseph Dudley, Jno. Win-throp, Wayte Winthrop, John Usher, John Green, Edward Randolph, Fra. Nicholson, Samuel Shrimpton, Esqrs.

Upon reading this day in Councill the Petition of Edward Randolph Esqr. pray-ing his Majesties grant of a certain tract of vacant and unappropiated land con-tayneing about seaven hundred acres lying between Spy Pond and Sanders Brook neere Watertown in the County of Middlesex, Ordered That the Sheriff of said County doe forthwith after re-turne hereof give public notice both in Cambridge and Watertown that if any person or persons have any clayme or pretence to the said land they appeare before his Excellency the Governour in Councill on Wednesday the seaventh of March next, then and there to shew forth the same, and why the said land may not be granted to the Petitioner as desired, of which he is not to faile and to make due return.

By order in Councill etc.

2. The Inhabitants of Cambridge Petition the Council

[Toppan and Goodrick, eds., Randolph Letters, IV, 211-13]

To his Excellency Sir Edmond Andros Knight Captain Generall and Governour in Cheife of his Majesties Territory and Dominion of New England and his Maj-esties Councill

The Petition and Address of his Maj-esties most Loyall Subjects, the In-habitants of Cambridge

In most humble wise sheweth:

In observance of the Councill's order sent unto us refferring unto those lands petitioned for by Edward Randolph, Esqr. wee humbly informe and certifie your Excellency and the Council that they are neither vacant nor unappro-priated Lands and are a part of those Lands granted by his Majesties Royall Charter under the Great Seale of Eng-land to the persons therein mentioned and by the Government and Company of the Massachusetts Bay to the Towne of Cambridge as the Records of the Gen-erall Court will shew and have been quietly possessed and improved by this Towne of Cambridge for more than fifty yeares. And was also purchased of the Indian Natives that claimed title thereto. And more perticularly as to those men-tioned by the Petitioner Scittuate and lying between Spy Pond and Sanders Brooke they were by allotment granted and measured and more than Forty yeares now past to sundry of the In-habitants of this Towne, and they have accordingly peaceably possessed and improved the same and are att this day Lawfully seized thereof. And for that other part Lying near to Water Towne

Lyne the Towne hath hitherto improved those Lands in common for Timber Fire wood and Pasture for all sorts of Cattle, the just interest of each person therein haveing been Legally settled more than forty yeares and the proprietors have accordingly respectively bought and sold their interests as they have seen meete. And for the secureing said Lands from Damage to ourselves by our neighbours of Watertowne the proprietors of said Lands have att their great Charge Erected a stone wall more than one mile in Length and made Provision of gates upon the high wayes as was needfull.

Wee doe also humbly Informe your Excellency and Councill that the Lands above Petitioned for are of soe great concernment to the Inhabitants of this Towne for their necessary Supplies of Timber fire wood and Pasture, that should wee bee Deprived thereof it would be the Inevitable Ruine of more than Eighty Familyes of his Majesties Subjects here settled who have spent their Strength and Estates in Confidence of their Indubitable right and peaceable injoyment thereof by virtue of his Majesties Royall Charter and to them Legally derived in manner as is above recited.

Wee Doe therefore Render to your Excellency and honourable Council our humble and thankfull acknowledgement of your respect to our Welfare (as well as to Justice and Equity) in giveing us this opportunity to Informe your Excellency and honours of our claime and just title to those Lands Petitioned for as above said and doe humbly pray that the Royall authority wherewith his Majesty have invested your Excellency for the Government of this part of his Dominion may putt a check upon your said Information and unreasonable request of the Petitioner for said Lands. And that your Petitioners may not be thence Illegally Ejected or Disturbed in their peaceable Enjoyment thereof, Contrary to his Late Majesties Declaration of the 26 July 1683 published upon the Issuing a Quo Warranto against the Late Charter of this Colony and to his present Majesties Gracious Declaration to all his Loveing Subjects for Liberty of Conscience and maintaining them in all their properties and possessions in any their Lands and propertyes whatsoever, the benefitt whereof wee humbly claime.

Your Petitioners are his Majesties most Loyall and your Excellencyes humble Servants and Supplyants in the name and by the order of the Inhabitants of Cambridge.

JOHN COOPER, WALTER HASTING, FRANCIS MOORE, JOHN JACKSON, SAMUELL ANDREW

9. Grievances Against the Governor, 1687-89

[A Narrative of the Proceedings of Sir Edmond Androsse and his Complices, Who Acted by an Illegal and Arbitrary Commission from the Late K[ing] James, during his Government in New England, by several Gentlemen who were of his Council (1691), in W. H. Whitmore, ed., The Andros Tracts (Prince Society, Publications, 5-7 [1868-74]), I, 135-47]

TO THE
READER.

————

The Particulars mentioned in the ensuing Narrative, are but a small part of the Grievances justly complained of by the People in New England, during their three years Oppression under Sir E.A. For a more full Account, the Reader is referred to the Justification of the Revolution in New England, where every particular exhibited against Sir Ed. and his Complices, by the Agents lately sent to *England,* is by the *Affidavits* of honest men confirmed. If some men find themselves thereby exposed to the just Resentments and Indignation of all true Christians, or true English-men, they must thank themselves for publishing such untrue Accounts as that which goes under the name of Captain *John Palmers,* and that scandalous Pamphlet called *N.E.'s Faction discovered,* supposed to be written by an Implacable Enemy of all good men, and a person that for Impudence and Lying has few Equals in the World. This which follows, being signed by several Gentlemen of great Integrity, who likewise had a particular knowledge of the things by them related, is therefore of unquestionable Credit. The Design in making of it thus publick, is to vindicate Their Majesties Loyal Subjects in *New-England,* and to give a true Representation of things unto those who have by false Relations been imposed on.

B. N. E. *Feb.* 4, 1691.

Having Received from Mr. *Addington* by order of the *Council and Representatives of the Massachusetts Colony* a signification of their desire; That whereas we were Members of the Late Council in the time of Sir *Edmund Androsses Government,* we would give some Information of the *Grievances and Maleadministrations* under the same. Upon consideration had thereof, and in answer thereto, we cannot but own and declare, that *not only ourselves and many others in the same station* (not now present to joyn with us) were of a long time much *dissatisfied* and *discouraged with very many of the Proceedings and Administrations in the said Government;* and had little reason to wonder that so great a number of the People were so too. It might well have been expected that the Governour (not so successful heretofore) notwithstanding the extraordinariness (to say no more) of many Clauses and Powers in his Commission; yea the rather and the more, because thereof would have cautioned and moderated the Execution of the same: But to our Great Trouble we found it very much otherwise. Many were the things that were accounted Irregular and Grievous therein, far from conducing to the Publick Weal of the Territory, and not a little to the disservice of the Crown, as tending rather to the disturbing and disaffecting of the Subjects here, than to the furtherance of that chearful Obedience, Loyalty, Love and Duty in them, which ought by all good means, to have been nourished and promoted. And of all this unhappiness, we must reckon the first step and in-let to be, that *the Governour did* so quickly neglect the great number of the Council, and *Chiefly adhere unto and Govern by the advice* only of a few others, the principal *of them Strangers to the Countrey, without Estates or Interest therein to oblige them, persons of known and declared Prejudices against us, and that had plainly laid their chiefest Designs and Hopes to make unreasonable profit of this poor People.* Innumerable were the evil Effects that from hence were continually growing up amongst us; *The Debates in Council were not so free as ought to have been,* but too much over-ruled, and a great deal of harshness continually expressed against Persons and Opinions that did not please. *The Greatest Rigour and Severity was too often used towards the soberest sort of People,* when any thing could be found or pretended against them, their humble submissions were little regarded, and *inexorable Persecutions ordered against them,* whilst in the mean time *the notorious viciousness and profaneness of others met not with the like discountenance,* but persons of such a character were put into places of business and trust. The long settled maintenance of the Publick Ministry, even from those that applied themselves to no other way of Worship, but continued ordinary hearers, could not be upheld by any act of Authority providing for the same, and Schools of Learning so well taken care of formerly, were in most cases fallen to decay, and many more such like might be reckoned up. But we shall more especially instance further in the particulars following, as not the least.

1. *And first;* It was as we thought a great slight put upon the Council, and to the prejudice of the good People of the Territory, That whereas at the Governours first coming a Committee appointed thereunto by himself, and a full Council had with great care and several weeks trouble revised a very considerable number of Orders and Laws collected out of the several Law-Books of these Colonies found by long experience very needful and agreeable to the good of these Plantations, which Laws so Collected and Revised, were again presented unto, and upon further advisement approved by the Governour and Council and passed. Yet upon the introducing Mr. *West* from *New-York* to be Deputy Secretary, they were, for what causes we know not, totally laid aside, and the People denied the benefit of them. And this Grievance was so much the greater, and a plainer Indication of the severity of some men in their Intended Management of things, because of good deliberation they had also passed an Order of Council, That until the Council should take further order, the several Justices, Town-Officers, and others should proceed according to former Usages, and such Local Laws in the several parts of this Dominion, as are not repugnant to the Laws of *England,* etc. Yet because by virtue of the said Order some in Authority have proceeded to put forth their power for the support of the Ministry, and some others did justifie themselves in some actions done by them that were not pleasing; hereupon when a discourse only, and some debate thereof had passed in Council, but *without any regular determination made,* and contrary to the express word of the said Order, *it was Entred in the Council-Book* concerning it, resolved that the same was only in Force till the next Session of the Council, and so determined as null of it self, and that none presume to act pursuant to such Laws as are or shall be made here.

2. *Whereas* the Act for the Continuing and Establishing of several Rates, Duties and Imposts, was one of the first of so great Moment that came out in Form under the Seal of the Territory, and was publickly proclaimed, we that were present have great cause to remember what trouble and dissatisfaction there was among Members of the Council concerning the same. As that Act was framed and urged upon us, *a very considerable number (and we believe we were the Major part) dissented* from and argued much against it. And tho the Governor expressed not a little heat and positiveness alledging his instructions, and held the Council together, unreasonably a very long time about it. Yet when we did at last break up we could not imagine that he could take the Bill to be agreed to; *Nevertheless it was the next day (to our wonderment) brought in fairly Engrossed in Parchment, and quickly Signed by the Governour without any counting of Voices* either then or the day before, which was the more needful because some did continue still to make their objections, others that had spoken against the Bill the day before, declaring their adherence to what they had then said; and many more under so great discouragement and discountenance, as was manifested sitting silent, which we are sure in the regular passing of Laws can never be reckoned for a consent.

3. *The Way* and Manner used afterwards of proposing and passing all Laws was very uncertain and unequal, not answerable to the Nature of so great a Power, nor to the largeness of the Territory that was to be obliged by them,

or to the Number of the Concellors appointed therein; for after a little while there were no set times appointed or given notice of for the making of Laws, that so the Members of the Council might attend in a fuller number to be helpful therein. Bills of the greatest concernment were usually first consulted and framed in private, and so unexpectedly brought into Council at any time, and then our work too was often under great disadvantages, not to advise freely and consult about the making of a Law thought necessary, but to maintain a Contest in opposition to a very inconvenient one, too far promoted and engaged in already; and above all, *there was never any fair way of taking and counting the number of the Councellors consenting and dissenting,* that so the Majority might be known in any matter that admitted of any considerable reasonings and debates, by reason whereof both Laws and other Orders and Resolutions might be set down as passed by the Council, which ought not to have been. And when it hath been (as often it was) expresly and earnestly prayed when matters of greater moment than ordinary were in hand, that the Debate and Resolution of them might be put off till a fuller Council of Members from other several parts of the Dominion might be Convened such motions were ever disaccepted, and entertained with no little displacency; *so that it might be too truly affirmed, that in effect four or five persons, and those not so favourably inclined and disposed as were to be wished for, bear the Rule over, and gave Law to a Territory the largest and most considerable of any belonging to the Dominion of the Crown.*

4. *In Pursuance* of this way and manner of passing Laws above expressed, there were two in special that came forth, which we are sure in fuller and freer Councils would have had a full stop put to them; *viz. First,* The Act for Regulating the Choice of select Men,

etc. wherein the Liberty of Towns to meet for the management of their Publick Affairs referring to their Common Lands, and all other their concernments, which they had enjoyed for so many years, to their great benefit, was most unreasonably restrained to once a year, and all other Convening of inhabitants as a Town Meeting, upon any pretence or colour whatsoever, was strictly forbidden: And the other Act was that intituled, An Act requiring all Masters of Ships or Vessels to give security, in which there were such restraints laid upon all persons from Transporting themselves freely (as their occasion might call) out of the Territory, That it would have been a meer Prison to all that should be found therein, and such Bond required of all Ships and Vessels (extending in the practice even to Shallops and Wood-Boats) as would quickly have intolerably discouraged, if not ruined the Trade thereof; and all without any other ordinary general benefit of the said Act, but the filling some mens Pockets with Fees: And (as it might be thought from the time of moving this Act, which was when Captain *Hutchinson* was already gone, and and Mr. *Mather was known to be intending for* England) *the obstructing of such mens going home as were likely there to make just Complaints, and seek Redress of Publick Grievances;* and when this act had been strenuously opposed in council here at *Boston,* where it was more than once vehemently urged, and as often denied, *it was carried as far as* New York, *and there an opportunity found for the obtaining of it.*

5. *The* great matter of Properties and Titles to our Lands is the next to be insisted on, His Majesty that granted the Charter did fully invest the Patentees with Right to the Soil throughout the whole Limits thereof, and here on the place, the Right of the Natives was honestly purchased from them. The Dis-

posal, Distribution, and Granting of Lands by the Patentees, who were also incorporated, and made a Body Politick, was in such a plain, ready, easie way, without any charge to the Planters, as in the Settlement of so large a Countrey was thought to be most agreeable: And so much of a publick spirit and design were those Noble Gentlemen, that (though well they might) they settled not one single Penny of service or acknowledgment to themselves and Heirs of any of their Grants, a thing so self-denying and worthy, that few Instances can be given of the like. All which notwithstanding, and the Possessions, Descents and Valuable Purchases of so many years that have passed since, *the Governour and those he adhered to, resolved and practised to make all mens Titles in effect quite null and void.* The purchasing of the Natives Right, was made nothing of, and next to a Ridicule. The Enjoyment and Improvement of Lands not inclosed, and especially if lying in common amongst many was denied to be possession; it was not enough that some men that thought it convenient, and were both willing and able, did take Confirmations of their Lands, the numbers of whom in time might have been a considerable gain to them; but *nothing would satisfie unless all in general might be compelled so to do; hence those that refused were declared Intruders upon His Majesty, and put in fear of having their Lands granted unto strangers.* Many were Solicited, and Encouraged to Petition for other mens Lands, and had a shameful Example set them by some of the chief Contrivers of all this Mischief. *When some men have Petitioned for a confirmation of their own Lands, a part of these only was offered to be granted to them, and another part denied.* Nor could any mans own Land be confirmed to him, without a particular Survey of every part and parcel of them first made, the great charges whereof, and of other Fees to be taken would have been to

most men Insupportable: *Yea it hath by some been computed that all the money in the Country would not suffice to patent the Lands therein contained.*

And yet further, a considerable quit-rent to the King was to be Imposed upon all Lands, though already a constant yearly Tax for the support of the Government had been laid on them.

And for all this most unreasonable vexation to a Laborious and Industrious people, the only Ground pretended was some defects and wants of form and due manner alledged to be in the way of the disposing and conveying of all Lands from the Patentees to the Townships and People here; which whatever it amounted to might have been easily remedied, either by an application and representation to the King for the obtaining a General settlement of all properties (which would have been highly Worthy and Generous for the Governour to have engaged in, on behalf of the People) or by some other ways that were proposed. But nothing but the way of particular Patenting as abovesaid could prevail. In prosecution whereof all Actions intended upon Informations of Intrusions in His Majesties behalf, or between old Proprietors and new Grantees must have had their Decision at the Ordinary Courts of Common Law here upon the Place where matters of Equity and of a Consideration Transcending all ordinary Cases could not have a proper Cognizance and due Influence in the Decision, Determination and Judgment.

6. *Though* sufficient Courts of Justice were appointed, and held in the several Counties for the Tryal of all Offenders, yet it *was too frequent upon more particular displeasure to fetch up persons from very remote Counties before the Governour and Council at Boston* (who were the highest, and a constant Court of Record and Judicature) not to receive their tryal but only to be examined there, and so remitted to an Inferior Court to be farther proceeded against.

The Grievance of which Court was exceeding great, for hereby not only the Charge was made Excessive upon such persons by the *notorious exactions of the Messenger,* the Secretaries Fees for Examination, *etc.* But these Examinations themselves were unreasonably strict, and rigorous and very unduely ensnaring to plain unexperienced men. *And* the Tryals of several, were by this means over-ruled to be at *Boston,* and not in the proper Counties, and were otherwise so far prejudged as to be rendered less equal.

The Extraordinary Oppressive Fees taken in all matters by indigent and exacting Officers, these were at the first for a long time arbitrarily imposed and required without any colour of an Establishment of them by the Council. Afterwards a Committee was appointed, to bring in a Table of Fees, that spent a long time without finishing any thing, the reason whereof was because some therein *especially the Deputy Secretary West,* insisted upon Fees much more extraordinary than some others could consent to. In conclusion; There was a Table of Fees drawn up to be presented to the Council, and signed by some of the Committee, one of whom, (whose Subscription is to this Paper) declaring expresly, that by his Signing he did no otherwise agree, but only that it might be presented to the Council, to do therein as they should see cause, who also when it was so presented to the Council, declared that many of the particulars in that Table contained, were unreasonable, and ought to be abated, and of this mind were many others. But the Entry after the usual manner was an approbation thereof.

Lastly. As to those *Great Jealousies and Suspicions of Sinister Designs in the Governour as to our Troubles by the Indians,* we have to say, That although divers things too uncertain, if not untrue have been too easily reported and spread concerning him, a practice which some of us have formerly with no little prejudice to ourselves discountenanced and borne Testimony against; yet *there have not wanted some other particulars that might give too great a ground for the same.* The principal of them (as far as we have any knowledge of things of that kind,) are these.

The Governours *Seizing and Taking away the Goods of Monsieur St.* Castine *of* Penopscot, the Summer before the War broke forth, which thing hath been esteemed not a little to have stirred up and furthered the succeeding Troubles. The Governours not hastening his Return to *Boston* when these Troubles were actually begun, but lengthening out his Tarrience in places so remote till the Hostility of the *Indians,* and the great Mischiefs thereof were too far advanced. That during his absence he was not pleased sufficiently to impower and instruct any to act things necessary for the safety of the out Plantations and the Prosecution and Suppression of the Enemy, tho' he had speedy and true Accounts from time to time sent him of all that happened. That all that was done to this purpose in a case of such necessity, either by the Lieutenant Governour, or by the Justices of the Peace, and Military Officers in many places, by securing and disarming of Neighbouring *Indians,* setting up Warding and Watching, Garrisoning several houses for the security of the Inhabitants, especially the Women and Children, in case of sudden Inroads and surprizings that might be, sending some relief of men to some places that were most in danger, and also what was done by those Members of the Council that were at *Boston,* in conjunction with the Commander in chief left in the Fort there, who raised and sent some Forces to *Casco-Bay,* where greatest harms were done. We say, that all that was thus done, was so extreamly disapproved of by the Governour upon his Return back from *Albany* and *New-York,* and an unaccountable displeasure manifested against all persons that had so acted, and that he was ready to call them to an account as high Offenders for the same, and refused a long time, tho' much solicited, to give any Order concerning the Souldiers sent to *Casco*, either for the continuance of them there, where they were very necessary, or for their dimission home. Unto all which may be added the Governours sending Messengers both *John Smith* the Quaker from *Albany*, and soon after Major *Macgregory* to *Keybeck* upon such Errands and Business as were not communicated and laid open to the Council. And further, *his Release and setting at liberty sundry* Indians *that were in hold, some of them known Enemies to the* English, and particularly objected against by several of the Council, and that without any exchange of our *English* Captives then in the Enemies hands.

These are the chief Matters which upon this occasion (without any undue Prejudice against any man, or design to justifie the defects of ourselves in the performance of our own shares of duty, but in answer to the desire signified to us as above) we have to set forth, professing truly that by such a state of things as we had the experience and feeling of, The Places that we held were rendred exceeding uneasie to us, and that out of a sincere respect to the Prosperity of these Their Majesties Plantations, we could not but be very desirous that through the Favour of God and our Superiors, all due Redress might in a good happy season be obtained; and the way of Governing *English* Subjects in Their Majesties Dominions without an Assembly of the Peoples Representatives banished out of a World for ever.

Boston in *New-England,*
  Jan. 27. 1690.

WILLIAM STOUGHTON,
THOMAS HINCKLEY,
WAIT WINTHROP,
BARTHOL. GEDNEY,
SAMUEL SHRIMPTON.

CHAPTER TWO

THE PATTERN OF REBELLION

THURSDAY morning, April 18, 1689, about eight o'clock, the sun well up, rebellion broke out in the narrow streets of Boston. By sundown that day the Governor, most of the high government officials, and the fort in Boston were in insurgent hands. The next day the two remaining points of resistance—a man-of-war in the harbor and the fort on Castle Island—were taken by the rebellious colonists.

All winter of 1688-89 New England had been in a turmoil about the rumored invasion of England by William of Orange. Up and down the Atlantic coast men waited anxiously for news of the outcome. But news, especially reliable news, was slow in coming. Boston could always count on being at least six weeks behind in news, more often three or four months. So it was that rumors flourished and tension mounted. Most of the population of Massachusetts was already convinced that Andros' government was an illegal tyranny. The excitement among many elements of colonial society rose to a pitch of hysteria while the people waited to hear the outcome of the fighting in England. By and large the leadership of Boston was quiet and self-disciplined. But all classes were afraid that Andros and his adherents would side with James II in any fight and might even turn the colony over to French Canada.

Andros had under his command two companies of redcoats. He could count on the frigate *Rose* under the command of the irascible Captain John George. Andros could also count on the active support of a handful of officeholders like Randolph who had come from England and a smaller handful of colonists who had from the start allied themselves with him.

During the early winter months of 1689 Indians, spurred on by the French to the north of them, began to attack outlying settlements in Maine. Andros sent most of his British regulars to man the frontier forts, and soon went himself at the head of a large force of Massachusetts farmers who had been drafted into service. The reactions of the discontented colonists to Andros' Indian policy were illogical, but none the less important. Andros was fiercely criticized for taking an army of settlers out on a bitter winter campaign. Although his military measures were eminently successful, he treated friendly Indians gently. Everywhere in the English colonies frontiersmen were likely to think that a good Indian was a dead Indian; they were indiscriminately brutal to all and often killed real or potential allies. Hence, even though Andros' actions against the enemy were effective, he was reviled for protecting loyal Indians and suspected of plotting to turn the colony over to the French. When he forbade Boston merchants to sell arms and ammunition to Indians, he won the merchants' enmity as well.

All these aspects of the Indian troubles contributed much to the crisis in March and early April. The threat on the frontier, the absence of regular troops from Boston, Andros' leniency toward friendly Indians, drafting Massachusetts boys into a winter campaign, the general atmosphere of armed men and fighting all increased immeasurably the readiness of many to seize arms themselves.

That a crisis was near at hand was apparent to all. The surviving record is very scanty about the immediate preparation for revolt. Samuel Mather, writing years later, said that the Puritan leaders—political, church, and merchant leaders—were frightened that some sort of rioting would break out. They themselves were decided on a policy of patience. But if the mob should get out of hand, they would try to step in, seize control, and justify the riots on behalf of William and Parliament (No. 10).

We know even less of the thoughts of the Governor and his aides. There were several small mutinies on Captain George's frigate *Rose*. At the end of March Andros smelled trouble and, leaving his troops on the Maine frontier, hurried back to Boston. At the water's edge below the fort was a small battery pointing out over the harbor. And riding out there was His Majesty's frigate, *Rose*.

Apparently a carpenter from the frigate, one Robert Small, a long-time troublemaker, put the spark of rebellion to the anxious town. Thursday morning a gang of armed men led by Small seized Captain George in Boston's North End. Within a few minutes the quiet business of the rural port town was shattered by armed mobs gathering in the streets. A dozen of Andros' officials were seized. Drums beat out the militia, which seems to have formed up in companies at the Town House in the center of Boston, although the militia seems not to have been a part of the insurrection at first. A mob of several thousand surrounded Fort Hill and forced the pickets back into the fort itself (No. 11).

At this point, about noon, the leadership of Puritan Boston gathered as they had agreed in the Town House. They met upstairs in the Council Room, and it was there that they announced to the crowd a "Declaration" justifying the revolt as an act of loyalty to William and the overthrow of an illegal and unjust government. They would await instructions from England.

The Declaration is a strange, florid, self-righteous document (No. 12). It justifies the rebellion in very general terms. Many of its arguments are demonstrably inaccurate from what we know of the history of Andros' administration. It seems certain that on April 18 Boston did not know definitely that William had been successful and was already installed on the throne of England. Otherwise the Declaration would have been specific on that point.

In the afternoon of the 18th the resistance of Andros, who had taken refuge in the fort, began to wear away. He was hopelessly outnumbered by the armed mob outside and must have known much less of what was going on than the men in the Town House. In some way which is not at all clear, because the best accounts differ, Andros went down to the Town House peacefully, but was arrested as soon as he got there. The dozen or so soldiers left in the fort were persuaded to surrender. All their leaders were captured. The next day the frigate and the fort on Castle Island were similarly persuaded to surrender, and by nightfall of the 19th the insurrection was complete (No. 13). Boston lay once more in the hands of its Puritans, who shortly after drafted an account giving their views of the revolt (No. 14).

Insurrection Accomplished

10. Samuel Mather's Account of the Preliminary to Revolt, April 1689

[Whitmore, ed., *Andros Tracts*, III, 145]

It was in the Month of April [1689] when we had News by the Edges concerning a Descent made upon *England* by the Prince of *Orange* for the Rescue of the Nation from Slavery and Popery; Then a Strange Disposition entred in the Body of our People to assert our *Liberties* against the Arbetrary Rulers that were fleecing them. But it was much feared by the more sensible Gentlemen at *Boston,* that an unruly Company of Soldiers who had newly deserted the Service in which they had bin employed for the Eastern War, by the gathering of their Friends to them to protect them from the Governor, who, they tho't intended nothing but Ruine to them; would make a great Stir and produce a *bloody Revolution.*

And therefore the principal Gentlemen in *Boston* met with Mr. MATHER to consult what was best to be done; and they all agreed, if possible, that they would extinguish all Essays in our People to an Insurrection; but that if the Country People to the Northward by any violent Motions push'd on the Matter so far as to make a *Revolution* unavoidable, *Then* to prevent the Shedding of *Blood* by an ungoverned Multitude, some of the Gentlemen present would appear in the Head of what Action should be done; and a *Declaration* was prepared accordingly.

On April 18, the People were so driving and furious, that unheaded they began to seize our public Oppressors, upon which the Gentlemen aforesaid found it necessary to appear, that by their Authority among the People the unhappy Tumults might be a little regulated. . . . Twas then Mr Mather appeared, [and] he set himself both *publickly* and *privately* to hinder the Peoples proceeding any further than to reserve the Criminals for the Justice of the *English* Parliament.

11. Samuel Prince's Account, April 22, 1689

[Prince to Thomas Hinckley, Boston, Apr. 22, 1689, Charles M. Andrews, ed., *Narratives of the Insurrections* (New York, 1915), 186-90]

Honored Sir,

THE consideration of my sending you a blank, wherein only the declaration was enclosed, seems to deserve a check, and constrains me to an apology, not having, at that time, so much as liberty granted me by the messenger to write two or three lines, whereby you might have understood the present state of things, which by this time you are doubtless acquainted withal; but, lest it should prove otherwise, I have now taken the pains to give a brief account.

I knew not any thing of what was intended, till it was begun; yet being at the north end of the town, where I saw boys run along the street with clubs in their hands, encouraging one another to fight, I began to mistrust what was intended; and, hasting towards the town-dock, I soon saw men running for their arms: but, ere I got to the Red Lion, I was told that Captain George and the master of the frigate was seized, and secured in Mr. Colman's house at the North End; and, when I came to the town-dock, I understood that Boolifant and some others with him were laid hold of; and then immediately the drums began to beat, and the people hasting and running, some with and some for arms, Young Dudley and Colonel Lidgit with some difficulty attained to the Fort. And, as I am informed, the poor boy cried very much; whom the Governor sent immediately on an errand, to request the four ministers, Mr. Joylife, and one or two more, to come to him at the Fort, pretending that by them he might still the people, not thinking it safe for him at that time to come to them; and they returned him the like answer. Now, by this time, all the persons whom they concluded not to be for their side were seized and secured, except some few that had hid themselves; which afterwards were found, and dealt by as the rest. The Governor, with Palmer, Randolph, Lidgit, West, and one or two more, were in the Fort. All the companies were soon rallied together at the Town House, where assembled Captain Wintroup, Shrimpton, Page, and many other substantial men, to consult of matters; in which time the old Governor came among them, at whose appearance there was a great shout by the soldiers.

Soon after, the king's jack was set up at the Fort, and a pair of colors at Beacon Hill: which gave notice to some thousands of soldiers on Charlestown side that the controversy was now to be ended; and multitudes would have been there, but that there was no need. The frigate, upon the tidings of the news, put out all her flags and pennants, and opened all her ports, and with all speed made ready for fight, under the command of the lieutenant—swearing that he would die before she should be taken; although the captain sent to him, that if he shot one shoot, or did any hurt, they would kill him, whom they had already seized. But he, not regarding that, continued under those resolutions all that day. Now, about four of clock in the afternoon, orders were given to go and demand the Fort; which hour the soldiers thought long for: and, had it not been just at that nick, the Governor and all the crew had made their escape on board the frigate—a barge being sent for them. But the soldiers, being so near, got the barge. The army divided, and part came up on the back side of the Fort, and part went underneath the hill to the lower battery, or sconce, where the red-coats were; who, immediately upon their approach, retired up the Fort to their master, who rebuked them for not firing at our soldiers, and, as I am informed, beat some of them. One of them, being a Dutchman, said to him, "What the Devil should I fight against a tousand men?" and so ran into the house.

When the soldiers came to the battery, or sconce, they presently turned the great guns about, and mounted them against the Fort, which did much daunt all those within; and were so void of fear, that I presume, had they within the Fort been resolute to have lost their lives in fight, they might have killed an hundred of us at once—being so thick together before the mouths of their cannons at the Fort, all loaden with small shot: but God prevented it. Then they demanded a surrender; which was denied them till Mr. West and another should first go to the Council, and, after their return, we should have an answer whether to fight or no. And accordingly they did: and, upon their return, they came forth, and went disarmed to the Town House; and from thence, some to the close jail, and he under a guard in Mr. Usher's house. The next day, they sent the two colonels to demand of him a surrender of the Castle, which he resolved not to give: but they told him, if he would not give it presently under hand and seal, that he must expect to be delivered up to the rage of the people, who doubtless would put him to death; so leaving him. But he sent and told them that he would, and did so; and so they went down, and it was surrendered to them with cursing. So they brought them away, and made Captain Fairwether commander in it. Now, by this time that the men came back from the Castle, all the guns, both in ships and batteries, were brought to bear against the frigate—which were enough to have shattered her to pieces at once—resolving to have her. But as it is incident to corrupt nature to lay the blame of our evil deeds anywhere rather than on ourselves, so Captain George casts all the blame now upon that devil Randolph, for, had it not been for him, he had never troubled this good people. So, earnestly soliciting that he might not be constrained to surrender the ship —for, by so doing, both himself and all his men should lose their wages, which otherwise would be recovered in England—giving leave to go on board, and strike the topmasts, close up the ports, and bring the sails ashore; and so they did. The country people came armed into the town in the afternoon, in such rage and heat, that it made us all tremble to think what would follow: for nothing would pacify them but he must be bound in chains or cords, and put in a more secure place, and that they would see done ere they went away, or else they would tear down the house where he was to the ground. And so, to satisfy them, he was guarded by them to the Fort. And I fear whether or no the matter of settling things under a new Government may not prove far more difficult than the getting from under the power of the former, except the Lord eminently appear in calming and quieting the disturbed spirits of people, whose duty certainly now is to condescend, comply, and every way study for peace. So prays the assured well-willer to New England's happiness,

S. P.

Counsellor Clark writ a very grateful letter to Mr. Bullifant, intimating what a faithful friend he had been to said Bullifant, and withal desiring said Bullifant, that if there should news come out of England of a change, which he hoped in God it never would (as to Government), that said Bullifant would do him the favor as to send him word with expedition, that so he might make his escape, living so dangerously in the midst of his enemies, who were even ready to devour him; and the merchants have gotten this pamphlet, and resolve forthwith to print it.—Farewell!

The Justification

12. The Boston Declaration of Grievances, April 18, 1689

[Andrews, ed., *Narratives of the Insurrections*, 175-82]

I. We have seen more than a decad of Years rolled away since the English World had the Discovery of an horrid Popish Plot; wherein the bloody Devotoes of Rome had in their Design and Prospect no less than the Extinction of the Protestant Religion: which mighty Work they called the utter subduing of a Pestilent Heresy; wherein (they said) there never were such Hopes of Success since the Death of Queen Mary, as now in our Days. And we were of all Men the most insensible, if we should apprehend a Countrey so remarkable for the true Profession and pure Exercise of the Protestant Religion as New-England is, wholly unconcerned in the Infamous Plot. To crush and break a Country so entirely and signally made up of Reformed Churches, and at length to involve it in the miseries of an utter Extirpation, must needs carry even a Supererogation of Merit with it among such as were intoxicated with a Bigotry inspired into them by the great Scarlet Whore.

II. To get us within the reach of the Desolation desired for us, it was no improper thing that we should first have our Charter vacated, and the Hedge which kept us from the wild Beasts of the Field, effectually broken down. The Accomplishment of this was hastned by the unwearied Sollicitations and slanderous Accusations of a Man, for his Malice and Falshood well known unto us all. Our Charter was with a most injurious Pretence (and scarce that) of Law, condemned before it was possible for us to appear at Westminster in the legal Defence of it; and without a fair leave to answer for our selves, concerning the Crimes falsly laid to our Charge, we were put under a President and Council, without any liberty for an Assembly, which the other American Plantations have, by a Commission from his Majesty.

III. The Commission was as Illegal for the Form of it, as the Way of obtaining it was Malicious and Unreasonable: yet we made no Resistance thereunto as we could easily have done; but chose to give all Mankind a Demonstration of our being a People sufficiently dutiful and loyal to our King: and this with yet more Satisfaction, because we took Pains to make our selves believe as much as ever we could of the Whedle then offer'd unto us; That his Magesty's Desire was no other than the happy Encrease and Advance of these Provinces by their more immediate Dependance on the Crown of England. And we were convinced of it by the Course immediately taken to damp and spoyl our Trade; whereof Decayes and Complaints presently filled all the Country; while in the mean time neither the Honour nor the Treasure of the King was at all advanced by this new Model of our Affairs, but a considerable Charge added unto the Crown.

IV. In little more than half a Year we saw this Commission superseded by another yet more absolute and Arbitrary, with which Sir Edmond Andross arrived as our Governour: who besides his Power, with the Advice and Consent of his Council, to make Laws and raise Taxes as he pleased, had also Authority by himself to Muster and Imploy all Persons residing in the Territory as occasion shall serve; and to transfer such Forces to any English Plantation in America, as occasion shall require. And several Companies of Souldiers were now brought from Europe, to support what was to be imposed upon us, not without repeated Menaces that some hundreds more were intended for us.

V. The Government was no sooner in these Hands, but Care was taken to load Preferments principally upon such Men as were Strangers to and Haters of the People: and every ones Observation hath noted, what Qualifications recommended a Man to publick Offices and Employments, only here and there a good Man was used, where others could not easily be had; the Governour himself, with Assertions now and then falling from him, made us jealous that it would be thought for his Majesties Interest, if this People were removed and another succeeded in their room: And his far-fetch'd Instruments that were growing rich among us, would gravely inform us, that it was not for his Majesties Interest that we should thrive. But of all our Oppressors we were chiefly squeez'd by a Crew of abject Persons fetched from New York, to be the Tools of the Adversary, standing at our right Hand; by these were extraordinary and intollerable Fees extorted from every one upon all Occasions, without any Rules but those of their own insatiable Avarice and Beggary; and even the probate of a Will must now cost as many Pounds perhaps as it did Shillings heretofore; nor could a small Volume contain the other Illegalities done by these Horse-leeches in the two or three Years that they have been sucking of us; and what Laws they made it was as impossible for us to know, as dangerous for us to break; but we shall leave the Men of Ipswich or Plimouth (among others) to tell the Story of the Kindness which has been shown them upon this Account. Doubtless a Land so ruled as once New-England was, has not without many Fears and Sighs beheld the wicked walking on every Side, and the vilest Men exalted.

VI. It was now plainly affirmed, both by some in open Council, and by the same in private Converse, that the People in New-England were all Slaves, and the only difference between them and Slaves is their not being bought and sold; and it was a Maxim delivered in open Court unto us by one of the Council, that we must not think the Priviledges of English men would follow us to the End of the World: Accordingly we have been treated with multiplied Contradictions to Magna Charta, the Rights of which we laid claim unto. Persons who did but peaceably object against the raising of Taxes without an Assembly, have been for it fined, some twenty, some thirty, and others fifty Pounds. Packt and pickt Juries have been very common things among us, when, under a pretended Form of Law, the Trouble of some honest and worthy Men has been aimed at: but when some of this Gang have been brought upon the Stage, for the most detestable Enormities that ever the Sun beheld, all Men have with Admiration seen what Methods have been taken that they might not be treated according to their Crimes. Without a Verdict, yea, without a Jury sometimes have People been fined most unrighteously; and some not of the meanest Quality have been kept in long and close Imprisonment without any the least Information appearing against them, or an Habeas Corpus allowed unto them. In short, when our Oppressors have been a little out of Mony, 'twas but pretending some Offence to be enquired into, and the most innocent of Men were continually put into no small Expence to answer the Demands of the Officers, who must have Mony of them, or a Prison for them, tho none could accuse them of any Misdemeanour.

VII. To plunge the poor People every where into deeper Incapacities, there was one very comprehensive Abuse given to us; Multitudes of pious and sober Men through the Land scrupled the Mode of Swearing on the Book, desiring that they might Swear with an uplifted Hand, agreeable to the ancient Custom of the Colony: and though we think we can prove that the Common Law amongst us (as well as in some other places under the English Crown) not only indulges, but even commands and enjoins the Rite of lifting the Hand in Swearing; yet they that had this Doubt, were still put by from serving upon any Juries; and many of them were most unaccountably Fined and Imprisoned. Thus one Grievance is a Trojan Horse, in the Belly of which it is not easy to recount how many insufferable Vexations have been contained.

VIII. Because these Things could not make us miserable fast enough, there was a notable Discovery made of we know not what flaw in all our Titles to our Lands; and tho, besides our purchase of them from the Natives, and besides our actual peacable unquestioned Possession of them for near

threescore Years, and besides the Promise of K. Charles II. in his Proclamation sent over to us in the Year 1683, That no Man here shall receive any Prejudice in his Free-hold or Estate, We had the Grant of our Lands, under the Seal of the Council of Plimouth: which Grant was Renewed and Confirmed unto us by King Charles I. under the Great Seal of England; and the General Court which consisted of the Patentees and their Associates, had made particular Grants hereof to the several Towns (though 'twas now deny'd by the Governour, that there was any such Thing as a Town) among us; to all which Grants the General Court annexed for the further securing of them, A General Act, published under the Seal of the Colony, in the Year 1684. Yet we were every day told, That no Man was owner of a Foot of Land in all the Colony. Accordingly, Writs of Intrusion began every where to be served on People, that after all their Sweat and their Cost upon their formerly purchased Lands, thought themselves Freeholders of what they had. And the Governor caused the Lands pertaining to these and those particular Men, to be measured out for his Creatures to take possession of; and the Right Owners, for pulling up the Stakes, have passed through Molestations enough to tire all the Patience in the World. They are more than a few, that were by Terrors driven to take Patents for their Lands at excessive rates, to save them from the next that might petition for them: and we fear that the forcing of the People at the Eastward hereunto, gave too much Rise to the late unhappy Invasion made by the Indians on them. Blanck Patents were got ready for the rest of us, to be sold at a Price, that all the Mony and Moveables in the Territory could scarce have paid. And several Towns in the Country had their Commons begg'd by Persons (even by some of the Council themselves) who have been privately encouraged thereunto, by those that sought for Occasions to impoverish a Land already Peeled, Meeted out and Trodden down.

IX. All the Council were not ingaged in these ill Actions, but those of them which were true Lovers of their Country were seldom admitted to, and seldomer consulted at the Debates which produced these unrighteous Things: Care was taken to keep them under Disadvantages; and the Governor, with five or six more, did what they would. We bore all these, and many more such Things, without making any attempt for any Relief; only Mr. Mather, purely of respect unto the Good of his Afflicted Country, undertook a Voyage into England; which when these Men suspected him to be preparing for, they used all manner of Craft and Rage, not only to interrupt his Voyage, but to ruin his Person too. God having through many Difficulties given him to arrive at Whitehall, the King, more than once or twice, promised him a certain Magna Charta for a speedy Redress of many Things which we were groaning under: and in the mean time said, That our Governor should be written unto, to forbear the Measures that he was upon. However, after this, we were injured in those very Things which were complained of; and besides what Wrong hath been done in our Civil Concerns, we suppose the Ministers and the Churches every where have seen our Sacred Concerns apace going after them: How they have been Discountenanced, has had a room in the Reflection of every Man, that is not a Stranger in our Israel.

X. And yet that our Calamity might not be terminated here, we are again Briar'd in the Perplexities of another Indian War; how, or why, is a mystery too deep for us to unfold. And tho' 'tis judged that our Indian Enemies are not above 100 in Number, yet an Army of One thousand English hath been raised for the Conquering of them; which Army of our poor Friends and Brethren now under Popish Commanders (for in the Army as well as in the Council, Papists are in Commission) has been under such a Conduct, that not one Indian hath been kill'd, but more English are supposed to have died through sickness and hardship, than we have Adversaries there alive; and the whole War hath been so managed, that we cannot but suspect in it a Branch of the Plot to bring us low; which we leave to be further enquir'd into in due time.

XI. We did nothing against these Proceedings, but only cry to our God; they have caused the cry of the Poor to come unto him, and he hears the cry of the Afflicted. We have been quiet hitherto, and so still we should have been, had not the Great God at this time laid us under a double engagement to do something for our Security: besides what we have in the strangely unanimous Inclination which our Countrymen by extreamest necessities are driven unto. For first, we are informed that the rest of the English America is alarmed with just and great Fears, that they may be attaqu'd by the French, who have lately ('tis said) already treated many of the English with worse then Turkish Cruelties; and while we are in equal Danger of being surprised by them, it is high time we should be better guarded, than we are like to be while the Government remains in the hands by which it hath been held of late. Moreover, we have understood, (though the Governour has taken all imaginable care to keep us all ignorant thereof) that the Almighty God hath been pleased to prosper the noble Undertaking of the Prince of Orange, to preserve the three Kingdoms from the horrible brinks of Popery and Slavery, and to bring to a condign Punishment those worst of Men, by whom English Liberties have been destroy'd; in compliance with which glorious Action we ought surely to follow the Patterns which the Nobility, Gentry and Commonalty in several parts of those Kingdoms have set before us, though they therein chiefly proposed to prevent what we already endure.

XII. We do therefore seize upon the Persons of those few ill Men which have been (next to our Sins) the grand Authors of our Miseries; resolving to secure them, for what Justice, Orders from his Highness with the English Parliament shall direct, lest, ere we are aware, we find (what we may fear, being on all sides in Danger) our selves to be by them given away to a Forreign Power, before such Orders can reach unto us; for which Orders we now humbly wait. In the mean time firmly believeing, that we have endeavoured nothing but what meer Duty to God and our Country calls for at our Hands: We commit our Enterprise unto the Blessing of Him, who hears the cry of the Oppressed, and advise all our Neighbours, for whom we have thus ventured our selves, to joyn with us in Prayers and all just Actions, for the Defence of the Land.

At the Town-House in Boston, April 18, 1689.

Sir,

Our Selves and many others the Inhabitants of this Town, and the Places adjacent, being surprized with the Peoples sudden taking of Arms; in the first motion whereof we were wholly ignorant, being driven by the present Accident, are necessitated to acquaint your Excellency, that for the quieting and securing of the People inhabiting in this Country from the imminent Dangers they many ways lie open and exposed to, and tendring your own Safety, We judge it necessary you forthwith surrender and deliver up the Government and Fortification, to be preserved and disposed according to Order and Direction from the Crown of England, which suddenly is expected may arrive; promising all security from violence to your Self or any of your Gentlemen or Souldiers in Person and Estate: Otherwise we are assured they will endeavour the taking of the Fortification by Storm, if any Opposition be made.

To Sir Edmond Andross Knight

WAITE WINTHROP.

SIMON BRADSTREET.

WILLIAM STOUGHTON.

SAMUEL SHRIMPTON.

BARTHOLOMEW GIDNEY.

WILLIAM BROWN.

THOMAS DANFORTH.

JOHN RICHARD.

ELISHA COOK.

ISAAC ADDINGTON.

JOHN NELSON.

ADAM WINTHROP.

PETER SERGEANT.

JOHN FOSTER.

DAVID WATERHOUSE.

13. Nathanael Byfield's Account of the Insurrection, April 29, 1689

[Nathanael Byfield, *An Account of the Late Revolution in New England* . . . (London, 1689), Andrews, ed., *Narratives of the Insurrections,* 170-75]

Gentlemen,

HERE being an opportunity of sending for London, by a Vessel that loaded at Long-Island, and for want of a Wind put in here; and not knowing that there will be the like from this Country suddenly, I am willing to give you some brief Account of the most remarkable Things that have hapned here within this Fortnight last past; concluding that till about that time, you will have received *per* Carter, a full Account of the management of Affairs here. Upon the Eighteenth Instant, about Eight of the Clock in the Morning, in Boston, it was reported at the South end of the Town, That at the North end they were all in Arms; and the like Report was at the

North end respecting the South end: Whereupon Captain John George was immediately seized, and about Nine of the Clock the Drums beat thorough the Town; and an Ensign was set up upon the Beacon. Then Mr. Bradstreet, Mr. Dantforth, Major Richards, Dr. Cooke, and Mr. Addington, etc. were brought to the Council-house by a Company of Soldiers under the Command of Captain Hill. The mean while the People in Arms did take up and put into Goal Justice Bullivant, Justice Foxcroft, Mr. Randolf, Sheriff Sherlock, Captain Ravenscroft, Captain White, Farewel, Broadbent, Crafford, Larkin, Smith, and many more, as also Mercey the then Goalkeeper, and put Scates the Bricklayer in his place. About Noon, in the Gallery at the Council-house, was read the Declaration here inclosed. Then a Message was sent to the Fort to Sir Edmund Andross, by Mr. Oliver and Mr. Eyres, signed by the Gentlemen then in the Council-Chamber, (which is here also inclosed); to inform him how unsafe he was like to be if he did not deliver up himself, and Fort and Government forthwith, which he was loath to do. By this time, being about two of the Clock (the Lecture being put by) the Town was generally in Arms, and so many of the Countrey came in, that there was twenty Companies in Boston, besides a great many that appeared at Charles Town that could not get over (some say fifteen hundred). There then came Information to the Soldiers, That a Boat was come from the Frigat that made towards the Fort, which made them haste thither, and come to the Sconce soon after the Boat got thither; and 'tis said that Governor Andross, and about half a score Gentlemen, were coming down out of the Fort; but the Boat being seized, wherein were small Arms, Hand-Granadoes, and a quantity of Match, the Governour and the rest went in again; whereupon Mr. John Nelson, who was at the head of the Soldiers, did demand the Fort and the Governor, who was loath to submit to them; but at length did come down, and was, with the Gentlemen that were with him, conveyed to the Council-house, where Mr. Bradstreet and the rest of the Gentlemen waited to receive him; to whom Mr. Stoughton first spake, telling him, He might thank himself for the present Disaster that had befallen him, etc. He was then confined for that Night to Mr. John Usher's House under strong Guards, and the next Day conveyed to the Fort, (where he yet remains, and with him Lieutenant Collonel Ledget) which is under the command of Mr. John Nelson; and at the Castle, which is under the Command of Mr. John Fairweather, is Mr. West, Mr. Graham, Mr. Palmer, and Captain Tryfroye. At that time Mr. Dudley was out upon the Circuit, and was holding a Court at Southold on Long-Island. And on the 21st Instant he arrived at Newport, where he heard the News. The next Day Letters came to him, advising him not to come home; he thereupon went over privately to Major Smith's at Naraganzett, and Advice is this Day come hither, that yesterday about a dozen young Men, most of their own Heads, went thither to demand him; and are gone with him down to Boston. We have also Advice, that on Fryday last towards Evening, Sir Edmond Andross did attempt to make an Escape in Woman's Apparel, and pass'd two Guards, and was stopped at the third, being discovered by his Shoes, not having changed them. We are here ready to blame you sometimes, that we have not to this Day received advice concerning the great Changes in England, and in particular how it is like to fair with us here; who do hope and believe that all these Things will work for our Good; and that you will not be wanting to promote the Good of a Country that stands in such need as New England does at this Day. The first Day of May, according to former Usage, is the Election Day at Road Island; and many do say they intend their Choice there then. I have not farther to trouble you with at present, but recommending you, and all our Affairs with you, to the Direction and Blessing of our most Gracious God, I remain

Gentlemen,
Your Most Humble
Servant at Command,
NATHANAEL BYFIELD

Bristol, April 29, 1689.

Through the Goodness of God, there hath been no Blood shed. Nath. Clark is in Plymouth Gaol, and John Smith in Gaol here, all waiting for News from England.

14. The Puritan Leaders Justify Their Actions, June 6, 1689

["An Account of the Late Revolutions in New England by A.B.," in Whitmore, ed., *Andros Tracts*, II, 191-202]

Sir,

Among the many matters of *Discourse* and *Wonder* at this day abroad in the World, the state of *New-England* cannot but be *One;* and of that, if I would not forfeit the Character which you allow me of your *Friend,* I must now give you some account. Since the *Illegal* Subversion of our Ancient Government, this *Great,* but *poor* people have been in the Hands of *men skilful to destroy,* and all our Concerns both Civil and Sacred, have suffered by the Arbitrary Oppressions of *Unreasonable Men.* I believe, no part of the *English America,* so powerful and united as *New-England* was, could have endured half so many Abuses as we have bin harrassed withal, with a tenth part of our *Patience;* but our *Conscience* was that which gave metal to our *Patience,* and kept us Quiet; for though our foul-mouth'd Enemies have treated us a *Rebellious,* because we are a *Religious* people, they may be pleased now to understand, That if we had not been *Religious,* we had long since been what they would, if they durst, have called *Rebellious.* The very *Form* of Government imposed upon us, was among *the worst of Treasons,* even a Treasonable Invasion of the Rights which the whole *English* Nation lays claim unto; every true *English-man* must justifie our Dissatisfaction at it,

and believe that we have not so much *Resisted the Ordinance of God,* as we have Resisted an intollerable Violation of His *Ordinance.*

But Sir, be pleased now to reflect upon our Declaration, and consider whether the Administration of this Government was not as Vexatious, as the *Constitution* of it was Illegal. Consider whether the whole Government was not become a *meer Engine,* a sort of *Machin* contriv'd only to enrich a crew of Abject Strangers, upon the Ruines of a miserable people. And yet, I am to tell you, That *scarce one half is told you.* The *Declaration* was composed so much in the Hurry of Action that it comprehends not all our *Grievances;* However, you may guess from the *Clawes* there pourtray'd, what sort of Creatures were devouring of us.

Sir, I own, that we *Argue simply* about the Affairs of Government; but we *Feel True.* I have sometimes challenged any man to mention so much as *One Thing* done by our Late Superiors for the welfare of the Country; a thousand things we all *Felt* every day doing for the Ruine of it; and as 'tis said, once when they had Divine Service among them, he that read it, being to read that Epistle, where, according to their Translation 'tis said, *Be Harbarous one to another:* By an unhappy mistake read it

Be Barbarous one to another: So we thought we *Felt* their continual Actings upon that mistaken Rule. However I confess (and I know not whether you will count it our *Honour* or our *Blemish*) we should have born the Grievances without any Attempts for our own Relief, but our own Supplications to the Great God; for our Applications to the Late King, our only remaining Remedy on earth, we had found ineffectual. But there happened one Provocation to our people more, which had more than an hundred in it, and such was their *Infirmity*, if you will call it so, that this they could not bear. A small Body of our *Eastern* Indians had begun a *War* upon us: the *Occasion of* which was as doubtful to us all at first, as the whole *Management* of it was afterwards mysterious. A Party of Indians which were affirm'd to belong unto that crew of Murderers were seiz'd by the *English;* but Governour *Andros* with many favours to them, ordered them to be set at Liberty again: and it's affirmed *Those* very men have done great part of the mischief sustained by us. An Army of near a *Thousand English* (and the flower of our Youth) was raised for the subduing of our Enemies, which I believe were much fewer than an *Hundred Indians.* This Army goes through the tedious Fatigues of a long and cold Winter, many scores of miles to the Northward; and underwent such Hardships that very many of our poor Souldiers perished on the Spot; and it is justly fear'd, That not a few more of them have got their bane, that they will never be strong men again: but not one Indian killed all the while: only Garrisons were here and there planted in the wild woods on a pretence, *To keep the Indians from Fishing;* which project of *Hedging in the Cuckow's,* our dull *New-Englanders* could not understand. It was further admirable to us, that though the Governour had been importun'd to take a much more *expedient,* and far less *Expensive* way of subduing our In-dian Enemies, he was thereto wholly unperswadeable. In the mean time the Country was wonderfully surprised, with Evidences coming in, from Indians and others, in several parts, which very Strangely concurred in their Testimonies, *That there was a Plot to bring in the Indians upon us;* and it was easy unto us to conceive, How *serviceable* another *Indian* War might have been to the Designs which we saw working for us. These Evidences were so far from being duly enquired into, that the *English-men,*—who had been inquisitive after them, were put unto all manner of trouble, and must have been destroyed if a Turn had not happend,—thought nothing in the World was more natural than the Agreement between such a *Plot* and the whole conduct of our *Eastern Affairs;* nor is there any contradiction in it in one of *Randolph's* Letters to *Blaithwait* which says *Nothing has been wanting in his Excellency to bring all things to a good posture; but this people are Rivetted in their Way, and I fear nothing but Necessity or Force will otherwise dispose them.* While these things were going on, by way of the *West-Indies* there arrived unto us a few small Intimations, That the Prince of *Orange* had prospered in his Noble Undertaking to rescue the *English* Nation from imminent POPERY and SLAVERY. But Sir *Edmond Adross* took all imaginable care to keep us ignorant of the News, which yet he himself could not be unacquainted with; and one that brought the Princes *Declaration* with him, was imprisoned for bringing Seditious and Treasonable Papers into the Country with him; and our Oppressors went on without *Fear* or *Wit,* in all the methods that could inflame the people to the highest exasperation. The Reports continually coming in from our *Eastern Army* now caused the Relations of those that were there perishing, here a little to bestir themselves; and they could not forbear forming themselves here and there in the Country unto some

Body, that they might consider what should be done for their poor Children, whom they thought bound for a bloody Sacrifice. While this was doing, the people of *Boston* were Alarmed with Suspicions buzz'd about the *Town,* by some belonging to the Ship, That the *Rose Frigat* now in our Harbour was intended to carry off our Late *Governour* for France, and to take any of our *English* Vessels that might be coming in unto us; and we apprehended our selves in the mean time very ill provided, if an Attacque from any of the *French* Fleet in the *West Indies* were perfidiously made upon us. 'T is impossible to express the Agonies which filled the minds of both Town and Country; but the consideration of the extream Ferment which we were boiling in, caused several very deserving Gentlemen in *Boston,* about the middle of *April,* to enter into a Consultation, how they might best serve the Distressed Land in its present Discomposures. They considered the *Directions* given in the Princes *Declarations* (of which at last we had stolen a sight) and the *Examples* which the whole Kingdom of *England* (as far we could learn) had set before us. They also considered, that the Governour being mov'd to call a General Council in this extraordinary juncture, instead of this, he never so much as called his Council here at hand to communicate unto them any part of the *Intelligence relating* to the Late Affairs in *England.* They likewise considered, That though they were above all things inclinable *to stay a little,* hoping that every day might bring some Orders from *England* for our safety, yet they could not undertake for such a Temper in all their provoked Neighbours. Wherefore they Resolved, That if either the outragious madness of our Foes, or the impatient motion of our Friends, did necessitate any Action, they would put themselves in the Head of it, and endeavour to prevent what ill effects an *Unform'd Tumult* might produce.

By that time the Eighteenth of *April* had given a few Hours of Light unto us, things were push'd on to such extremities that *Bostons* part in Action seem'd loudly enough and hastily called for. Accordingly, the Captain of the Frigat being then on Shoar, it was determined that he must be made incapable either to *Obstruct,* or to *Revenge* the Action, by *Firing* on, or *Sailing* from the Town; him therefore, they immediately seized. There were not very many acquainted with the measures that were to be taken; but the Action was now begun, and the Rumour of it running like Lightning through the Town, all sorts of people were presently inspired with the most unanimous Resolution, I believe, that was ever seen. *Drums* were beaten, and the whole Town was immediately up in *Arms.*

The first work done, was by small parties here and there about the *Town* to seize upon these unworthy Men who by repeated Extortions and Abuses had made themselves the objects of *Universal Hatred* and Indignation. *These* were many of them secured and confined; but the principal of them, at the *First Noise* of the Action, fled into the Garrison on *Fort-Hill,* where the *Governours* Lodgings were; a place *very* Commodiously *Scituated* to Command the whole Town, but not sufficiently *Fortify'd.*

The Army had no sooner got well together, but a Declaration was Read unto them, unto which they gave an Assent by a very considerable Shout. And upon this, the Gentlemen with such as had come in to their Assistance in the *Townhouse,* apprehending the Resolutions of the people, drew up a short Letter to Sir *Edmond Andross,* and dispatched away a couple of their Number with it; the whole armed Body attend them unto the *Fortification,* whither they Marched with all the Alacrity in the world, and yet with so composed a *Sobriety,* that I question whether *America* has ever seen what might equal it. It was expected, That the *Garrison* might make some Resistance: but they intended to be Owners of it within one-half hour, or perish in the Attempt. When they were just come to beset the Fort, they met the Governour and his Creatures, going down the Hill to the Man-of-Wars *Pinace*, which was come to fetch them off; had they not come thither just at that Neck of time, our Adversaries would have got down to the Castle, which is a League below the Town; and in spite of us all, the Frigat would have gone unto them: but our *Houses* on shore and our *Vessels* at Sea, must have paid all the satisfaction they could have demanded of us. However, now at the sight of our Forces, the Gentlemen ran back into their Hold; whither the two Gentlemen our Messengers, now advancing, were presented at by the Red-coat Centinels; our Souldiers warned them on pain of-Death, to forbear firing; upon which they fled into the Fort, and (as 'tis affirmed) had very terrible Reprimands, *for not firing on them*. The Gentlemen being admitted, Sir *Edmond Andross* read what was written to him, and now better understanding his own circumstances, there was a safe conduct given to him, and he with his Associates were brought into the Chamber where he had formerly himself been hatching the Things that now procur'd his more humble Appearance there. *He* was treated with all the Respect that could be due unto his Character; but he was confined for that Night unto the House of the Late Treasurer, with Guards upon him; and the *Rest* had their several confinements alotted unto them in such places as were most agreeable to their Quality. With much ado, the Governour gave Order for the surrender of the Fort; and the ceremonies of the surrender were performed by Secretary *Randolph*, the very man whose lyes and clamours and malicious unwearied Applications had the greatest influence in the overthrow of our former Government.

All the Country round about now began to flock in, and by the next day some Thousands of Horse and Foot were come in from the Towns Adjacent, to express the unanimous content they took in the *Action*, and offer their utmost Assistance in what yet remained for the compleating of it. The obtaining of the Castle was the main thing that yet called for our cares; but after some stomachful Reluctances the Late Governour gave Order also for the surrender of *That*, and himself was by the people removed unto the Fort to be kept as a Prisoner there. Thus was the Action managed; and through the singular Providence of God, not one mans Life was lost in the whole Undertaking: There was no *Bloodshed*, nor so much as any *Plunder* committed in all the *Action;* and setting aside the intemperate Speeches of some inconsiderable men (if there were any such) the people generally gave a Demonstration, That they designed nothing but the securing of some great Malefactors, for the Justice which a course of Law would expose them to, and they were loath to treate them with any incivility beyond the bare keeping of them in sufficient custody. No man underwent any Confinement, but such as the people counted the Enemies of the *Prince* of *Orange,* and of our *English Liberties;* it was not any passion for the Service of the *Church of England,* that exposed any man to hardship; no, even some of that Communion did appear in their Arms to assist the enterprize; tho' the Worship of the Church of *England* had the disadvantage with us, that most of our Late Oppressors were the great and sole Pillars of it there. The principal Delinquents being now in durance, and the Frigat secured for the Crown of *England,* our main difficulty was yet behind: Namely what Form we should put our selves into, that the Peace might be kept among us.

A great part of the *Country* was for an immediate Reassumption of our old Government, conceiving that the vacating of our *Charter* was a most illegal and injurious thing, and that tho' *a Form of Law* had cast us out of it, yet we might now return to it at least as a *Vacuum Domicilium*. Others were of the Opinion, That since Judgment was entred against our *Charter*, and we did not know what Consequence a *wrong step* at this time might have, therefore 'twas best for the Affairs of the Country to continue in the Hands of a *Committee for the Conservation of the Peace*, till the daily expected Directions from *England* should arrive unto us. The latter Expedient was condescended unto, but the Sword yet continued in every man's hands, and for divers weeks the Colony continued without any pretence to *Civil Government;* yet thro' the mercy of God, all things were under such good Inclinations among us, that every man gave himself the Laws of good Neighbourhood, and little or nothing extravagant was all that while done, besides the seizure of a few more persons who had made themselves obnoxious to the Displeasure of the People. The Gentlemen of the Committee laid their Country under great Obligations by their Studies for *the Conservation of our Peace*, and it mostly consisted of such as were ever worthy of our esteem. It was made up of them whose Hap 'twas to be in the Head of the late Action; but there were added unto them the most of our old Magistrates, who had not so far concerned themselves in the Affair. Our former Governour, the Honourable *Simon Bradstreet*, Esq; was Chosen by them for their President: Who tho' he be well towards Ninety Years of Age, has his *Intellectual Force hardly abated*, but retains a vigour and Wisdom that would recommend a younger man to the Government of a greater Colony.

But when the Day which our ancient *Charter* appoints for our Anniversary *Election* drew near, our people grew more and more set upon a Return to the *Basis* on which our *Charter* formerly had placed us; and of those who were thus disposed, some were for an *Election* on the proper Day; others judged that could not be so honestly attended, because a whole County in the *Colony* was too far to have a *Vote* in it, and they therefore were for a Re-assumption the Day following. These *Two* Opinions, with a *Third* which was for the continuing of their *Committee* just as it was, filled the Country; and very potent Numbers espoused each of these three opinions: only we all agreed in joyful expectations of having our *Charter* restored unto us. This Variety of Apprehension was the occasion of much needless Discourse and of many Heart burnings that might as well have been spared. But the Towns on the Eighth and Ninth of May sent in their Representatives at the Desire of the *Committee* to adjust the matters that concerned a further Necessary Settlement; and after many Debates and some Delays they came to this Temper: That our Ancient *Magistrates* should apply themselves unto the *Conservation of our Peace*, and exercise what acts of *Government* the Emergencies might make needful for us, and thus wait for further Directions from the Authority of *England*.

The Country being put into this posture, all things tended unto a good settlement both of *Minds* and *Things;* which were again too much disturbed by a Fire, too justly fear'd to be maliciously kindled (by some that made themselves parties to our Late Enemies) in the N ********** whereby *Four Houses* were consumed, but perhaps more than **** Thousand *Spirits* inflamed into an Heat that was hardly Governable. But our people being in a good measure again composed, the World mov'd on in its old orderly pace, until the last week in May when two Ships arrived unto us from *England* with more perfect *News* than we had yet been owners of; the first effect thereof was, our Proclaiming of King *William* and Queen *Mary*, with such a Joy, Splendour, Appearance and Unanimity, as had never before been seen in these Territories. The other Colonies are now settling on their old Foundations; and *We,* according to the Advice now brought us, hasten to put our selves into such a condition as may best answer the performance of our Allegiance to their Majesties.

SIR,

This Relation of our State will doubtless give New-England *an interest in the Prayers of all Good Men to whom you* *shall Communicate it: And Yours I hope will not be wanting for the Wellfare of*

Sir,

Your Servant

A.B.

Boston, June 6.
    1689

The foregoing Account being very carefully and critically Examined, by divers very Worthy and Faithful Gentlemen, was advised to be Published for the preventing of *False Reports:* And is to be Sold at the *London-Coffee-House.*

CHAPTER THREE

THE CONSEQUENCES OF REBELLION

R EVOLUTION in Boston was almost absurdly easy. What to do next, however, was not at all clear. First, a Council of Safety was created from twenty-two prominent settlers, mostly from Boston and many of them merchants. This executive body strove to quiet and disperse the mobs which lingered on for many months and which seem to have presented a constant threat to the authority of the self-appointed government. The Council of Safety summoned representatives from the towns to decide on some form of interim government until directions came from England. And finally it set up machinery to prepare indictments against Andros and his colleagues. In all their actions the council members were eagerly hopeful that the revolt should win the approval of the new government in England.

Many of the settlers, particularly the well-to-do, wished that the Council of Safety would remain in control until Parliament or the new King should authorize a new colonial government. Most people believed that the old Massachusetts charter would be restored, however, and when the representatives from the towns had assembled, it was apparent that the large majority favored an immediate resumption of the old government without waiting for approval from London. By the end of May 1689 this was done. The Governor and Assistants of 1685 were called back to office, although many of them were more than a little reluctant to resume their functions without higher authority.

Meanwhile, the work of preparing indictments against those who had participated in Andros' government went ahead quickly. Each township was asked to draw up papers of grievances (No. 15). These were collected at the county level and forwarded to a central office in Boston, where the mass of material was sorted and analyzed by a Committee of Seven; in addition to depositions against Andros' colleagues, the extensive papers of Edward Randolph were seized and carefully analyzed for incriminating evidence (No. 16).

It was much easier to collect these accusations than it was to re-establish stable government. Most of the troops sent out to the Maine frontier by Andros deserted and came home. The frontier was left undefended and the results there were disastrous. Many frontier communities were evacuated altogether, and such prosperous and economically important centers as Exeter, New Hampshire, the heart of the lumber industry, were greatly reduced. In Massachusetts itself men refused to recognize the revolutionary government or the authority of its courts, and the Naval Officer appointed by the interim government was powerless. The port of Boston experienced a flurry of activity as the Navigation Acts were ignored and both smugglers and pirates made it a headquarters (No. 17).

In an extravagant gesture of loyalty to England the government launched an attack on the French community at Port Royal on the Bay of Fundy. The expedition found support from merchants anticipating booty and churchmen eager to strike a blow against the Papists. But it was expensive. The Boston government levied thirty-two times the usual pre-1686 tax. Sheriffs ordered to collect the tax were rebuffed by many. Revenue from customs dropped. Massachusetts for the first time issued paper fiat money.

Beset on every side with distrust and lack of cooperation, almost every responsible group within the colony, whether favorable to the revolt or not, urgently wrote London to send directions for establishing legitimate government in New England.

Meanwhile, in London itself the consequences of the Glorious Revolution were being ironed out. Always dilatory in attending to colonial needs, London was even slower now. Not until 1691 was order made out of chaos. And then it was the same colonial bureaucracy which had been forming since 1660 that called the tune.

That bureaucracy was dominated by William Blathwayt, Secretary of War and Clerk to the Lords of Trade, and Sir Robert Southwell, a commissioner of the customs. Neither man took a favorable view of the revolutions in America (No. 18). They wanted as soon as possible to reestablish a stable colonial government which could be effectually controlled from London. Already England was at war with France on the continent. There was little interest in launching a campaign against the French in America too. The bureaucracy in London was struggling to maintain its own authority against decentralizing forces in England and did not want to return the colonial governments to the virtual independence which had existed in 1660.

Increase Mather, one of Boston's leading Puritan clergymen, had been in London since 1688 as an unofficial agent for Massachusetts, seeking the return of the old charter. After the revolt the colony sent three official agents to join him. They arrived together with Andros and several other men taken prisoner in April 1689. The agents, however, were unable to substantiate the indictments against these men, who were soon exonerated, and many of whom were returned again to colonial service by the Crown (No. 19). Mather almost succeeded in getting the old charter restored by slipping it in with a bill in Parliament to restore English borough charters. But the bill failed when Parliament was prorogued.

In the end, largely through Mather's efforts, a new charter was granted to Massachusetts in 1691 (No. 20). It was radically different from the old charter, however; there was to be a representative legislature, but the governor was to be appointed by the King. The franchise was in the future to be based on property rather than on church membership (No. 21). In many other details the new charter marked the end of the seventeenth-century, church-oriented community and the beginning of a more worldly, eighteenth-century colony. This charter of 1691 remained with slight alterations the basis of Massachusetts government until the critical years immediately before the revolution of 1775.

The Indictment of the Dominion of New England

15. The Grievances of the Township of Lynn, May 24, 1689

[Massachusetts Archives, XXXV, 183]

At Lynn the 24th May 1689

Upon a Signification from Captain Jonathan Coxwin of the Committee of the County of Essex to make Inquiry into the Grievances Suffered under the late Government, That it is expressed that this Towne or any Inhabitant therein that have been agrieved or burthened, Doe manifest the same under theire hand to the Committee aforesaid, or to Captain Jonathan Coxwin, to make knowne the same. Wee the Committee chosen by the Inhabitants of Lynn on the 20th of May 1689, to Consider of the signification abovesaid, and to drawe up what grievances and burthens we have sustained by the late

Government etc., Doe declare Viz: that this poore Towne of Lynn have sustained greate rong and Dammage by the late said Government. In that our orderly honest and Just Rights in a tract of Land within the bounds of Lynn, (called Nahants) that hath been Injoyed, Possessed, Built upon and Improved, by fencing, Planting and Pasturing etc. by the Township of Lynn well onward to sixty yeares, And yet by the Unjurious, unjust and Covetous Humors of some very ill minded persons, Upon Petitions preferred as Mr. Randolph first and Mary Dassin of Boston in the Second place, when Mr. Randolph could not make his Petition true and valid, Then he throweth in

Mary Dassin her Petition, for the same Lands and as unjustly founded as Mr. Randolphs. But on theire two Petitions and Vaine Pretences, We the poor people of Lynn have been by orders from the Governor and Councill Called, Summoned and ordered, to appeare at Boston and to shew and make good title to said Lands, before Sir Edmond Andros and his Councill at one sitting, and a second sitting, and soe a third, and a fourth, to our greate loss and expence of tyme and monyes, and no advantage nor benefitt to us because of delayes and Procrastinations to Scrue our monyes out of our hands and to make us pay with a vengeance for such writings as we must be constrained to take forth. And thus we have been greived and oppressed and put to loss Cost and Damage neere one Hundred Pounds and never the better, noo Justice done us. And at last put upon a threatned necessity of Pattening our own old injoyed properties and a denyall of our Rights in any of our Commons allwayes Injoyed, but now Called Kings Lands, and wee denyed to be any Towne, Thus we have been perplexed, vexed and oppressed and Impoverished, and except

the Lord had rought for us, whose name we bless and give thanks to, the worthy Gentlemen, his Instruments wee had been, the worst of bondmen. Furthermore by the late Government, we were debarred of our Constant liberty of Towne meetings, but once in a yeare whereby we could not meete to consult of defending our rights in the Premisses because it should be charged with riott, and also of keeping a watch for our Security from any dangers we had too just cause to feare which was our greate griefe and burthen.

signed OLIVER PURCHASE Cleric per order of or in the name of the Towne and Committee

and our abuses by the profane farmers of Excise. and our sons neighbours and servants Impressed and sent out in remote Winter Season.

And Constrained thereunto, and all Sufferings And we understand not upon what grounds.

Boston in New England. Jan. 24. 1689.

Sworn by MR. OLIVER PURCHASE. Before THOMAS DANFORTH. Deputy Governor.

16. The Committee of Seven's Charges against Dominion Officials, 1689

A. THE CHARGES AGAINST SIR EDMUND ANDROS, GOVERNOR

[Whitmore, ed., *Andros Tracts*, I, 150-51]

SIR EDMUND ANDROS, *Late Governour, matter against him by*

I.N.A.

1. Mr. John Wise minister, John Andrews senr., Robt. Kinsman, Wm. Goodhew Junr., Tho. French. These prove their damage for their being unwilling for Sir Edmund Andros rayseing mony on the people without the consent of the people, but Improved upon Contrary to Magna Carta.

6. Tho. Patch: about illegall and excessive charges, (in file G.)

9. Jos. Quilter: about excessive charges in proveing a will, (in file D.)

10. Samuel Howlet: about sending him to Prison without a mittimus and great charges.

13. Jos. Wood: about threatning to hang him, etc.

14. David Foulton: and Tho. Clark: about the Cruelty of Sir Edmunds officers to Souldiers Eastward.

15. John Dresser: about his great suffering in the Ipswich business.

17. John Hovie: about his suffering for he knew not what.

16. John Wood: about his suffering for being against paying Rates without an Assembly.

23. John Sibley about his fine before the Councel.

24. John Higgeson, minister and Capt. Step. Seawall about Sir Edmund Andros his affirming that all the lands in New England were the Kings and not the peoples, etc.

25. Wm. Bond, Esq: about an Indian said to have received a Ring from Sir Edmund Andros which Indian was a known enemie to the English, etc.

26. Thomas Brown and 5 more of Sudbury: about John James, Indians' saying of his owne voluntary minde that the Governour was a rogue and had hired the Indians to kill the English, and in particular had hired Wahawhy (the English bitter enemie) and had given him a Ring for his Commission, which Enemie Indian was afterwards Imprisoned by the English; and set at Liberty by Sir Edmund Andros and became a bitter enemie to the English, and was a Commander of a great partie that did fight against the English and kill some.

28. John Langford and Ben. Majery, sweare that severall French men on board a French man of warr Eastward said that there were 10 french men of warr come out of France to come to Boston in New England to take the Country in possession for the King of France and that Sir Edmund Andros had sent for them to that end etc.

29. Joshua Conant: to dito purpose etc.

30. Phillip Hilliard: to dito thing.

31. Tho. Atchinson: Ja. Cooke and Michaell Chapleman, about the Frenchs comeing here.

33. Sir Edmund Andros: his Arbitrary Commission.

32. Sam. Wright and 6 men more, about Sir Edmund Andros how he bid his Sergeant when they went upon the long march, to kill them Souldiers that were not able, or unwilling to tr[avel.]

[3]4. Sir Edmund Andros his etc: Act for Rayseing mony by Rate, duties, and Impost, on the [people?] without their Representatives Consent.

35. An Act for Masters of Ships not to carry off persons without a ticket, and about their often entring into bonds, etc.

37. Watanum and David (Two Indians) swear about Sir Edmund Andros that he gave the Mohocks two bushells of wompum Peague, and three cart loads of goods to Ingage them to fight against the English.

38. Edw. Randolphs letter to Povey informing that Sir Edmund doth all he cann to bring the people to quitt Rent.

41. Henry Kerly and Tho. How: about their being threatned to be hanged if etc. when they were keeping watch against the Indians, Soone after the Indians had killed 5 English.

42. Lenox Beverly his deposition against Sir Edmund Andros entertaineing four enemie Indians in the English Fourt two dayes and sending them away with powder and bullets, in the time of warr, and that when the Indians wanted it Extreamly.

The like in 109.

45. Nath. Saltonstal Esq: his oath about illegall proceedings against him without a cause.

47. Wm. Hutchins his oath about Sir Edmund Andros illegall proceedings and Intollerable fineing him and excessive charges.

48. Emmerson and Whitaker, their deposition about Sir Edmund Andros his Millitary officers unhumaine destroying of souldiers that were here Imprest.

51. His warrant in Councill to Confine Major Appleton to the common prison and that without any crime done by him, a most hellish way to undoe men.

52. Tho. French and John Harris, their letter about the Ipswich mens voating, against Sir Edmunds Rayseing mony contrary to the liberty of Free born English Subjects.

53. The Towne of Lynns Complaynt against Sir Edmund, etc.

7. Simon Stacy: about his being illegally dealt withall. (In file B.)

B. THE CHARGES AGAINST JOSEPH DUDLEY, MEMBER OF THE COUNCIL

[Whitmore, ed., *Andros Tracts*, I, 158-59]

73. Coppie of twelve of his owne Letters, which declare his Malitious Spirrit, and manifest his Treacherous minde against the Massachusetts Colloney, Chiefly to Augment his fortune and Avenge himselfe for being left out of the Majestry—did he not break his freemans oath.

76. The Selectmen and Constable of the Towne of Salisburys Complaint, wherein are notorious things mentioned to have been done against them.

78. Jos. Dudley hath his name sett to the Writt to bring the Revd. Charles Morton to a tryall out of the County he did and doth live in which is contrary to Law (in file H.)

79. Edward Randolph Esqr: in his letter to Mr. Blathwait Complayns of Mr. Dudley his encroachment on all and every side and that he hath so contrived the matter that Capt. George hath Received above £200 mony which belonged to him, and that the said Dudley as President with Capt. George carry all as they please to the great dissatisfaction of the Members of the Councill, and he sayes Sober men are abused by the false President.

85. The case of Charlestown men about his more then Ordinary unjustly as he was Chief Judge, Judgeing fineing and granting of executions against them, after such an illegall manner of proceeding countrary unto the Law of England, and the Law made here by the Governor and Councill whereof himselfe was one, and makeing a pack horse of the law as if it must attend him and George Farewell his child (the Attourney) as they pleased, for some when they falsly accused of a pretended Riotous matter they would bring no Inditement against them, and when they answered to their call in Court, time after time, they would say nothing to them, nor would not suffer them to Speak at another time, and called them from County to County, and would not suffer them to have a Jury, and above a yeare after, sent out Executions against them, altho before that they did not know so much that there was any Judgment of Court against them etc. (in file A.)

86. Esqr. Johnson and Fr. Kendall, about President Dudley and his Councill writeing a mittimus and Committing them to the Marshall, Because they would not Swear that the said President and Councill were a lawfull Government whereas their Commission was an Arbutrary Commission contrary to Magna Carta.

And being examined by said President Dudley, about the Act and adjournment of the Generall Court, and when he did see they would not Confess etc. then the said Dudley said that Act and ajournment would cost some men their lives etc.

88. James Lowdens Complaint for his unjust dealing with him, in binding him over without a cause, and in Court three times, and then saying nothing to him and after he as Cheif Judge brake up Court with Oh Yez. that all should depart untill further summoned, yet without any further summons, or hearing at all about a yeare after, ishsued out Execution against him, from another County for £5 fine, and £12: 18: 4: charges for prosecution, and so sent him to prison.

90. Sam. Weed and Jno. and Ben. Steephens testimony about John Weeds being fourced to [pay?] fees and charges for that he could not possibly doe.

C. The Charges Against Edward Randolph, Secretary and Registrar

[Whitmore, ed., *Andros Tracts*, I, 161]

1. John Wise Minister, John Andrews Senr: Robt. Kinsman, Wm. Goodhew Junr., and Tho. French Swears to their damage sustained from Edward Randolph, as one of their Judges, for their being unwilling that Sir Edmund Andros and his Councill should Rayse mony without the consent of the people (in file A.)

11. Wm. Howlet, as the last above (in file B.)

21. Caleb Boynton, about paying excessive charges in the Ipswich case (in file B.)

27. His letter, dated Aug: 23: 1686: against the Country to my Lord Treasurer, about rayseing great Revenues by Quitt Rents.   P. quintesence of Injustice to N. E.

40. His letter to the Lords of the Committee against this Country.

41. Henry Kerley and Tho. How, about their being threatned to be hanged if etc. when they were keeping watch against the Indians soon after the Indians had killed 5 English (in file A.)

43. His letter to the Arch Bishop of Canterbury against Governor Hinkley, Mr. Dudley and severall other Majestrates etc. and about takeing away the mony gathered in England for the Preaching of the Gospell among the Indians.

53. The Town of Lynns Complaint (in file A.)

77. The Proprietors of Nahant in Lynn, about his unjust molesting them about their Land which they had possessed 49 yeares,—and here by the way note, That none of the petitioners for other mens lands, never went to Settle a Town in the wild Wilderness unmade use of out of a Township, this would not have brought grist enough to Sir Edmund and his Creaturs Mills.

80. Mr. Wm. Blaithwaits letter of the 22d October 1687, to him saying, that there being but one thing wanting to sett all right at Boston, where he hath but one rock to avoyd which he ought to be awarr of, he means his letting them come within him, after which they will easily give him the Cornish hug [these words shews Mr. Blathwait to be Bostons under hand enemie] and that Edw. Randolph Esqr. was then Secretly carrying on an ill designe against New England.

100. Jarvis Ballard—about his unjustly takeing away his goods that was apprized at £113: 7: 0: and makeing him pay £140: to Redeem them.

110. His petitioning to Sir Edmund for Nahant Land in Lynn, he putt the People to great charge, and if he had gott it, it would have undone many.

Note that two of the old Pattentees were Interested in Common with the Lynn People in Nahant Lands viz. Major Humphreys and Mr. Johnson etc. (in file A.)

D. The Charges Against John West, Deputy Secretary

[Whitmore, ed., *Andros Tracts*, I, 163-64]

2. Neh. Jewet, his Excessive damage, for being unwilling, and against Rayseing mony by Arbitrary power (in file B) and that against Magna Carta.

4. Andrew Sergent, about illegall Fees for Probate of a will.

8. Caleb Kemball about excessive charges to Settle an Estate.

9. Jos. Quilter about excessive charges in the probate of a Will.

11. Wm. Howlett about excessive charges for being against Raysing money without the consent of the people (in file B).

12. John How about West saying, it would not be for the Kings Interest untill this Country were in another Peoples hands.

21. Caleb Boynton, about paying excessive charges in the Ipswich busines (in file B).

24. The Reverend John Higgeson, and Capt. Step. Seawall about Mr. West saying that all the lands in New England were the Kings and not the peoples etc. (in file A.)

27. In file C: Mr. West is called by Esqr. Randolph more Arbutrary then the Great Turk—the letter is Randolphs writeing tho' not Signed.

39. Edw. Randolph Esqr. letter to Mr. Povey dated January 24th: 1687 accuseing Mr. West for extorting what fees he pleases to the great oppressing of the people and that it Renders the present Government greivious.

45. Major Nath. Saltonstall his oath about takeing illegall fees of him (in file A).

46. Jno. and Christopher Osgood about

illegall fees (in file A).

60. Wm. Coleman about illegall proceedings against him (in file B).

70. Capt. Jos. Lynes about his telling him when he petitioned for a pattent for his whole Lands, that he must have so many pattents as there were Countyes that he had land in, if not townes (in file A).

71. Math. Salter about Judge Palmer and Mr. John West Deputy Secretary their Examining him how he came by his lands, he haveing told them all along down to the purchase of it from the native Indians, then they told him that such a title would not do but he must take a pattent for it, and if they would not, then they would Seize upon what he had, and burne his house, and carry him to Yorke, and Exchequor him for a Rebbell, he then told them he never heard nor read that any King or Prince would take away any Subjects lands, which had been passed forty or fifty yeares, and sell it or give it to any other person, then they called him many bad names, and threatned to cane him, and at the last fourced him to take a pattent for the which he was fourced to pay them two pounds tenn shillings in mony, that was hard to gett, (in file No. E.)

E. The Charges Against John Palmer, Judge

[Whitmore, ed., *Andros Tracts*, I, 165-66]

44. Ezekiell Woodward, his oath, about his illegall Judgment contrary to a verditt. (in file B.)

60. Wm. Coleman, about illegall proceedings against him. (in file B.) Judge Palmer was one of the Judges that gave Judgment against, and gave Deer Island to King James—notwithstanding King James gave Sir Edmund Andros no power in his Commission to medle with any land, but wast land.

And noat that Deer Island was not wast land, but Improved for a great

many yeares, about 40: to the use of a free Schoole.

67. Caleb Moodey about false Imprisonment and £40: damage.

68. Joseph Bailey about dito and £30: ——— damage.

70. Capt. Joseph Lynes, about his being fourced out of his own County by a writt about his land in the County where he lives, being contrary to the Law of England and the Law made here by Sir Edmund and his Councill (in file A.)

71. Matthew Salter about Judge John

Palmer and Mr. John West Deputy Secretary their examining him how he came by his lands, he haveing told them all along down to the purchase of it from the natives, they told him that such a title would not doe, but he must take a pattent for it, and if he would not they would Seize upon what he had, and burn his house, and carry him away to Yorke, and Exchequor him for a Rebbell, he then told them that he never heard nor read that any King or Prince would take away any Subjects lands, which had been possessed 40 or fifty yeares, and Sell it or give it to any other person, then he was called many bad names, and threatned to be caned, and at last fourced him to take a pattent, for the which he was fourced to pay them two pounds ten shillings in mony that was hard to gett.

79. Edw. Randolph Esqr. in his letter to Mr. Blathwait, complains of Palmer and West about their hostile takeing of wines from Penopscutt in Nova Scotia belonging to the french, and that he fears it will occation warr between them and the English (in file No. B.)

83. Judge Palmers Signing Excessive bills of Cost.

106. Edw. Randolph Esqr. in his letter to Mr. Povey dated January 21th 1688 gives an account of Mr. West and Palmer, how they had their Emisaries among the poore people at Pemiquid and Dartmouth, and had frighted them into takeing of leases produceing unto them, a Commission from Coll. Dongon, to dispose of all the Lands to who ever would take leases at 5s a hundred Acres quit Rent, and that they had past about 140 leases, and some had 800 and some 1000 acres and all paid £2: 10: 0: for passing their grants for 100 acres of wood land, and 20 acres of Meddow where ever it could be found, and that this bred a great mischeif among the people few or none haveing their land measured or marked, West and Palmer was in hast and gott what they could, and that the people had been very much oppressed by it.

And at this time Capt. Palmer and Mr. West laid out to themselves such large lotts, and Mr. Grayham altho' not there had a childs pourtion, he thinks some of them have 8 or 10000 acres but heares not of one penny rent comeing in to the King, and that 5s. a hundred acres was only a sham put upon the people.

And about Coll. Dongan and his agents West and Palmer, to teare all in peeces that was Setled and granted at Pemiquid by Sir Edmund Andros was not well, and that they placed and displaced at Pleasure, and that they were as Arbutrary as the great Turk.

And some of the first Setlers of the Eastern Country, they denied grants of their own lands, and gave the poore peoples lands among themselves (in file A.)

Problems of the Revolutionary Government

17. The Attempt to Form an Interim Government

A. Edward Randolph Writes to England from the Boston Jail, July 20, 1689

[Randolph to William Blathwayt, Common Gaol, N. Algeires in New England, July 20, 1689, Toppan and Goodrick, eds., *Randolph Letters*, VI, 289-92]

Sir

Who would have questioned but the poeple who 13 weekes ago pulld down a Setled Government and erected their Old one should be quiett and subject to it, but nothing lesse; here is a violent and bloudy zeal stird up in the Rabble acted and managed by the preachers. So that when ever they have a design of mischeife, tis done upon their first direction: I have wrote in my letter to Capt. nicholson sent by Robin the Governors servant that Mr. Dudley upon his request to the Councill obtained leave to be confind to his house at Roxbery: 6 of the Representatives told the Governor and Councill t'was their Assent also: you have No. 1. a Duplicate of it. as also of the Bond No. 2: upon which he went on the 13th instant home: before 10 aclock that night a Rabble of above 150 men calling at Mr. Bradstreets house first to know by what order Mr. Dudley was out of Goal and calling him old Rogue) went to Mr. Dudley house: broak down his Fence fetchd him to the Goal kept him at the Gate 2 houres. then left him under the care of a Constable. munday the 15th. One Deering well known to Mr. Usher and Capt. Nicholson. with one Winsloe who married his daughter were sent to the prison for being head of that Rabble and the better to pretend their dislike of his action and that they would not send any to Goal they frame a mittimus No. 3: he had not continued in Goal above 2 houres. but the Governor under pretence of busines sends for the Keeper and in the meane tyme a Constable fetches Deering out of Goal: his son in Law was baild out by Bradstreets direction and made head of the faction and Rabble Munday night following. when the women boyes and negros sett upon Paiges house broak all the Windowes and Mr Dudley for feare left the house conveyed himselfe but not unseen to Coll. Legett: being discovered to be there great care was taken to gett him to Goal. One of his Baile Colonel Shrimpton being afraid his house would be pulld down by the Rabble should Mr. Dudley make his escape used his arguments to have him returne to goal: but nothing more does demonstrate the inability of the Government to defend their own act and the power of the Rabble do upon all such suddaine Emergencyes exercise then Mr. Bradstreetes letter to Mr. Dudley No. 4 and that would hardly secure him from being committed himselfe nay they were in such feare he would be gone. that an Order was prepared to be published by beat of Drum to make it treason for any person whatever to harbour him or conceal him.

One Georg Wells a Sayler and of Cape Ann was observed to be very busy in the Riott. he was brought to Goal. about 12 a clock on Monday night but lett out with his companions the next day upon humbling themselves to the Councill: he and his Company 6 or 7 men are all saylers aboard John Updike Master of the Ketch which brings this letter. It were well they were all sent for examined and sent back to Boston to be punishd. I inclose to you a Copy of an Order for a fast. No. 5: wee very much feare the dire effects of their fasting.

The paper No. 6: is a Copy of a Warrant and execution served upon an honest man of Our Church now in Goal. because he will not pay a fine of 4 lb. nor Go to the Indian Warr. Severall other poore men are here also upon the same Reason. they know no Authority they have to presse men and see no way how they shall be paid some having been abroad this whole last Wintr without one penny for their service: The Capts. in Boston presse good house keepers of whom they have 4 . 5 : and 6 lb. a man to provide a man for them: the money being received. they presse any poor man and give him 20 s. or if he will not go they will gett 4 lb of him before he comes out of Goal: this is the better part of their methods to gett poor men to serve against the Enemye.

I send you a booke putt out by young Mather. the Epistle to Mr Winthrop showes what great hopes the church men had of his turning Rebell to serve their Turn: this Mather had a meeting of Armd men at his house the night before they entred upon their strange worke. he has shewed his Christian Spiritt in his Appendix: calculated for one Georg Keith a Quaker of whom Capt. Nicholson and Mr. Usher can give an account and of the falcityes contained therein. I intreat you to communicate these papers and booke to Capt. Nicholson Mr. Usher and Mr. Ratcliffe for I have not tyme nor any perticular busines to write to them. pray peruse that letter to the Marquis of Hallifax: if you think it more proper to adresse it to any other of the Lords of the Councill you may please to putt it under another cover and direction: I wish all happines to you and your Lady. wee think it long to have no shipps from England. Mr. Mather has wrote to his freinds here that he stopd the Circular letter with their Majesties declaration to continue all Officers in their respective places: which wee heare is sent to all other of his Majesties Plantations. my service to Sir Robt. Sowthwell and to Mr. Povey: I am Sir.

your most humble and
fast freind
ED RANDOLPH

my service to Capt.
Nicholson I have wrote to
him severall letters.

B. Randolph Reports More from New England, October 8, 1689

[Randolph to William Blathwayt, Common Gaol in Boston, Oct. 8, 1689, Toppan and Goodrick, eds., *Randolph Letters*, VI, 296-303]

Sir:

Since writing the inclosed a Duplicate whereof I have sent to the Lords of the Committee of trade by way of Barbados: wee have had a fort at Oyster River neer Exiter taken by the Indians and 18 Christians kild and carried away prisoners: Great care has been taken and at last agreed to by the Commissioners of the united Colonyes: vizt. this: Plymouth and Connecticott: to send out men against the Indians: this has from severall townes raised and 6: or 700 men they say are marchd against the enemy: but lye in Garrison in the remaining Townes in the Province of Main and eate up such corn and Cattle as yet have escaped the Enemy: which done I expect to have them return. N. Plymouth sent out 50 English and above 100 Indians under Capt. Church he accidentally landed at Casco when the

Indians were designd to take that town and fort: they report for the Creditt of the matter that he had kild 50 or 60 enemyes: Its certaine the English lost and were wounded 15 or 16: and not one Indian Scalp yet seen of those many kild: tho' they make wonders of this to animate the poeple. I am well assured they sommers work is at an End: wee expect their return: and demand for their pay: of this the Government are sensible: and their Treasurer Phillips has issued out his Warrants to raise a Rate upon the People: No. 1: (a plaine demonstration that they are in actuall possession and administration of their charter Government) but the poeple deny their power to raise money and to keepe courts as appeares by Mr. Graves his paper No: 2: he is a Justice of the peace born in the Country and a very sober Gent: upon the Councills notice of his paper they send for him Capt: Sprag and others of Charles Town they appear and openly acknowledg their paper (as in Mr. Graves his paper. No. 3 upon this they order them to be sent to Cambridg Goal: they refused to go told them they had no power to send them to Goal. Sprag who had tyme to give in bond for his appearance or go to Goal: came next day to Mr. Addington and told him he came on purpose to disown their power: would go home and if any man came forceably into his house he woud kill him: the Councill with representatives are now mett but dare do nothing with them. The men of Charles town and of severall townes there abouts threatning to pull down the Goal if they put them in: I inclose also a larg discourse wrote by a very sober Gent to prevent the poeple of Connecticotts assuming their Government. Hee is a man of such note that his paper has very much affected the poeple. So that this Colony are now made very inclining to Sir Edmund Andros; and say if they must pay any money it shall be by order from him who has a legall Authority: this paper will be printed and dispersd in the Government. the printed paper sent also: has been newly sett a foot. the poeple begin to think of shifting for themselves and are laying the blame upon those who drew them in. Agents have been sent from this Government to Albany to treat with the Maques Indians to invite them down to fall upon Our Eastern Indians: They allowed 300 lb. towards the charge of this Expedition and for presents made to them at Albany: their Errand and Successe you have in an abstract of Coll. Byards letter to Mr. West which I here with send you. Nine Maques are come to Boston: they are treated with thanks and entertainment at the publick charge: they enquire for Sir Edmund Andros: and these poeple having by their inviting them heither discovered their weaknes and ill treatment of the Governor are indeed inviting them to fall upon the Christians about Albany so soon as they have concluded with the french: the discourse in that letter confirmes to you the oppertunity of our driving the french out of their forts setled by them by force amongst the 5 Nations of Indians: and had Sir Edmund Andros been at Liberty wee had been Masters of all the bever Trade as well to the Eastward which the french now have and of that at Albany, where I heare has been a great Trade with the Indians this yeare, and nothing but our present distractions will make these Indians high and despise us: you may please to remember that in my letters sent you from N: York last yeare I acquainted you of the Indians and English kild by the french Indians in Northfeild and about Springfeild: which occasioned an alarum thro this whole Country: which was the effects of the Maques Indians falling a little before upon the french: and now the Indians having as in Coll: Byards letter made so great havock of them they have ordred their french Indians to fall upon us. And accordingly they have kild 3 Christians living 3 miles off Scaneidity a very good fortifyed town

20 miles from Albany: and the Dutch at Albany are so apprehensive, that the french intend to fall upon them this winter that the Mayor sent to Jacob Leisler Cheife of the Rebells at New York for Ammunition etc: to defend themselves: instead whereof he sends to Mr. Bradstreet for ammunition of all sorts and promises upon Honor to repay him and if he cannot spare him what he writes for but to send him one Tonn of Saltpeter: Bradstreet sends him word he has but 8: Barrels powder in the stores: and that what ever accident should happen they had not here above 60 Barreles of pouder in publick and private stores: I well remember Sir Edmund Andros carried with him to N. York last yeare from hence above 60 Barrells of pouder: Armes and plenty of all stores of Warr: and supplyed albany from thence sufficiently (for till he came to that place they had not one Round of pouder for the guns in the fort: nor a Ladle or a Spung fitt to use.) New Yorke was as much wanting but refitted by him: at Boston about 200 Barrells powder: above 200 small Arms Byanetts Swords etc: proportionable. But the Arms stores and every thing which belonged to the King are all imbezled: so that I am well assured should the french make as briske an assault upon this town but with 500 good men as they did at St. Christophers with a greater number they would carry the place: in the account of the Indians taking of pemmaquid. I write you they were well armd and supplyed by all necessaryes from the french: and its very true for they were supplyed about may and the Maques fell upon them some weekes after else wee had heard of them in our Eastern parts long before this tyme: those Indians keep up the forts. wee dare not looke towards them: they say there were 3 or 400 of them gott to Casco: they will lye still till our men are returnd home:

Wee have in Salem a pyrate : of a ship of 24 Guns 24 peteraras : 75 men (but takes in more dayly from hence) a dutch man he pretends to be but has no Commission has brought in a prize from the Banks of N.foundland he comes and takes in Boston and Salem: Capt. Georg is still at an Anchor in the Harbour they had rather be ruined by pyrates then trust him with their sayles: as to the Acts of Trade (Mr. Bradstreet calls one Tho. Hill Navall Officer but he nor his Officer signifye any thing) they are laid asleepe One vessell of 148 Hoggsd of tobacco came heither from Maryland (where bond was given to go to Engd. directly) onely to stop a leake:the Owners turnd out the Master because he would proceed his voyage : and have arested the Cargo pretending a Debt upon it : they will unload it and send it abroad : a Ketch is now gone for Bilboa loaden with fish and tobacco : a ketch lately from Maryland tobacco loaden belonging to Boston came in to this port her Master had like wise given bond there : but he left the ketch here and another Master went in her to Scotland or Holland : and for Brandee and oyle wee have plenty brought in our vessells from N:foundland. my Officers went to seize a vessell loaden with Oyle and Brandee by assistance of General Bradstreets warrant the Constable laught at them and the Master would not let them go aboard : Hill : Bradstreets officer seized upon a Barrell Brandee : the Owner an Inhabitant told Bradstreet if he did not order the delivery of it to him . he would bring 100 men and putt him out of his Government (I could give you more of these instances:) telling him they had putt Sir Ed: Andros and me in prison for hindring their trading . and they would not suffer him to do it : I have wrote here of to the Commissioners: of the Customs. By what I have wrote you it plainely appeares this Country is in very ill circumstances : they know not how to keep the poeple in quiett: much longer finding no charter (as was promised) come : nor no power from England to govern them. Wee looke earnestly for releife and force from England else wee are likely to continue our Stations all this winter : some are for letting us out. others feare the poeple will putt them in who were the occasions of this trouble and (I feare) ruine to this Country, which without speedy Orders from home will unavoidably fall upon it : the Governor is troubled most barbarously in a Ground Room in the Castle very small . no chimney . Every Raine falls makes a floud under his bed. They intend if possible to kill him with Cold and extreamity of cruelty : but I hope God will preserve him and us from the malice and base degenerate treatment of professing Cowards : were they men they would abominate to use a slave as they imperiously use him dayly : I question not your care and sincere resentment of their inhumane actions and that in good tyme wee shall be taken care of. I send this by Mr. Wallis who will be able to say many things more perticulerly of the Eastern Country . being concernd with Sir William Warren about the Masts for the Navy. my humble service to Sir Robt. Sowthwell and to all my freinds I am Sir your most obliged servant.

ED RANDOLPH

English Reaction to Rebellion

18. The London Civil Servant's View, March 23, 1689

[[Sir Robert Southwell?] to the Earl of Nottingham, Mar. 23, 1689, Blathwayt Papers, BL 418, Huntington Library, San Marino, Calif.]

My Lord

This serves only for a short generall Notion of our Interest in the West-Indies. Our Islands are Barbados and Nevis, Half St. Christophers, Antego, Monserrat and Jamaica, Bermudos and a part of New-foundland.

On the Continent Carolina, Virginia, Mary Land, Pensylvania, New Jersey, New York, New England and some Parts in Hudsons Bay. of all which Dominions your Lordship will have some short account in a Paper from Mr. Blathwayts.

There may be in these Parts about 3, or 400,000 subjects that furnish a full third part of the whole Trade and Navigation of England. Here is a great Nursery of Our Sea Men, and the Kings Customs depend mightily thereon. But as most of that Trade lyes now under some Damp by the Late heavy Impositions on Sugar and Tobacco, and consequently a great discontent among those People, soe if New England be restored to the usurped Priviledges they had in 1660 and the old Proprietors of New Jersey, New York and other Islands and Places to what they pretend, It will soe Confound the Present settlement in those Parts, and their Dependance on England, that 'tis hard to say where the Mischeif will stopp, or how farr the Act of Navigation will be over throwne thereby. Yett with such Power and Ardour is this Designe carryed on and by those who perhapps suspect not the Intention of the Republicans who sollicite them, that no Man dares open his Mouth to the Contrary for feare of being Crusht. Mr. Blathwayt, who best knows the truth and state of things dares not speake more then he has done, unless to his Majesty and my Lord Danby, and to your Lordship alone. And 'tis of vast Importance that an hour were sett apart to have this thing made plaine, before it runns on in Parliament beyond Redresse.

The Dutch footing on the Continent is only at Surinam, a Place of Ill Aire, much exposed to the Danger of the Natives. The product is only brown sugar and some woods for dying. Mons'r Summerdike a private undertaker sent a Governour lately over with about 7 or 800 men, most of them of the poor French. And tho' his Governour was cutt off by a Mutiny, yett the Interest is restored again.

They have alsoe the Island of Curasaw neer the Main with about 5 or 6000 Inhabitants thereon. They there drive a forbidden Trade among the Spanish Governors which is soe much at Mercy, that 7 of their shipps were taken and confiscated the last yeare. Yett this is a considerable Mart unto them; and the Spaniards doe by agreement take from them about 3000 Negroes a yeare; but this also is uncertain, since they sometimes take their Negroes from Jamaica or else where as they can best Establish their Contracts.

The Dutch have only besides two Little paltry Islands called Statia and Sabia, which lye soe neare our Charibbee Islands, as they Pilferr a Trade among Us to the hurt of our Act of Navigation.

The French footing is first in the Island of Tobago, which they have lately possesst, and is considerable for a very good Haven, and lying Windward to all our Islands,. Their Next is Martinigo, which is their Capitall for force and People. Then Guadalupe, Half St. Christophers, and Severall small Islands thereabout. Their Bucaniers possess one Side of Hispaniola; and their Fishermen have a Large Tract of Newfound Land, and their Fishing is Considerable.

Then upon the Main they have Nova Scotia, which wee very slightly yeilded by Treaty unto them about 1664. Then Canada and all the Territory thereabout; whereof the Principall Towne is Quebec; and they have lately usurped upon Us some of the Factorys at Hudsons Bay.

They have always given Countenance to their Interest and Trade in these Parts by 5 or 6 Frigotts constantly among them, whereas Wee have scarce one sloop to the Leeward Islands, and but one small Frigatt to Jamaica, which is now coming home with the Dutchess of Albermarle. But as wee have there Large Territory and much Disperst, soe are Wee thereby the more Lyable and exposed to Danger, unless wee have a Mastering force at Sea, for this is the soul of power in those Parts. And if a Warr break out with France, 'tis indispensable in as much as things lye there so Intermixt betweene Us, that in all probability they who will venter to strike first may carry all.

But 'tis manifest that in all the Parts above mentioned the English have already the Governing Trade. The French are there but as great Interlopers, and the Dutch as small ones; While the Spaniard both in his Islands and his Continent lyes there as the great Carcass, upon which all the rest doe prey.

There is noe doubt but if the Dutch had more footing, they might prove more Noxious to England hereafter, by Engrossing the Trade, then if such footing remained as it is, in the Hands of the French. And therefore as to the Business which your Lordship has now in charge, namely how to regulate a Conjunction of our Forces with Holland as to common Defence or the Offence of Our Enemie there. 'Tis first plaine that if Wee desire only to Secure Our Selves, Wee then ought to rayse the Dutch Proportion to as much as wee can. But if wee foresee that our Preparations are likely to be farr superiour to those of our Enemies, and that Wee may easily conquer, then ought wee to desire but little of their Aid, that they may have but little of the spoile. Yet to me it appears wee have already but too much Territory abroad, and to gett more, were but to drain England of People and to loose at home. Whereas the Dutch footing is hitherto soe small, and they have soe many French Protestants at Command, that it would import them highly to have more, whereof England in time might feele the smart.

Soe that when I consider the Vast Expence and Preparations which must be necessary for acquisition in those Parts and how Little It will import Us. Alsoe how Impossible It is to make any Calculation of our owne state abroad while New England is going to be turned into a Common Wealth, to coine Money, To destroy our Act of Navigation, and to shake off all Dependance but what they think fitt. And that New York, New Jersey, etc. shall returne to their old Intended Proprietors. All is hereby at such uncertainty, that as 'tis Scarce Pos-

sible to adjust with Holland in the Quotas of Preparation, soe will it be hard to please them in this Matter at all, since their true Interest seemes to be for Conquest, while ours is for bare defence and the keeping of what already Wee have.

I wish your Lordship with the Earle of Danby would persuade his Majesty to assigne one hour to heare Mr. Blathwayt nakedly Expose the State of this Western Dominion before the Proceedings in Parliament runn too farr, and that the Crown be irreparably damnifyed thereby, which is humbly submitted by

My Lord, your [Sir Robert Southwell?]

19. Massachusetts' Agent Describes Events in London, October 16, 1690

[Elisha Cooke to Simon Bradstreet, London, Oct. 16, 1690, Mass. Hist. Soc., *Proceedings*, 45 (1912), 644-54]

HONORABLE SIR,

After an exceeding stormy and every way dangerous passage of six weekes and six dayes thro Gods wonderfull mercy we arrived at Bristoll March 30th in the evening, and that night by the Post advised Mr. Mather therof; April I Mr. Palmer, Sherlock, Farewell, Pepoon, and others of their passengers came to Bristoll also from some place in Wales, by whom we understood that Mr. Bant was arrived at Scillie and had disposed of his passengers. Some went from on board his into another ship at sea, others he let go off at Scillie, and all had their libertie to go where they pleased, of which Mr. Nicholson can give account, so carefully did he observe your orders. April 3 their coach day we set out from Bristol and came hither the 5th in the evening, and immediately I went to Mr. Mather's lodgings and there found our papers, we taking up at an Inn at first. Mr. Mather advised Sir Henry Ashhurst of our arrival, who was so exceeding kind that the next morning he sent his coach to the Inn desiring me and

Mr. Oakes to keep the sabbath with him at Mr. Baxter's meeting and dine with him; this day Mr. Dudley came to towne, Mr. Randolph the day before us, Sir Edmund and others the day after. Monday with Sir Henry Ashhurst we went to Whitehall to the Earle of Shrewsberry, delivered your honors letter, and prayd his favor to gaine us an opportunity to wait on his Majestie, and the next morning being ushered by him, presented the Colonies Address to his Majestie at his Court at Kensington, which after being read to him by Sir H. Ashhurst he was pleased graciously to accept and sayd he would consider it: we went immediately to the Queenes Lodgings with the Address, but she being then indisposed, which continued some time, that Address was not presented till the 21th, and then being ushered by her Majesties Chamberlain, the Marquis of Winchester, and the Address read to her by Sir H. Ashhurst, her Majestie was pleased to say to us she would be kind to N. England, and as kind as the King; there being in that

Address, as your honor may remember, an intimation of the King's kindness. But to return to the 8th Aprill, being upon the Exchange just before we went to Kensington with the Address, we met with a Notification from the Lords of the Committee for Trade and Plantations, intimating that they expected our attendance on their Lordships at the Council Chamber the Thursday following about the business of N. England, and respecting his Majesties Letter of Command for sending over Sir Edmund Andros and others, that were under Restraint there. At the time we appeared, when their Lordships told us that some Gentlemen were lately come from N. E., and that Sir Edmund Andros and others that had been sent over according to his Majesties Command had moved for their discharge, that they might attend their particular business; their Lordships desired us, if we had any thing to object against them, to lay it before their Lordships, and also inquired whither we had any Credentials, and who the persons were that were therby impowered, for that their names ought to be upon Record there. We answered that we had brought Credentials, but had them not there, and that we had also brought some testimonies of matter of fact respecting Sir Edmund Andros and others, which we hoped would sufficiently vindicate the proceedings of the present Government in N. E. against them; but we were some of us but just arrived and all of us strangers to the proceedings of that Honorable Board, and therefore prayed that we might appeare and answer by our Council, and that time might be allowed them to peruse our papers, and then to draw up what might be proper. The Lord President replyed the request was very reasonable, and after taking our Names in writing beginning with Sir H. Ashurst and so on by the Secretary Mr. Blathwait, we were desired to withdraw, and soon after called in and told by my Lord President that their Lordships had ordered that we should appeare again that day seven night, being the 17th Aprill, with our Council, two of a side, and no more, and in the meane time should leave with the Secretary our Objections in writing on the Munday following (being the 14th day), that so Sir Edmund might have time to answer them, and that at our next appearing we should bring our Credentials. At the time appointed Mr. Humphryes, our solicitor, carryed the Objections to Mr. Blathwait: but when the Objections were drawne up a discourse was raysed among ourselves about the signing of them, upon which our Council being consulted sayd there was indeed no need to sign them, their Lordships having taken our names already and recorded them with our Quality, and because we were properly but upon the Defensive side (the King's Command to send over Sir Edmund, and also this meeting of the Committee being both at his sollicitation), our business was therfore to offer the Reasons of the confinement of Sir Edmund Andros and his Crew, setting forth their Male Administrations of the Government, and thereby vindicate the people in the matter of the Revolution. After delivering the Objections I assisted Mr. Humphryes in drawing up the Brieff, and proceeded so farr therin as he thought their Lordships would have patience to heare at one sitting, coppeys of which are herewith sent. On the 17th day we appeared at the Council Chamber, Mr. Blathwait then calling us each by name under the Character of the N. E. Agents: And after our appearance was observed we acquainted their Lordships that we had entertained Sir John Somers and Mr. Ward as our Council, and prayed they might be heard in behalfe of the Colonie. Then our Council proceed[ed] and acquainted their Lordships that according to the Order of that Honorable Board the Matters objected against Sir Edmund Andros and the other Gentlemen with him were delivered to Mr. Blathwaite the Munday before, and supposed the partyes concerned had taken coppyes thereof. Sir George Treby and Sir Robert Sawyer appearing as Council on the other side sayd they had; and then Sir George began as it were by way of complaint, and sayd they had been imprisoned and very hardly dealt with for a considerable time, and thereby put to great Costs and damages and the like. Sir John Somers replying said, It's true we are properly in this Case on the defensive part, and if these Gentlemen have any thing to charge us with we shall be ready to answere them.

Then Sir Robert Sawyer (the quondam Kings Atturney that prosecuted the Quo Warrantos and Scire facias against the Colonie) verry fiercely enumerated the pretended Crimes that Mr. Randolph had formerly suggested against the Country, and for which he sayd a Quo Warranto and Scire facias had been issued out and Judgment thereupon given against them, and their Charter declared forfeited, and that they deserved far greater punishment than meerly the loss of their Charter Priviledges; but in the close of this stormy Harangue (to prevent his receiving any answer) acknowledged that what he had sayd was forreign to the present Case; whereupon one of the Lords sayd, let us keep to the present matter before us. And then Mr. Blathwat the Secretary was ordered to read the paper of Objections against Sir Edmd. Andros, etc., which after his acquainting the Board when and of whom he received it, he read; then our Council declared that they were ready, and came prepared to prove all or any of those Articles, as their Lordships should please to appoint. Then they were ordered to proceed, and the first Article being read again, and Sir Edmund asked what he sayd to the first part of it relating to the Proclamation, he peremptorily denyed that any such Proclamation was ever emitted by him, and the rest of his Accomplices shewed their Assent to what he sayd by

their Reverence to the Board, when he had done speaking. Then the printed Proclamation was produced and delivered to the Board, which most plainly proved the charge, and that under his owne and his Secretary Wests hands: then Sir John Somers proceed[ed] and sayd, we will now prove the second part of the first Article, viz. that Sir Edmd. Andros endeavoured to stifle the news of his present Majesties landing, and caused him that carryed his Declaration thither to be imprisoned as bringing a seditious and treasonable paper; and to prove this, here is first the testimony of the verry person that was imprisoned, which we pray may be read: then the Lord President sayd, but who are they that make these Objections; who was answered that we appear here in behalfe of the Country that imploy us, and are ready to proceed in proving them. Lord President. But who imprisoned Sir Edmd. Andros and the rest? Sir J. Somers. The Country, my Lord, the people of the place, who being under the oppression of an arbitrary Government did there as we did here, arose as one man and tooke the oppertunity from the News they had of the Revolution here to free themselves from such a yoake, and also secure the country for their present Majesties. Sir Robert Sawyer, with heat and noyse. You say it was done by the people, but it was by the Rabble spirited by the faction to overthrow the Government. Sir J. Somers. It was done just as it was here by a general concurrence of the people of all degrees, and if you will say the Revolution here was done by the Rabble, you may. Mr. Ward. They acted like Englishmen and good subjects, and showed their good affection and loyalty to the English Interest and their present Majesties in securing that country to the Crowne of England, and are no more to blame in that matter than we here in England. Lord P. You say it was done by the country and by the people, that is nobody. Let us see A. B. C. D. the persons that will make it their owne case, and make this charge, that we may know who we have to do with, for that Paper is not signed by anybody. Sir J. S[omers]. We are my Lord in behalfe of the Country, and are imployed by the Colonie to manage their concern as such, and not in the behalfe of any particular persons. That is not our business; and we are ready to prove all these Objections, if your Lordships please, or such of them as your Lordships shall please to order. Then one of the Agents standing just behind the Council to whisper them as there might be occasion, sayd to Sir J. S[omers], if the stick be for that the paper of Objections is not signed by the Agents, we will some of us signe it now immediately, but he replyed no, we are in our way, and have attended the direction of the Board; and if they will bring it off thus, they may. Lord P. but who are these persons, we were told that you had Credentials. Sir J. S[omers]. Yes, my Lord, and here they are, then opened your Commission and offered it to be read. Lord P. Who is it from? Mr. Ward. The Colonie of the Massachusetts, my Lord, and under their seale, which plainly showes the persons that are impowered and by whome, but if the designe be to make particular men espouse this matter as their owne Case, and so render themselves lyable to personal Actions, that would be most unreasonable and unjust, it being the concerne of the Colonie, and not of any particular persons. Lord P. You say true, and may be sure that no such thing would be countenanced by this Honorable Board. Then one of the Lords sayd, I perceive the Revolution was there as it was here, by the unanimous agreement of the people. For who seized and imprisoned the late Lord Chancellor? Who seized the Lords such and such, naming several, and secured the Garrison at Hull, etc. I think we understand the matter well enough, and see no reason why we may not goe forward in hearing the proof.

Another spoke to the same purpose, and added that the people were to be commended for what they had done, and desired they might proceed in the proof. Lord P. applying himselfe to the Agents sayd, Gentlemen, here has been a pretty deale of time spent. My Lords will give his Majestie a true and impartial Account of what has been sayd on both sides, and waite his Majesties further pleasure in the matter, and you may withdraw for the present. The verry next day we were told by a person of good intelligence, that Sir Edmund and the rest of them were dismissed their Attendance at Court, and the day after, vizt. the 19th, that they would be introduced by some body to kiss the King's hand, which honor tis sayd they and Mr. Lidgett had the Munday or Tuesday following: the Thursday after, being the 24th, the Lords of the Committee made their Report to the King in Council, which his Majestie was pleased to approve, and then ordered the matter to be dismissed, and Sir Edmund and the rest discharged, and set at liberty, as you will find by the Coppy. Afterward we pursued our great business, the settlement of the Government, which most friends judged would best be effected by a new Grant: we came in a verry ill time for our business. The Parliament being sitting, and the King preparing for his Expedition into Ireland; However we were in great hopes of effecting it before his departure, but by an unaccountable providence were delayed therein, and so prevented by loosing the verry season. May 25th at night, Mr. Shrimpton came to towne with your honors packet, having laine at Scillie three weekes. The next day we endeavored to present the Address, but his Majestie being extreame busy in his preparations for Ireland, could not be come at; therefore least that and the Express directed to the Earle of Shrewsbury (who was then sick and had also desired to lay downe his place) at the Earle of Nottingham, then and still the only principal Secretary of State, his Office. On the 28th day a Notification was sent us to the Exchange from the Lords of the Committee for Trade, etc., directed as per the Coppy, to attend their Lordships the next day. We went up accordingly, accompanyed with several Gentlemen of good quality, and friends to N. E., an Account of which dayes Action and of the several letters from N. E. then read at the Board, your Honor may have from Mr. Shrimpton, Mr. Heath Nicholson and others, which to write would swell this too large. But your Honors will (I believe) have a more full Account thereof by a friend. In the close of this hearing Sir Edmund Andros presented a large paper to the Board, what preceeded being I suppose the more advantagiously to usher in this, which he calls an Account of the forces raysed in N. E. for the Defence of the Country against the Indians, etc., setting forth his care and paines taken for the security of the Country, and that by reason of the Revolution all his measures were broken, the Forts deserted, souldiers debauched and returned home, and thereupon the Country destroyed by the Enemy, etc., as per the Coppy appears. The next day our Answer (Coppy whereof you also have) was drawne up, and the day following we carryed it to the Lord President's Lodgings and acquainted his Lordship that our Answer to Sir Edmund's paper was ready, and prayed to know when we might lay it before their Lordships, who told us that the Committee would not sit till the King was gone; who went June the 4th, and therefore sometime afterwards leaft our Answer with Mr. Blathwayt, Secretary to the Committee. June the 12th, upon the Exchange we were served with a [summons] directed to one of their Majestie's Messengers to attend the Lords of the Council the 14th Instant, etc. See the Coppy. That day we attended with some Gentlemen with us, but were not called, but at last referred to the 19th. And then Mr. Ran-

dolph offered a large complaint against the present Government of N. E. of their Irregular trade since the Revolution, with a prayer therein for his continuance in the Office of Collector, etc. See the Coppy, which being read was followed with long harangues from two of the Commissioners of the Customes, setting forth that it was the manner of New England men so to trade under their former Government, and that unless the King did send them a Governor again they would never be brought to a due observance of the acts of trade, making large speeches to that purpose, and withall commending Mr. Randolphs care and diligence in his office. We prayed a copy of Mr. Randolph's paper, that we might give our answer thereto, which we doubted not would be to their Lordships full satisfaction, whereupon we were ordered to appeare the next Council day, being the 25th June, vid. Order of Council. An Answer was immediately drawne, and we attended with it that day expecting to be called. The Council once calling for us inquired by the officer at the door whither we were ready with our Answer. We told him we were, but others were called in: at night we were called into the Council Chamber, and told by my Lord President, that they had not time to heare us then, but would take in our Answer that Mr. Randolph might have a coppy of it, and that all parties concerned were ordered to attend the Council July the 2d, and then he sayd they would come to a settlement of the matter. That day also we attended till or within night, having several times given notice that we were attend[ing], to be heard upon our Answer to Mr. Randolphs paper; but the Council brake up without any Order concerning it, and so were dismissed *sine die:* so that neither our Answer to Sir Edmunds nor that to Mr. Randolphs Account were ever read publickly. Captain Sampson came not hither with his ship til October 9th, who drowned your Honors letters to your Agents when he saw he must be taken. Sir, there has been a wonderfull omission of Returning the Coppys of the Bonds of ship Masters according to the Acts of Trade, which I could no wayes excuse, but by the hopes they were drowned; therefore please to order Mr. Addington to be your Honors Monitor for the future, for great advantage is taken against us therby. It will be also N. E's Interest that Colonel Sloughter the present Governor of New York be very civilly treated, who 'tis sayd is a true English man and came over with the King from Holland on that Account, and its most probable may have orders to inspect Matters with you, and make his Report hither: its therefore necessary that he have a right information of things, and the true state of the Country, and that before his understanding be vitiated by the poyson of your N. E. toryes, which doubtless they will endeavor to Instill. Sir, I am heartily sorry that my country men have been so unkind to themselves and to your Honor (which I observe in their Election) as [to] deprive themselves and you at such a time, of such helping hands as were both able and willing to serve them: to my certain knowledge Major Richards was a true, faithfull and willing Drudg to his Country from the time of the Revolution till my departure, and is still I doubt not so kind as to give his advice and counsell in all your arduous and difficult matters, tho deprived of his vote therein, and so Mr. Shrimpton: I doubt there was not that due regard had to the Rules of the Charter as ought to be; the due observation wherof would be as well our Interest as security. It was our great unhappyness that your Honors Advice, given the day after the Revolution, for settling the Government on its first and proper Basis was not then attended; and is the opinion of the thinking men on this side the water. Sir, upon Mr. Shrimptons coming to towne we bespake the making of 500 armes in hope to have despatched Welsteed as soon as they

were made, but he not coming hither till June the 9th and the French Fleet coming into the Channell within few days after and continuing Masters therof and so of the seas till about the middle of August, when they returned home, and after that a strict Embargo here till our Fleet was fitted and still continuing, prevented his despatch so long that it was judged not safe to venture with his sloop in the winter, and is therefore layd up, and the Armes shipt on Captain Prince going on Account of several Merchants, and in part on Account of the Colonie; powder also goes on several ships as Merchandize which we perswaded several friends to ship who do it more to serve the Country than for their owne proffit, and Mr. Welsteed is going passenger in Captain Browne. Captain Martin either carelessly or wilfully ran his ship on shoare with his sheet Anchor at the Bow at Margarets August 31, bulged her on the Rocks, made her a wreck and sold her, having much dammaged his sayls and what else was perishable: he had insured his ship, yet keeps out of sight, and its thought so much of his business is knowne that he will verry hardly gett his money of the Insurers, your fifty pound Bill to be sure will faile being payd by him, tho I believe it may be recovered at home, of which more hereafter when better informed. Sir, since the Kings coming home we have been endeavoring to effect our main Concerne, but the great and general concerns of the Nation respecting the present warr, and the preparation for the next Campaign and summers Fleet crowd out our comparatively small one, the Parliament being sitting and busyed about that Affaire. We have good encouragement given us by several, but the Issue is with the Lord. It seems to me strange that Plymouth Colonie make no application to his Majestie in all this yeare. They had like to have put into Colonel Sloughter's Commission and annexed to N. York Government; pray Sir, to give my service to

Governor Hinckley with information therof; my hearty service to Madame Bradstreet, praying her to be kind to the poor widowlike Gentlewoman at my house; the same Mr. Danforth and the rest of the Gentlemen of the Council, begging the continuance of your prayers for, Sir, your Honors most humble servant

ELISHA COOKE.

Sir, yours per Blake who is arrived in some part of Scotland is received this day being the 18th October.

I know your Honor will be surprised at the sight of this letter being in halfe sheets of which I am not a little ashamed, but the truth is that after I had writt it Mr. O[akes] came into the Chamber in the evening and wanting halfe a sheet of paper splitt this, thinking it had been cleane paper, for which he has reason to beg pardon, it being just before it should have been sealed and delivered to Mr. Heath just going and therfore could not be transscribed. I have herewith also sent Coppyes of Petitions from some Gentlemen in Charlestowne, etc. [Endorsed] October 10 1690. E. C. to Gov. Bradstreet.

Winning a New Charter

20. The Role of Increase Mather, 1691

[Hall, ed., "The Autobiography of Increase Mather," Amer. Antiq. Soc., *Proceedings*, 71 (1962), Pt. 2, 335-37]

The King was in Holland when I had this discourse with the Queen, (1691), but returned to London that moneth. I was very desirous once more to plead with the King and to begg his favor to New England. The Earle of devonshire spoke to the King praying I might have Access to his Majesty. On April. 28. I was admitted into his bedchamber. What then passed was as followeth. Mather. I most humbly thank your Majesty, in that you were graciously pleased to signify to my Lord Devonshire, That I might have leave to wayt on your Majesty in the behalfe of New England. None of your subjects are or can be more in your Interest than they are. Nor are there any that do pray more for your long life, and happy reign and the success of your Armes. King. Sir, what do you desire I should do for them? Mather. May it please your Majesty that they may be restored to their auncient priviledges, and that their settlement may be expedited. They have an humble confidence that through your Majesties goodness they shall be made happy in having their auncient priviledges restored to them, which will cause your subjects there to be your servants forever. And your Name will then be great and famous in those ends of the earth unto all posterity. Your Majesty has bin graciously pleased to referr the consideration of this affair to the two Chief Justices with the Attorney and Sollicitor general. We only pray humbly, that what they have thought reasonable for us to desire may be granted by your Majesty. King. I expect within 2 or 3 dayes to have a Report from the Committee of Lords for Plantations, and then shall see what may be done. Mather. Your Majesties subjects have bin willing to venture their lives to inlarge your dominions. That expedition against Canada was a great and a noble undertaking, and they are willing to do the like again, if encouraged by your Majesty. May it please your Majesty in your great wisedom to consider the circumstances of that people. As in your wisedom you have considered the circumstances of England and of Scotland. In New England they differ from other plantations. They are such as are called congregational men and Presbyterians. So that such a Governor will not suit with the people of New England as may be very proper for the other English plantations.

Having thus spoken, I bowed to the King and Hee immediatly went out of his bedchamber into his closet.

Two dayes after this the Council mett at Whitehall. The King then declared that the Agents of New England should nominate a person to him to be their Governor, who might, in respect of his perswasion in matters of Religion, be sutable for them. I remember a Lord (some time after) sayd, that the reason of the Kings so expressing Himselfe, was the Impression which the words I had spoken to him but two dayes before, had made upon his spirit.

The King returned to Holland again within two dayes after this. Nevertheless before Hee went, the Archbishop of Canterbury, and Mr Charleton did on my desires sollicit and pray his Majesty to be kind to New England.

October. 23. The King being newly returned to England again, the Earle of Nottingham introduced me to him, only to kiss his hand, and bid him welcome to England again. The King when Hee first saw me, smiled on me, and stepped aside to me, graciously telling me that Hee was glad to see me.

Altho I had not obtained all for New England which I desired and to my utmost endeavor to get for them, I thought it my duty to Thank, not only God, but the King for what kindness had bin shewed to that people. And I therefore proposed to the Earle of Nottingham, that Hee would please again to introduce me to his Majesty, which Hee very readily did, on Novbr. 4. the King then being in the secretary of states office, none present but my Lord Nottingham and the Earles of devon, and Portland. I then sayd, I do in the behalfe of New England most humbly thank your Majesty in that you have bin pleased by a charter to restore English liberties to them, to confirm them in their properties, and to grant them some peculiar priviledges. I doubt not but that your subjects there will demean themselves with that dutyfull affection and loyalty to your Majesty, as that you will see cause to inlarge your Royal favors towards them. And I do most humbly thank your Majesty in that you have bin pleased to give Leave to those that are concerned for New England to nominate their Governor. Sir William Phips has bin nominated by us at the Council Board. Hee has done a good Service for the Crown by inlarging your dominions and reducing Nova Scotia to your obedience. I know that Hee will Faithfully serve your Majesty to the utmost of his capacity, and if your Majesty shall think fit to confirm him in that place, it will be a further obligation on your subjects there. The King Replyed, I shall take that Colony under my protection, and do what is in me for their encouragement, And shall take what concerns the Government there into my consideration.

21. The Massachusetts Charter of 1691

[Thorpe, *Federal and State Constitutions*, III, 1877-83]

And Wee doe further for Us Our Heires and Successors Will Establish and ordeyne that from henceforth for ever there shall be one Goverour One Leiutenant or Deputy Governour and One Secretary of Our said Province or Territory to be from time to time appointed and Commissionated by Us Our Heires and Successors and Eight and Twenty Assistants or Councillors to be advising and assisting to the Governour of Our said Province or Territory for the time being as by these presents is hereafter directed and appointed which said Councillors or Assistants are to be Constituted Elected and Chosen in such forme and manner as hereafter in these presents is expressed. . . . *And further* Wee Will and by these presents for Us Our Heires and Successors doe ordeyne and Grant that there shall and may be convened held and kept by the Governour for the time being upon every last Wednesday in the Moneth of May every yeare for ever and at all such other times as the Governour of Our said Province shall think fitt and appoint a great and Generall Court of Assembly Which said Great and Generall Court of Assembly shall consist of the Governour and Councill or Assistants for the time being and of such Freeholders of Our said Province or Territory as shall be from time to time elected or deputed by the Major parte of the Freeholders and other Inhabitants of the respective Townes and Places who shall be present at such Elections Each of the said Townes and Places being hereby impowered to Elect and Depute Two Persons and noe more to serve for and represent them respectively in the said Great and Generall Court or Assembly To which Great and Generall Court or Assembly to be held as a foresaid Wee doe hereby for Us Our Heires and Successors give and grant full power and authority from time to time to direct appoint and declare what Number each County Towne and Place shall Elect and Depute to serve for and represent them respectively in the said Great and Generall Court or Assembly *Provided* always that noe Freeholder or other Person shall have a Vote in the Election of Members to serve in any Greate and Generall Court or Assembly to be held

as aforesaid who at the time of such Election shall not have an estate of Freehold in Land within Our said Province or Territory to the value of Forty Shillings per Annum at the least or other estate to the value of Forty pounds Sterl' And that every Person who shall be soe elected shall before he sitt or Act in the said Great and Generall Court or Assembly take the Oaths mentioned in an Act of Parliament made in the first yeare of Our Reigne Entituled an Act for abrogateing of the Oaths of Allegiance and Supremacy and appointing other Oaths and thereby appointed to be taken instead of the Oaths of Allegiance and Supremacy and shall make Repeat and Subscribe the Declaration mentioned in the said Act before the Governour and Lieutenant or Deputy Governor or any two of the Assistants for the time being who shall be thereunto authorized and Appointed by Our said Governour and that the Governour for the time being shall have full power and Authority from time to time as he shall Judge necessary to adjourne Prorogue and dissolve all Great and Generall Courts or Assemblyes met and convened as aforesaid And Our Will and Pleasure is and Wee doe hereby for Us Our Heires and Successors Grant Establish and Ordeyne that yearly once in every yeare for ever hereafter the aforesaid Number of Eight and Twenty Councillors or Assistants shall be by the Generall Court or Assembly newly chosen that is to say Eighteen at least of the Inhabitants or of Proprietors of Lands within the Territory formerly called the Collony of Massachusetts Bay and four at the least of the Inhabitants of or Proprietors of Lands within the Territory formerly called New Plymouth and three at the least of the Inhabitants of or Proprietors of Land within the Territory formerly called the Province of Main and one at the least of the Inhabitants of or Proprietors of Land within the Territory lying between the River of Sagadahoc and Nova Scotia

And that the said Councillors or Assistants or any of them shall or may at any time hereafter be removed or displaced from their respective Places or Trust of Councillors or Assistants by any Great or Generall Court or Assembly And that if any of the said Councillors or Assistants shall happen to dye or be removed as aforesaid before the Generall day of Election That then and in every such Case the Great and Generall Court or Assembly at their first sitting may proceed to a New Election of one or more Councillors or Assistants in the roome or place of such Councillors or Assistants soe dying or removed And Wee doe further Grant and Ordeyne that it shall and may be lawfull for the said Governour with the advice and consent of the Councill or Assistants from time to time to nominate and appoint Judges Commissioners of Oyer and Terminer Sheriffs Provosts Marshalls Justices of the Peace and other Officers to Our Councill and Courts of Justice belonging *Provided* always that noe such Nomination or Appointment of Officers be made without notice first given or summons issued out seaven dayes before such Nomination or Appointment unto such of the said Councillors or Assistants as shall be at that time resideing within Our said Province . . . *And further* Our Will and Pleasure is and Wee doe hereby for Us Our Heires and Successors Grant Establish and Ordaine That all and every of the Subjects of Us Our Heires and Successors which shall goe to and Inhabit within Our said Province and Territory and every of their Children which shall happen to be born there or on the Seas in goeing thither or returning from thence shall have and enjoy all Libertyes and Immunities of Free and naturall Subjects within any of the Dominions of Us Our Heires and Successors to all Intents Constructions and purposes whatsoever as if they and every of them were borne within this Our *Realme* of England and for the greater Ease and Encouragement of Our Loveing Subjects Inhabiting our said Province or Territory of the Massachusetts Bay and of such as shall come to Inhabit there Wee doe by these presents for us Our heires and Successors Grant Establish and Ordaine that for ever hereafter there shall be a liberty of Conscience allowed in the Worshipp of God to all Christians (Except Papists) Inhabiting or which shall Inhabit or be Resident within our said Province or Territory . . .

And wee doe of our further Grace certaine knowledge and meer motion Grant Establish and Ordaine for Us our heires and Successors that the great and Generall Court or Assembly of our said Province or Territory for the time being Convened as aforesaid shall for ever have full Power and Authority to Erect and Constitute Judicatories and Courts of Record or other Courts to be held in the name of Us Our heires and successors for the Hearing Trying and Determining of all manner of Crimes Offences Pleas Processes Plaints Actions Matters Causes and things whatsoever ariseing or happening within Our said Province or Territory or between persons Inhabiting or resideing there whether the same be Criminall or Civill and whether the said Crimes be Capitall or not Capitall and whether the said Pleas be Reall personall or mixt and for the awarding and makeing out of Execution thereupon To which Courts and Judicatories wee doe hereby for us our heires and Successors Give and Grant full power and Authority from time to time to Administer oathes for the better Discovery of Truth in any matter in Controversy or depending before them *And* wee doe for us Our Heires and Successors Grant Establish and Ordaine that the Governor of our said Province or Territory for the time being with the Councill or Assistants may doe execute or performe all that is necessary for the Probate of Wills and Granting of Administrations for touching or concerning any Interest or Estate which any person or persons shall have within our said Province or Territory . . .

And we doe further for us our Heires and Successors Give and Grant to the said Governor and the great and Generall Court or Assembly of our said Province or Territory for the time being full power and Authority from time to time to make ordaine and establish all manner of wholsome and reasonable Orders Laws Statutes and Ordinances Directions and Instructions either with penalties or without (soe as the same be not repugnant or contrary to the Lawes of this our Realme of England) as they shall Judge to be for the good and welfare of our said Province or Territory And for the Government and Ordering thereof and of the People Inhabiting or who shall Inhabit the same and for the necessary support and Defence of the Government thereof *And* wee doe for us our Heires and Successors Give and grant that the said Generall Court or Assembly shall have full power and Authority to name and settle annually all Civill Officers within the said Province such Officers Excepted the Election and Constitution of whome wee have by these presents reserved to us Our Heires and Successors or to the Governor of our said Province for the time being and to Settforth the severall Duties Powers and Lymitts of every such Officer to be appointed by the said Generall Court or Assembly and the formes of such Oathes not repugnant to the Lawes and Statutes of this our Realme of England as shall be respectively Administered unto them for the Execution of their severall Offices and places And alsoe to impose Fines mulcts Imprisonments and other Punishments And to impose and leavy proportionable and reasonable Assessments Rates and Taxes upon the Estates and Persons of all and

every the Proprietors and Inhabitants of our said Province or Territory . . . *Provided* alwaies and Wee doe by these presents for us Our Heires and Successors Establish and Ordaine that in the frameing and passing of all such Orders Laws Statutes and Ordinances and in all Elections and Acts of Government whatsoever to be passed made or done by the said Generall Court or Assembly or in Councill the Governor of our said Province or Territory of the Massachusetts Bay in New England for the time being shall have the Negative voice and that without his consent or Approbation signified and declared in Writeing no such Orders Laws Statutes Ordinances Elections or other Acts of Government whatsoever soe to be made passed or done by the said Generall Assembly or in Councill shall be of any Force effect or validity anything herein contained to the contrary in anywise notwithstanding *And* wee doe for us Our Heires and Successors Establish and Ordaine that the said Orders Laws Statutes and Ordinances be by the first opportunity after the makeing thereof sent or Transmitted unto us Our Heires and Successors under the Publique Seale to be appointed by us for Our or their approbation or Disallowance And that incase all or any of them shall at any time within the space of three years next after the same shall have presented to us our Heires and Successors in Our or their Privy Councill be disallowed and rejected and soe signified by us Our Heires and Successors under our or their Signe Manuall and Signett or by or in our or their Privy Councill unto the Governor for the time being then such and soe many of them as shall be soe disallowed and r[e]jected shall thenceforth cease and determine and become utterly void and of none effect.

PART II

LEISLER'S REBELLION IN NEW YORK

CANADA

St. Lawrence River

Richelieu River

NEW YORK 1689

Lake Champlain

Lake Oneida

Mohawk River

NEW
HAMPSHIR

Schenectady
Albany

Hudson River

RENSSELAERSWYCK

MASSACHUSET

UNSETTLED BOUNDARY

ULSTER

DUTCHESS

PENNSYLVANIA

CONNECTICU

ORANGE

WESTCHESTER

EAST
AND
WEST
JERSEY

NEW
YORK

SUFFOLK

RICHMOND

KINGS

QUEENS

CHAPTER FOUR

SEEDS OF DISCONTENT

THE "Protestant Wind" which carried William of Orange to the throne of England in 1688 was to have momentous repercussions in the American colonies. In New York, it set in motion a series of events which shaped the character of the colony's politics for decades, becoming the touchstone in all things pertaining to government, and even warping the normal problems of administration and leadership. The consequences of the two years between 1689 and 1691 can only be suggested by the violence of the interpretations which have been made of them over the succeeding centuries.

Contemporary accounts of the Rebellion are replete with allegations as to the motives, ambitions, and characters of the participants. The author of one account refers to his rival as "a monster begat by an incubus on a Scotch Witch," and proceeds from there to let loose his venomed pen. These, of course, were propaganda pieces designed to fight current battles, and their virulence reflects the magnitude of the stakes involved. An outsider could write in 1695: "I do believe that there were some of either side who sought in what they did their own advantage, many who truly did intend his Majesties service and many who blindly followed the leading men." But not until half a century later could a New Yorker view these events judiciously and proclaim that "nothing could be more egregiously foolish, than the conduct of both parties, who by their intestine divisions, threw the province into convulsions, and sowed the seeds of mutual hatred and animosity, which for a long time after, greatly embarrassed the public affairs of the colony."

The period of calm appraisal was short-lived, for by the nineteenth century historians were again looking upon these events as the precursors of their own problems. John R. Brodhead, writing in the 1860's, saw the earlier conflict through spectacles distorted by the bitter struggle then raging in the nation, and the Leislerians, to him, were rabble-rousers and dangerous oppressors of liberty. The weight of his scholarship gave his interpretation authority, and it was incorporated in the comprehensive study published by Herbert L. Osgood in the early twentieth century. This view was shortly challenged, however, by Mrs. Schuyler Van Rensselaer, and her interpretation was seconded later by Charles M. Andrews. In our own time, the pendulum has swung full, and the Leislerians have been treated as the advance agents of modern democracy.

There is no doubt that the events of 1689-91 have provoked controversy and divergent interpretations, but the question remains why this should be so. What did the news of William of Orange's invasion and of James II's forced abdication really mean to New Yorkers? What were the latent forces unleashed in the colony by the events in the mother country? And what was there about the conflict in New York that should have created such disagreement as to its meaning and significance?

The explanation can best be found within the context of two main themes which dominated the colony at the arrival of the "soe strange news" of the Glorious Revolution. The first is the underlying tension created by the transformation of a Dutch trading company outpost into a ducal proprietary and then a royal colony; the second is the imposition on the colony of a rigid framework which did not allow the flexibility essential in any growing society, the channel through which one group can strive to displace another in the struggle for power.

The quarter century following the English conquest of 1664 was clearly a transitional period. Beginning with the polyglot base of nationalities and religions inherited from the Dutch, the English gradually imposed their own forms on the colony. Administrative methods and legal codes were changed, large landed estates were converted from patroonships to manors, municipal corporate rights were codified, and English religious institutions were fostered.

As things English gradually supplanted those of Dutch origin, there were bound to be points of controversy, areas of discontent, and these were accentuated by the economic decline that began in the 1670's and continued throughout the period (No. 22). Various causes were ascribed by the colonial authorities for the depression—territorial losses to other colonies, interference by neighboring areas in New York's trade, external pressures from French Canada, and, as the local merchants sometimes hinted, the growth of imperial trade regulations (Nos. 24 and 25) —and they attempted to alleviate the problem through the creation of monopolies and the transmission of appeals to the English authorities (No. 23). But no relief was forthcoming.

Complicating the colony's economic distress was the desire of the proprietor, the Duke of York, heir presumptive to the throne, to make New York financially self-supporting if not profitable. This goal became less attainable by the mid-1680's as hostility increased between New York and its French and Indian neighbors to the north. However, the Duke's fiscal hopes finally led him to authorize a legislative assembly in return for a promise by the colonists that they would assume a greater share of the financial burden of governing the colony (No. 26).

These rapid alterations and economic uncertainties did afford an opportunity for shrewd individuals to gain power, prestige, and governmental positions. Men such as Nicholas Bayard, Stephanus Van Cortlandt, Frederick Philipse, and Robert Livingston laid the foundations of their fortunes during these troublesome times. But their rise to high stations was not unchallenged. Abraham De Peyster, Gerardus Beekman, Samuel Staats, Abraham Gouverneur, and Jacob Leisler stood on just slightly lower rungs of the ladder in the colony's economic, social, and political life, and they aspired to a higher place.

Individuals such as these were largely responsible for forcing the Duke's hand on the matter of a representative assembly. To them, the legislature was a logical path for advancement. But once James, Duke of York, ascended the throne in 1685 as James II, things quickly changed. The King first abolished the Assembly and then incorporated the colony into the Dominion of New England (No. 27). The rigidity thus introduced into New York meant that those who had already attained power were confirmed in their places and those whose ambitions were still unfulfilled found their way blocked. The path to preferment lay no longer in the local agencies of government, but rather in the complex and autocratic machinery of the Dominion at best, and at worst in the machinations which occurred within the precincts of Whitehall.

This then was the situation which made the administration of Sir Edmund Andros so intolerable to many New Yorkers, which made the prospects of overthrowing the Dominion government so attractive. When those in power proved timid and hesitant about embracing the Glorious Revolution, the discontented thought they had found a way to restore the *status quo* as it had existed in the better days of Governor Thomas Dongan.

Although repressed ambitions certainly provided the leadership of the rebellion, it required popular backing to succeed. And it is here that the long-term grievances and the immediate fears came into play. High taxes, monopolies, and economic difficulties combined with an unrealistic dread of a French-Indian-Catholic plot against the safety of Protestant New York to inflame the populace (No. 28). Thus the news of the Glorious Revolution brought together a series of problems, no one of which was violent by itself, but in combination became an explosive force which was to wrack the colony for years.

Economic Depression

22. Indices of Economic Difficulty

A. NEW YORK CITY PROPERTY VALUATIONS, 1676-88

[*Minutes of the Common Council of the City of New York, 1675-1776*, 8 vols. (New York, 1905), I, 29-37, 169, 201]

1676 assessment of	£103,457	1688 assessment of	78,231
1685 assessment of	75,694		

B. SIZE AND PRICE OF WHITE BREAD LOAVES, 1677-91

[*Minutes of Common Council*, I, 65, 161, 173, 195, 202, 227, 256]

October 17, 1677	32 ozs.	3-2/3d.	December 22, 1688	16 ozs.	1½d.
April 30, 1685	12 ozs.	2d.	May 9, 1691	16 ozs.	1½d.
January 8, 1685/6	12 ozs.	1-2/3d.	November 26, 1691	14 ozs.	1½d.
March 24, 1687/8	14 ozs.	1½d.			

23. Controversies Over Monopolistic Privileges

A. PETITION OF THE ALBANY MERCHANTS, APRIL 30, 1679

[Arnold J. F. Van Laer, ed., *Minutes of the Court of Albany, Rensselaerswyck and Schenectady, 1668-1685*, 3 vols. (Albany, 1926-32), II, 406-8]

The underwritten petitioners . . . have heard read or seen posted a certain order in council issued at New York on the 21st of this month, providing that no merchants at Albany whatsoever are to do any business or carry on any trade overseas, which is greatly tending to the prejudice and loss, yes, the entire ruin of this place, being contrary to all laws and statutes and very detrimental to the prosperity of this place and its inhabitants, it being a matter which heretofore has never been questioned, but a privilege which has always been enjoyed in all parts of His Royal Highness's territories, upon payment of such imposts and custom duties as it has pleased His Royal Highness or his lieutenants to impose upon them, which they have never refused to pay, but on the contrary have always paid in proportion to their ability, yes, even more than those of New York have paid.

Secondly, this privilege, being the principal one, was unquestionably confirmed among others by the Right Honorable General Sir Edmund Andross upon his arrival, as may be seen from the first and second order, and more particularly renewed and granted in the month of June of the year 1676, when there was a discussion with his honor about the said matter. Also, that those of New York infringe on our rights and privileges by making opportunity to trade with the Indians, about which the burghers of this city presented a humble petition to the governor, who made thereon the following apostil: "All the former privileges are confirmed and no one may trade with the Christians by the small measure [i.e., retail], or in any manner with the Indians, unless he be a burgher or freeman."

Furthermore, it is to be observed that:

1. The trade with the Indians daily weakens and diminishes, being in the hands of 20 or 30 persons, and can not possibly support this place or its inhabitants.

2. Many of the inhabitants have made their arrangements and preparations to ship flour, wheat and other grain across the sea, in order to bring trade and prosperity into this place and the colony, seeing that if they take the same to New York they can not get more for it than the merchants there are willing to give, as can be shown by several examples.

3. It is an ancient privilege of the inhabitants of this city to trade over seas, as can be shown sufficiently by the letters of denization granted by the former governors to some of the inhabitants here.

4. If none of the inhabitants of Albany may be over sea merchants or traders, they will have to sell their beavers at such low prices as those of New York will be pleased to give, and consequently pay for all their merchandise, both Indian and Christian trading goods, as much as those of New York may be pleased to demand, in which case they will not be in a position to attract the Indians, who may then easily go to Canada and deprive this place of the trade, which can not be of any advantage to the colony, but will tend to the considerable loss, detriment, and prejudice of Albany.

5. It will be a great loss to us and our children after us if we are deprived of such statutes and privileges. Yes, many of the inhabitants who can neither trade nor do any manual labor will have to leave, also to the great prejudice of mechanics in every respect.

6. As to the inspection of flour, we trust that no fraud has ever been discovered about the flour which has been shipped from here anywhere since Albany obtained the privilege in the year 1677. If the flour which goes thither must be dumped and repacked and then lie there until the merchants please to buy it, we having no privilege to ship it, it will tend to our great loss and the ruin of the entire place.

7. Truly, Albany should be encouraged by the extension of her privileges rather than that the same should be abridged or that she should be totally deprived thereof, lying at the extreme limit of the colony in the west, in great peril, as is well known to every one. Yes, in case of fire alarm or in times of war (which may God prevent) with Christians as well as Indians, we must immediately bear the brunt and risk our lives and property in defense, whereas many private merchants, who perhaps greatly envy us in this matter, are exposed to little risk.

8. Truly, no right minded persons can be of opinion that the abridgment of our privileges can be of any benefit or profit to the colony. We have taken the oath of supremacy and allegiance, which many in the colony have not taken in that manner. We therefore claim and appropriate to ourselves all such privileges which any others of his Majesty's subjects in this colony can claim or appropriate to themselves.

B. THE GOVERNOR'S RESPONSE AND ALBANY'S REACTION, MAY 19, 1679

[Van Laer, ed., *Minutes of the Court of Albany*, II, 413]

There was read in court the order in council of the 6th instant in answer to a certain letter . . . recommending to his honor the contents of a certain petition presented to us by the inhabitants of this city and colony [i.e., Albany], requesting that they might have the privilege and freedom of trading overseas, which recommendation was resented by his honor, so that the matter as a whole is suspended and for the present is to remain as ordered, etc.

And . . . his honor suggests two things, to wit:

1. Whether we prefer a general privilege and freedom to trade and do business overseas;

2. Or whether we desire a special privilege regarding the trade with the Indians. . . .

All of which having been duly considered and deliberated upon by us [i.e., Albany magistrates] it is unanimously resolved to refer the entire matter to his honor, the governor general, to do therein as his honor in his wisdom and sound judgment shall see fit, which no doubt will tend to the preservation and benefit of the place. And we shall await his honor's resolution in the aforesaid matter.

C. NEW YORK CITY ARGUES FOR ITS MONOPOLY, APRIL 6, 1684

[Mayor and Aldermen of New York to Lt. Gov. Thomas Dongan, Apr. 6, 1684, *Minutes of Common Council*, I, 149-50]

This city being the metropolis of the province hath from time to time been the main support thereof, the flourishing or decay of which doth influence all its parts, and by its industry in trade and traffic maintained by its number of inhabitants hath gained credit and reputation abroad, by whose means alone all foreigner's commerce and shipping is drawed hither.

That the manufacture of flour and bread, for so we consent it may be properly termed, hath been and is the chief support of the trade and traffic to and from this city and maintenance of its inhabitants of all degrees, and if used and practised in other parts of the province must of necessity lessen our trade and consequently the number of our inhabitants employed therein.

All other parts of the province have some particular advantage and way of living, as Long Island by husbandry and whaling, Esopus being the fat of the land by tillage, Albany by Indian trade and husbandry, this city [has] no other advantage or way of living but by traffic and dependence . . . on [one] another chiefly upheld by the manufacture of flour and bread.

To us it is evident that had all parts of the province equal liberty to make flour and bread, no part thereof would be advantaged thereby, but the trade so dispersed that it would be much impaired if not wholly lost, and the value of flour and bread less to the farmer than now his corn is, the price of which is kept up by the industry of the inhabitants of this city who first made it a commodity abroad, gained it reputation, and are only proper to continue both.

So that the establishing the making of flour and bread in this city only takes nothing from other parts of the province, but removed or admitted in other parts will be the apparent ruin and decay of the same. . . . How necessary it is to maintain and encourage [a city], the want of so well a situated and such a number of inhabitants so incorporated in Virginia, Maryland and other neighboring parts may sufficiently demonstrate, who though [they] have the same advantages from the fruits and produce of the earth, for want thereof can not accrue to that benefit in trade by husbandry as this province hath and doth enjoy by the means and encouragement of this city only.

D. LEISLER ATTACKS MONOPOLIES, APRIL 24, 1690

[Commissioners of Statutory Revision, *The Colonial Laws of New York from the Year 1664 to the Revolution*, 5 vols. (Albany, 1894), I, 218]

An Act to raise throughout the whole gouvernment three pence in every pound reall and personall [property] to be paid the first of June and that all townes and places should have equall freedom to boult and bake and to transport where they please directly to what place or country they think it fitt, anything their places afford, and that the one place should have no more privileges than the other.

E. POPULARITY OF LEISLER'S ANTI-MONOPOLY STAND, APRIL 14, 1690

[Robert Livingston to Sir Edmund Andros, Apr. 14, 1690, O'Callaghan, ed., *Documents Relative to Colonial New York*, III, 708]

I was in hopes Your Excellency should have heard the newes of the distroying Schenectady by the French and Indians before your departure that your Excellency might [have] the more hastned their motion at Whitehall for our setlement. On the 9th of February last a Company of 250 French and Indians came upon that place when they all were alseep about 11 aClock at night, and kill'd and destroyed 60 men women and children, carryed 27 men and boys prisoners and burnt the towne. . . . The people of that Towne were so bygotted to Leisler that they would not obey any of the Magistrates neither would they entertain the souldiers sent thither by the [Albany] Convention. . . .

Thus had Leisler perverted that poor people by his seditious letters now founde all bloody upon Schenectady streets, with the notions of a free trade, boalting etc. and thus they are destroyed; they would not watch, and wher Captain Sander commanded, there they threatened to burn him upon the fire, if he came upon the garde.

24. New York Attacked by "Little Artifices," February 9, 1693

[The Mayor and Council of New York to Gov. Benjamin Fletcher, Feb. 9, 1693, *Minutes of Common Council*, I, 311-13]

[We] . . . doe with all Submission presume to Acquaint your Excellency that as itt has been the Sentiments of all your Excellencys Predecessors . . . as well as the Interest of the Crown That Trafique and Comerce (the foundation of Riches as well as the increase and Support of Empire) Should be Singularly

Encouraged att this place (which by its Natural Scituation is Convenient for trade and Navigation), They were therefore pleased to publish and bestow many Priviledges and Franchises upon Such as would come, Settle and Inhabitt here, for the propagation and Increase of trade and Comerce, which gave Incouragement to the Inhabitants of this Citty to Transport themselves from their Native Country, hoping thereby to Advance the Interest of the Crown, and increase Trafique and Navigation. . . . Whereupon the Inhabitants of this their Majesties Citty were Induced with uncessant Labour, great Charge and expence to enrich this barren soile, and Supply Some naturall defects thereof with Art and Industry for the Suitable Accomodation of trade and Shipping, not doubting but this, their Endeavors, would have Convinced all the Other Inhabitants of this Province (who have had great Advantage by the Improvement of this Citty) that what has been done and Invented by the Citizens of this Citty was for the Publick and Common good of the whole Province as well as for the advancement and interest of the Crown. But may itt Please your Excellency

This City noe Sooner began to make A figure in trade and grow in Reputation beyond the Seas, but itt became the envy of our Adjacent Neighbors who did not cease by all their little Artifices to Interupt our trade, but also did reproach us with many false Sugestions which, together with the Insinuations of particular persons for their own private Lucre and gain, did procure Considerable branches of the Government to be lopped off; and Still not Contented with that Devastation, [they] were restless until wee were Swallowed up by that unhappy Annexation to New England, whereby our Traffique not only drooped, but all that was dear and Valuable amongst us wholly destroy'd. That Ignorance which did then Spread itt Self throughout the Province [Leisler's antimonopoly stand] hath since dropped Some Seeds which now begin to Sprout again, who will not be Contented with any thing Except all the Principles of trade be reduced to Confusion and every Planters Hutt throughout the Province become A Markett for flower and biskett (the only Staple Commodity of the Province) and on which the whole trade and Revenue doth depend. For that purpose, May itt Please your Excellency, they have Sett up bolting Mills in the Country in Contempt of former Orders Restraining the Same, and have Commenced Suits att Law against the Citty officers for ascertaining the Rights thereof, which hath been A long time depending att the Supream Court and, after long Consideration and Advicement of the Judges thereupon, att last declared in favour of the Citty. . . . Now May itt please your Excellency, many Proffitts and great Advantages hath allways Accrued to the whole Province by the Improvements and Industry of the Citty, and particularly the whole Income of the Revenue doth Cheifly Rely upon the trade thereof. Besides the fifth part of the Charge of the whole Province and often the fourth [part] has been paid by this City during this Present Warr, all which will Certainly Sink if the Cittizens be Interrupted in the enjoyment of their former Franchises and Priviledges, Itt being Impossible by any Art or Invention of man for this City to Support itt Self and maintain its Inhabitants Except by trade and Comerce which were the Causes of its foundation. And the possession thereof, together with all Such Priviledges and usages needfull for their Support hath allways been Ratified and Confirmed by the Respective Governors, your Excellencys Predecessors. May itt Please your Excellency
. . . to take the decaying State of this afflicted City into your favourable Consideration, and become their effectual Patron and Protector, under whose Influence itt Can only flourish.
Your Excellencys Petitioners do therefore humbly pray

That your Excellency would be pleased to Order their Majesties Grant of Confirmation of their Charter, and that the Sole and only bolting of flower and [baking of] biskett for Transportation may be Confirmed to this Citty as formerly.

25. Geographical Expansion for Economic Survival

A. Coveting the Jersey Market, March 7, 1684

[Mayor and Aldermen of New York to Lt. Gov. Thomas Dongan, Mar. 7, 1684, *Minutes of Common Council*, I, 130-31]

The Inhabitants of this . . . Citty were Induced with uncessant Labour, great Charge And Expence to Cultivate the Barren Soyle And Suply Some Naturall Defects of the place with Art and Industry for the Conveniency And Accomodation of Trade And Shipping, hopeing that this . . . would have . . . Encouraged our Posterity to Improve the Same, Methods which without Doubt would have been Accomplished if the Unhappy Seperation of East Jersey had not Occured which must necessarily Diverte the Trade of this Province, as this Years Experiance doth Sufficiently Demonstrate. The Partes which before Brought Considerable Yearly Trade To this Citty being not Only furnished And Supplyed By their Imediate Traffique And Commerce to And from Europe And Other Partes without Paying the Dutyes And Accknowledgments Due And Payable to his Royall Highness Or Observeing what [is] Required by the Acts of Navigation . . . but much of the Produce of the Remainder of this, his Royal Highness Province, by Reason of their Neer Scituation, is Drawed to them And the Indian Trade which before was of Considerable Benefitt And Advantage to this City is Likewise Removed thither to the great Loss, Hinderance, And Decay . . . of many of our Inhabitants, besides the Apparant Loss, Prejudice, and Spoyl of his Royall Highness Revenues. . . .

Wee doe humbley Suplycate your Honor That . . . you would Represent the Same unto his Royall Highness In behalfe of this Citty And Desire that East-Jersey may be ReAnnexed to this Province Againe by Purchase Or Other wayes.

B. Governor Dongan's Expansionism, February 22, 1687

[Dongan's Report to the Privy Council on the State of the Province, Feb. 22, 1687, O'Callaghan, ed., *Documents Relative to Colonial New York*, III, 391-93]

And then if his Majesty were further pleased . . . to add to this Government Connecticut and Rhode Island, Connecticut being so conveniently situate . . . to us and soe inconvenient for the people of Boston by reason of its being upwards of two hundred miles distance from thence. Besides Connecticut, as it now is, takes away from us almost all the land of Value that lies adjoyning to Hudsons River and the best part of the River itself. Besides as wee find by experience, if that place bee not annexed to this Government it will bee impossible to make any thing considerable of his Majesty's Customs and Revenue in

Long Island. They [of Connecticut] carry away without entring all our [whale] Oyles which is the greatest part of what wee have to make returns from this place. And from Albany and that way up the river our Beaver and Peltry.

This Government too has an undoubted right to it by Charter. . . . And indeed if the form of the Government bee altered [by revocation of Connecticut's charter], their people will rather choose to come under this than that Government of Boston [i.e., Dominion of New England]. . . .

And as for East Jersey, it being situate on the other side of Hudsons River and between us and where the river disembogues itself into the sea, paying noe Custom and having likewise the advantage of having better land and most of the Settlers there out of this Government. Wee are like to bee deserted by a great many of our Merchants whoe intend to settle there if not annexed to this Government.

Last year two or three ships came in there with goods and I am sure that that Country cannot, noe not with the help of West Jersey, consume one thousand lbs. [sterling] in goods in two years soe that the rest of these Goods must have been run into this Government without paying his Majesty's Customs, and indeed theres noe possibility of preventing it.

And as for Beaver and Peltry, its impossible to hinder its being carried thither. The Indians value not the length of their journey soe as they can come to a good market which those people can better afford them than wee, they paying noe Custom nor Excise inwards or outwards.

An other inconveniency by the Governments remaining as it does is that privateers and others can come within Sandy Hook and take what Provisions and Goods they please from that Side. Alsoe very often shipps bound to this place break bulk there and run their Goods into that Colony with intent af-

terwards to import the same privately and at more leisure into this Province notwithstanding their Oath. . . .

If the Proprietors [of East Jersey] would rightly consider it, they would find it their own Interest that that place should bee annexed to this Government, for they are at a greater charge for maintaining the present Government than the whole Profits of the Province. . . .

We in this Government look upon that Bay that runs into the Sea at Sandy Hook to bee Hudsons River. Therefore there being a clause in my Instructions directing mee that I cause all vessels that come into Hudsons River to Enter at New York, I desire to know whether his Majesty intends thereby those Vessels that come within Sandy-Hook, the people of East Jersey pretending a right to the River soe farr as their Province extends which is eighteen miles up the River to the Northward of this Place.

West Jersey remaining as it does will be noe less inconvenient to this Government for the same reasons as East Jersey, they both making but one Neck of Land and that soe near situate to us that its more for their convenience to have commerce here than anywhere else, and under those circumstances that if there were a Warr either with Christians or Indians they would not bee able to defend themselves without the assistance of this Government.

To bee short, there is an absolute necessity those Provinces and that of Connecticut bee annexed.

The three lower Countys of Pennsylvania have been a dependency on this Place and a great many of the Inhabitants persons that removed thither from this Government, and I doe not beleive it was his Majesty's intention to annex it to Pennsylvania nor to have it subject to the same Laws, it being the Kings own Land. The doing whereof by Mr. Penn there has been of great detriment to this Place in hindring the Tobacco to come hither as formerly, for then there came two shipps for one that comes now, Beaver and Peltry taking up but small Stowage in Shipps.

And indeed it were in my opinion very necessary for the advantage of this Place and increase of his Majestys Revenues that it were soe ordered that the Tobacco of these Countrys may bee imported hither without paying there the duty of one Peny per Pound. . . . Then wee should not bee at such streights for returns, their Trade would much increase, and this Place become a Magazin for the Neighbouring Pro-vinces, and care taken that the Tobacco bee duly returned to England, whereas now a great part of it goes another way and soe its very necessary that the Collector of this Place should be Collector of that River for the enumerated commoditys. And wee will have such regard to the advantage of this Port that wee'l suffer noe fraud to bee committed there nor noe Tobacco to be exported but what goes either directly for England or this Place.

C. EDWARD RANDOLPH CRITICIZES NEW YORK'S EXPANSIONISM, NOVEMBER 23, 1687

[Randolph to William Blathwayt, Nov. 23, 1687, Blathwayt Papers, I, Colonial Williamsburg, Inc.]

Those of Connecticutt who above all things Dreaded to be joind to New York, though they were very highly Courted by Colonel Dongan who depended upon his great interest at Court. He wanted that Colony for he has so squeezed the people of New York That they are very hardly able to live, and as many as can leave the place. Some come hither [i.e., Boston] who are not very Gratefull; others are turnd planters in Jarsey, and very few English left [in New York].

The Political Problem

26. The Reluctant Creation of Representative Government

A. THE DUKE OF YORK'S DISLIKE FOR POPULAR LEGISLATURES, APRIL 6, 1675

[The Duke of York to Sir Edmund Andros, Apr. 6, 1675, O'Callaghan, ed., *Documents Relative to Colonial New York*, III, 230]

First then, touching Generall Assemblyes which the people there seeme desirous of in imitation of their neighbour Colonies, I thinke you have done well to discourage any motion of that kind, both as being not at all comprehended in your Instructions nor indeed consistent with the forme of government already established, nor necessary for the ease or redresse of any greivance that may happen, since that may be as easily obtained by any petition or other addresse to you at their Generall Assizes (which is once a yeare) where the same persons (as Justices) are usually present, who in all probability would be theire Representatives if another constitution were allowed.

B. The Duke of York on the "Dangerous Consequence" of Assemblies, January 28, 1676

[The Duke of York to Lt. Gov. Edmund Andros, Jan. 28, 1676, O'Callaghan, ed., *Documents Relative to Colonial New York*, III, 235]

I have formerly writt to you touching Assemblyes in those countreys and have since observed what severall of your lattest letters hint about that matter. But unless you had offered what qualifications are usuall and proper to such Assemblyes, I cannot but suspect they would be of dangerous consequence, nothing being more knowne then the aptness of such bodyes to assume to themselves many priviledges which prove destructive to, or very oft disturbe, the peace of the government wherein they are allowed. Neither doe I see any use of them which is not as well provided for whilest you and your Councell governe according to the laws established (thereby preserving every man's property inviolate) and whilest all things that need redresse may be sure of finding it, either at the Quarter Sessions or by other legall and ordinary wayes, or lastly by appeale to myselfe. But howsoever if you continue of the same opinion, I shall be ready to consider of any proposalls you shall send to that purpose.

C. The Duke of York Conditionally Grants an Assembly, March 28, 1682

[The Duke of York to Lt. Anthony Brockholes, Commander in Chief, Mar. 28, 1682, O'Callaghan, ed., *Documents Relative to Colonial New York*, III, 317-18]

I have had an account of the result of divers meetings of my Commissioners touching the state of affayres at New Yorke, but untill I come to London (which I doubt will not be till this ship is sailed), I cannot perfect those resolutions which I shall take thereupon; only for the present, in confirmation of what my Secretary lately wrote to you, I send to tell you that I intend to establish such a forme of government at New Yorke as shall have all the advantages and priviledges to the inhabitants and traders there which His Majesty's other plantations in America doe enjoy, particularly in the chooseing of an Assembly, and in all other things as nere as may be agreable to the laws of England. But then I shall expect that the Countrey of New Yorke and its Dependencyes shall provide some certaine fonds for the necessary support of the government and garrison, and for dischargeing the arreares which are or shalbe incurred since the obstructions that have lately beene to the collection of the publique revenue there. Wherefore you are to use all dilligence to induce the people there of best note and estates to dispose them selves and their freinds to a cheerfull complyance in this point, and you may assure them that what soever shalbe thus raysed shalbe applyed to those publique uses.

D. William Penn Reports New York's Reaction, October 21, 1682

[Penn to William Blathwayt, Oct. 21, 1682, Blathwayt Papers, VI, Colonial Williamsburg, Inc.]

I am now at New York, where I last night persuaded all Partys to lett fall their Animositys, which they promest, and since the Duke has named another Governor to think of ways how to maintain their charge in consideration of the priviledges the duke had on those terms assured them they should enjoy. I must needs say that the fault I find upon Sir Edmund Andros is sometimes an over eager and too pressing an execution of his powers.

27. The Death of Representative Government

A. James II's Instructions to Gov. Thomas Dongan, May 29, 1686

[O'Callaghan, ed., *Documents Relative to Colonial New York*, III, 370]

12. And whereas wee have been presented with a Bill or Charter passed in the late Assembly of New York containing several Franchises, privileges, and Immunitys mentioned to be granted to the Inhabitants of our said province. You are to Declare Our Will and pleasure that the said Bill or Charter of Franchises bee forthwith repealed and disallowed, as the same is hereby Repealed, determined, and made void. But you are nevertheless with our said Council to continue the Dutys and Impositions therein mentioned to bee raised untill you shall with the consent of the Council settle such Taxes and Impositions as shall be sufficient for the support of our Government of New York.

13. And our further will and pleasure is that all other Laws, Statutes, and Ordinances already made within Our said Province of New York shall continue and bee in full force and vigor soe far forth as they doe not in any wise contradict, impeach, or derogate from this Commission or the Orders and Instructions herewith given you till you shall, with the advice of our Council, pass other Laws in our Name for the good government of our said Province, which you are to doe with all convenient speed. . . .

16. And you are to observe in the passing of Laws that the Stile of Enacting the same By the Governor and Council bee henceforth used and noe other.

B. New York Incorporated into the Dominion, April 7, 1688

[James II's Commission of Sir Edmund Andros, Apr. 7, 1688, O'Callaghan, ed., *Documents Relative to Colonial New York*, III, 537-38]

To our trusty and welbeloved Sir Edmund Andros Knight Greeting: Whereas by our Commission . . . wee have constituted and appointed you to be our Captain Generall and Governor in Cheif in and over all that part of our territory and dominion of New England in America. . . . And whereas since that time Wee have thought it necessary for our service and for the better protection and security of our subjects in those parts to join and annex to our said Government the neighboring Colonies of Road Island and Connecticutt, our Province of New York and East and West Jersey with the territories thereunto belonging, as wee do hereby join, annex, and unite the same to our said government and dominion of New England. . . .

Wee do hereby give and grant unto you full power and authority, by and with the advice and consent of our said Councill or the major part of them, to make constitute and ordain lawes statutes and ordinances for the public peace welfare and good government of our said territory and dominion and of the people and inhabitants thereof, and such others as shall resort thereto, and for the benefit of us, our heires, and successors. Which said lawes statutes and ordinances are to be, as near as conveniently may be, agreeable to the lawes and statutes of this our kingdom of England: Provided that all such lawes statutes and ordinances of what nature or duration soever, be within three months, or sooner, after the making of the same, transmitted unto Us under our Seal of New England, for our allowance or disapprobation of them, as also duplicates thereof by the next conveyance.

And Wee do by these presents give and grant unto you full power and authority by and with the advise and consent of our said Councill, or the major part of them, to impose assess and raise and levy such rates and taxes as you shall find necessary for the support of the government . . . to be collected and levyed and to be imployed to the uses aforesaid in such manner as you and our said Councill or the major part of them shall seem most equall and reasonable.

C. Edward Randolph on New York's Inclusion in the Dominion, September 12, 1688

[Randolph to William Blathwayt, Sept. 12, 1688, Blathwayt Papers, I, Colonial Williamsburg, Inc.]

Colonel Dongan . . . sends his answeare highly reflecting upon the governor and abuses the Councill, Saying his Excellencys privat Malice against him was the Sole Cause why the account was not passed and thereby his Majesties Service obstructed. Saying with all that he had made all the government easy for his excellence with little charg to the King. 'Tis Trew, if to impoverish the people, to leave the forts unprovided of all necessary Stores, not one ounce of powdre in the fort at Albany at the Governors coming thither, and the fort at New York is wholy out of Repair, be to make a Governor Easye, this is Certainly So. For all is either Sold or traded away. Wee find the french Governor has been too hard in all his proceedings for Colonel Dongan. He keepes his Indians in armes who have by his order kild 6 Christians and 4 Indians in the Collony of Connecticott since the Cessation and wrote to Colonel Dongan that they should not lay Down their Armes till the Senecas give him assurance of their complying with his terms, and to this day continues the fort of Cadarachqui in his possession, lying in the best part of our Indian country.

The Religious Situation

28. The Religious Complexion of New York

A. Jacob Leisler's Orthodoxy, August 23, 1676

[Van Laer, ed., *Minutes of the Court of Albany*, II, 146-48]

Domine Nicolaus Van Renselaer, plaintiff, against Mr Jacob Leyselaer and Jacob Milburn, defendants. . . .

The plaintiff states in writing that the defendant, Leyselaer, in derision ventured to boast that he could preach as well as Domine Renselaer, and that in other places he divulged that he was not orthodox but heterodox in his preaching, whereby his person, studies, preaching and the talents graciously granted to him by God are brought into contempt and the good and faithful hearts of the resident members are disturbed and alienated, he having furthermore misrepresented his sermons, as appears from his glosses, annotation and false memoranda made in church, consisting of some points which the plaintiff challenges and refutes by an affidavit of 12 trustworthy members of this congregation, whereas the defendant has failed to adduce any testimony of witnesses. He further submits that Reynier Schaets, as a member of the church, can not testify against his pastor. Likewise, that Zarah Van Borsum, who is a blood relation, is also objectionable and that Damhouder's *Praxis*, in chap. 50 of his criminal procedure, teaches that women who testify may be challenged in criminal proceedings instituted in criminal cases.

As to the accusations and slander of Jacob Milburn, his own witness, Reynier Schaets, invalidates his allegations.

The plaintiff says further that the defendants can not do so with any decency, citing on that subject some passages of the Scriptures, and consequently that it appears therefrom that the passionate words, blasphemies and slander uttered by them are inspired by a hatred conceived against him.

He therefore concludes that the defendants, Leyselaer and Milburn, for the slanderous remarks, glosses, annotations and false accusations regarding the preaching of Domine Nic. v. Renselaer, made by them against his person and the dignity of his office, ought to make honorable and profitable amends; consequently, he requests that their honors may be pleased to examine and compare the documents and the evidence as the crime committed deserves and to render such judgment in the matter as the truth and justice require in a case of slander of a minister of Jesus Christ, begun contrary to the tranquility, peace and harmony of this good congregation, all *cum expensis*.

The defendants request an English translation of the plaintiff's declaration, to serve them when the occasion presents itself. . . .

Mr Jacob Milburn states and submits that it is a matter of grave importance with which they are charged and that it not only renders them suspect before men, but that their conscience, soul and salvation depend upon it. He therefore requests that Domine Renselaer give security in the sum of £1000 sterling, declaring that he [Milburn] has that much in his possession, in order that he may be compelled to make good his accusation.

Mr Jacob Leyselaer, for the reason aforesaid, likewise demands of the plaintiff security in the sum of £5000 sterling and offers to swear that his person and capital are worth that much. . . .

The honorable court, having heard the parties, order the plaintiff to give sufficient security in the sum of £1500 sterling, to wit, £1000 for Leyselaer and £500 for Milburn to the end that he may make good his accusation and charge against the defendants.

B. Celebrating the Birth of a Catholic Prince of Wales, October 2, 1688

[Edward Randolph to William Blathwayt, Oct. 2, 1688, Blathwayt Papers, I, Colonial Williamsburg, Inc.]

I cannot omitt to acquaint you that upon the newes Sent us from Boston by Captain Nicholson of the Birth of the Prince of Wales (it being the 27 of August last) about 6 in the Evening his Excellence immediately went to the fort, Colonel Dongan sent for all the Councell, the Mayor, and Aldermen and invited all that would Come to drinke the princes health, which, upon his Excellencys beginning it, all the Great Gunns in the fort were fired, volleys of small shott from his Majesty's two Companys answearing them. And then all the Shipps in the harbour firred off their Gunns. The people every where drinking and crying out God Save The Prince of Wales. During this Entertainment in the fort a Very larg Bonfire was made before the fort gate where his Excellence and all the Councill dranke the princes health, and instead of Conduits were severall pipes of wine, the heads knockd out, which plentifully supplyed the whole Company running From one pipe to another, Burning their hatts and cloathes with Full potts and peales of Huzzars all night long, some by choise, others by necessity, keeping their ground till morning. The next day a publick day of thanks Giving was ordered to be kept thro the whole Government. . . . A fortnight after in the remotest parts in our passage to Albany, about halfe way on Hudsons River, his Excellence went a Shoare and all that were able made 3 great fires and Carried plenty of wine and provisions of all Sorts which were dressd on the land, and most part of that night was spent in drinking the princes health and firing Gunns, and that high Land Called the Princes Point. . . . Upon the Sunday fortnight his Excellence, being at Albany, after church went to the Fort with all the Council and the Cheife Merchants, with the Mayor and Aldermen of that Citty and beginning the princes health, the Great Gunns were fired off: 3 volleys from the Souldiers in the fort which were answeared from the fort by the water side and followed by the vessells in the River. Then all the Company were treated at a very plentifull Dinner—that the Jolly Dutchmen might not want a Supper, a whole Ox was roasted and two very Larg Bonfires made to Entertain the numerous guests never before so feasted by wholesale, and the Easier to wash down their roast beefe, barrells of very stout beere Stood every wheare ready broachd at the head for men, women, and children to drink or drown as they pleased. From thence wee followed his Excellence to his house where he had ordered a great supper to be made ready and nothing but God blesse the prince and drinking his health and loud acclamations were heard that night.

CHAPTER FIVE

THE PATTERN OF REBELLION

AS an integral part of the Dominion of New England since 1688, New York was nominally under the control of Governor-General Sir Edmund Andros stationed in Boston. But the problems of distance and communication, together with the colony's vulnerability to attack from French Canada, made it necessary that the actual command be exercised by Lieutenant Governor Francis Nicholson and the councilors resident in the immediate area—Stephanus Van Cortlandt, Frederick Philipse, and Nicholas Bayard.

When these leaders in New York City learned in March 1689 of William of Orange's invasion of England, they were perplexed as to its meaning. Their immediate reaction was to suppress the news for fear of its consequences upon a population discontented and uneasy (No. 29 A). But such news could be kept secret just so long, and by the end of April word had leaked out that Sir Edmund Andros and most of his official family had been imprisoned in Boston. Nicholson was now in a quandary—his legal source of authority was cut off, and he could only assume the government of the Dominion in the event of Andros' death or absence, neither of which had occurred. Moreover, should he take over the government, he had to have a quorum of five councilors, and only three were available to him. His government had become *de facto* rather than *de jure,* and it was questionable whether he could maintain his authority in New York. Nevertheless, Lieutenant Governor Nicholson attempted to win support by consulting New York leaders on measures to maintain "the quietness of the people and security of the government" (No. 29 B).

The caliber and resiliency of Nicholson's administration was soon tested by a series of events beginning in Suffolk, Westchester, and Queens counties, and quickly spreading to New York City (Nos. 30-31). Developments in London and Boston served as catalysts, and the Lieutenant Governor was incapable of handling the popular reactions in New York. As the citizens took full advantage of the opportunity to express their grievances, Nicholson found the situation intolerable (No. 32). Finally, on May 30, he reached the breaking point, and destroyed the last vestige of his own authority by his hot-headed threat to burn the town if the people's attitude did not change. The citizens rose in anger, marched on the fort, and were admitted by Lieutenant Hendrick Cuyler of the militia.

The rebellion had begun. The militia refused to obey the commands of their colonel, councilor Nicholas Bayard, and the militia captains assumed command of the fort, each serving in turn. No suggestion was made, either by those who had risen or by those who were displaced, that any one individual led or formulated the uprising. Not until June 2 did any one of the captains achieve individual prominence, and that occurred only when Bayard refused to act upon rumors of the arrival of a French invasion fleet. Jacob Leisler took temporary control, but he remained thereafter only one of several captains acting in unison (No. 33).

Nicholson, who had been completely repudiated by the people, next violated his earlier instructions from the Crown and departed for England (No. 34). He entrusted the government to the three councilors who had also been repudiated. To fill the governmental void the militia captains called a council of safety into being. Delegates attended from Westchester, Kings, and Queens counties, New York City, Staten Island, Kingston (Esopus) in Ulster County, and Hackensack and Elizabethtown in New Jersey. This group on June 28 appointed Leisler as permanent captain of the fort and later, on August 15, granted him the title and authority of commander-in-chief.

From the moment of his elevation, Leisler wielded his power in an arbitrary manner to accomplish his purposes. He reconstructed the fort in New York City and acquired the supplies necessary for the colony's defense. He also incarcerated those alleged to be enemies of Protestantism, conducted municipal elections in New York City to remove his opponents from their last official positions, and attempted to extend his authority over Albany.

Given the long-standing and delicate relationship which existed between the Albany burghers and the Iroquois, Leisler's effort to take control of this area was bound to create friction. The town's leaders had not reacted strongly to either the incarceration of Andros or the flight of Nicholson, but neither had they any love for the New York City rebels, one of whose goals was sure to be the elimination of the town's coveted monopoly of the Indian trade. But control of Indian affairs was vital to the colony because the Iroquois provided its first perimeter of defense. Thus a stalemate developed: Albany supported the cause of the Glorious Revolution but refused to accept Jacob Leisler as King William's agent. Not until the French and Indians massacred the population of the neighboring town of Schenectady and the Connecticut authorities withdrew their forces from the town did Albany capitulate to Leisler.

On December 10, 1689, a letter from the Privy Council arrived in New York, containing royal instructions directed to "Francis Nicholson Esqre. . . . and in his absence to such as for the time being take care for preserving the Peace and administering the Laws." Leisler quickly seized it and announced that the Crown had recognized him as Lieutenant Governor (No. 35 A). His claim to this authority, although accepted by modern scholars, aroused violent controversy at the time (No. 35 B).

Leisler immediately converted his supporters into a royal council, and then operated as though he had the full backing of Whitehall. One of his most important problems, of course, was to raise funds for the colony's defense. Since he himself had denied the legality of the old revenue laws enacted by Andros, he issued writs for a new Assembly in February 1690. At the same time, he wisely understood that New York could not singlehandedly deal with the French menace in Canada, and he called an intercolonial conference to meet in New York City in May. Massachusetts, Plymouth, and Connecticut sent delegates, and Virginia and Maryland promised whatever aid they could spare.

The conferees agreed upon a land invasion of Canada and assigned the major responsibility to New York because Massachusetts was preparing a naval assault. Although the delegates also agreed that Leisler should name the commander of the land expedition, the Albany leaders, cooperating with the Connecticut authorities, finally forced him to name Major-General Fitz-John Winthrop of New Haven. When the expedition failed, the major reasons were disease, inadequate supplies, and lack of Indian support, but the venture nevertheless brought bitter recriminations between Leisler and the Connecticut authorities.

By the fall of 1690, Leisler's star was dimming. The failure of the Canadian attack, the government's repressive measures, its inability to remedy the underlying grievances of the people, all led to a growing disenchantment. At the same time came word of the appointment of a new royal governor, Henry Sloughter, and the group whom Leisler had displaced took new hope. Sloughter was a good friend of those in England who had close contacts with the old leadership of the colony, and as early as October 1690 he had decided that New York's government was "at present held by a rabble." When the royal authorities left the matter of Leisler's fate to the new governor's discretion, therefore, it was clear that the revolutionary leadership was doomed.

Prelude to Revolt

29. The Sudden News of Revolution

A. Nicholson Keeps the News Secret, March 1, 1689

["Minutes of the Councell att New Yorke," Mar. 1, 1689, "Documents Relating to the Administration of Jacob Leisler," New-York Historical Society, *Collections*, 1 (1868), 241-42]

This day . . . brought unto the Lieutenant Gouvernor Nicholson, a letter from Captain John Blackwell Gouvernor of Pennsylvania with a copy off an examination off one Zachariah Whitepaine lately come from England. The substance off which Examination is that the Prince off Orange had invaded England and severall other transactions there. . . .

Resolved, that for the prevention off any tumult and the divulging of soe strange news, The said letters [also brought by the messenger] be opened to see if they contained the same substance off England's being invaded, which was forthwith done. . . . [Several] contained the same news which made this Board give the more creditt to itt.

B. Governor Nicholson Consults the Leaders of New York, April 27, 1689

["Minutes of the Councell att New Yorke," Apr. 27, 1689, "Documents Relating to the Administration of Jacob Leisler," N.-Y. Hist. Soc., *Collections*, 1 (1868), 245]

Upon hearing the Revolutions att Boston and rumors of war from abroad between England and [the] French and the number off the Councill being soe few, considring the necessity that all affairs ought to be put in good order, the peace kept, and gouvernement secured from invasion abroad.

Its ordered and resolved,

That the Mayor, Aldermen, and Common Councell with the Chief military officers be called together this afternoone to meet the Lieutenant Gouvernor and Councill att the Towne Hall, there to advise whatt needful is to be done in this troublesome times for the quietnesse

off the people and security off the Gouvernment.

And some of the Councell informing the Gouvernor of the jealousies and fears off the Inhabitants of this Citty by reason of the small number off soldiers in the Fortt, and most of them infirme and old and thatt it would bee demanded by some off the Captains off the militia That some off their soldiers might keep the guard in the Fortt, to prevent the same, it was resolved to propose the same to them To shew our willingnesse to defend the fortt, Citty and Gouvernmentt against any common enemy.

30. Evidences of Discontent

A. Suffolk County Freeholders' Declaration, May 3, 1689

[O'Callaghan, ed., *Documents Relative to Colonial New York*, III, 577]

1st. Being alarmed by a printed declaration at Boston the 18th last of the Gentlemen Marchants and country adjacent, manifesting the grounds of their seizing the Governor and Government into their hands, wishing all others their neighbours to follow them, and [by] our Country of England's example for securing our English nations liberties and propertyes from Popery and Slavery, and from the Intented invasion of a foraign French design, and [by the] more than Turkish crueltys by relation already acted upon severall of our nation. . . . And we being persons . . . who have groaned under the heavy burdens imposed upon us by an arbitrary power for a considerable time together, without the lest molestation on our parts, and being under the like circumstances of being invaded by a forraign ennemy [about] which the other English America[ns] is alarmed, which moved us to do something at this time for our own self preservation, being without any to depend on at present till it pleases God to order better.

2ndly. Therefor we esteem it our bounden duty to use all lawful endeavours for securing our head quarters of New York and Albany forts, and all other fortifications, and the same to put into the hands of those whom we can confide in, till further order from the parliament in England.

3dly. We also think it our duty to use our best endeavours for the redemption and securing of all such moneyes as has been lately extorted from us by the aforesaid power; as also to secure all those persons reputed to be the ennemyes of the peace and prosperity of our country and the fundamental laws of our English nation, as aforesaid till further orders.

Lastly. We firmly beleive that herein we have endeavoured nothing less than what mere duty to God and our country doth call for at our hands, committing our enterprise to his blessing, and desire all our neighbours to join with us in praises and all just actions for the prosperity and safety of our country from all approaching dangers.

B. Queens County in an Uproar, May 9, 1689

["Minutes of the Councell att New Yorke," May 9, 1689, "Documents Relating to the Administration of Jacob Leisler," N.-Y. Hist Soc., *Collections*, 1 (1868), 254-55]

Major Thomas Willett and Captain John Jackson appeared and acquainted the gouvernor and Councell that the men in Queens County that have been with Colonel Thomas Dongan in the late expedition at Albany are all in armes and the whole county in an uproar, desiring that they might be paid money being raised for that purpose, etc.

After mature deliberation for quieting the minds off the people and securing and keeping the peace of the gouvernement it is ordered that . . . Mr. Matthew Plowman [collector of the colony] . . . pay unto Captain Jackson aforesaid the sume of one hundred and sixteen pounds thirteene shillings, being the arrears due to the men that ware prest out off said

County. But hearing that said County had paid unto the Collector aforesaid But fourty two pounds tenn shillings and three pence on account of their Tax it is further ordered Thatt . . . the Justices of said County . . . call the severall Collectors before them . . . and to give them an order to pay unto Captain John Jackson aforesaid the sume of seaventy foure pounds two shillings six pence halfe penny which with the fourty two pounds tenn shillings and three pence aforesaid compleats the whole sume off one hundred sixteen pounds thirteen shillings halfe penny.

C. Jealousies of the Indians near Albany, May 12, 1689

["Minutes of the Councell at New Yorke," May 12, 1689, "Documents Relating to the Administration of Jacob Leisler," N.-Y. Hist. Soc., *Collections,* 1 (1868), 256-58]

This morning the Lieutenant Gouvernor received a letter from the Mayor att Albany, That the Indians had gott some jealousies in their heads which if not prevented might cause greatt mischieff, it is therefore thought fitt to send them the following letter, vizt.

New Yorcke, 12 May, 1689.

Gentlemen,

This morning came to our hands by these bearers a letter from the Mayor att Albany acquainting us off the affaires off the Inhabitants off thatt County in regard off the Indians, occasioned by the jealousies raised amongst them that Gouvernor Andros last winter att the Eastward had agreed with those off Canada to destroy the five cantons nations [i.e., Iroquois]. Wee have cause to beleeve that those jealousies are come over to them by some ill affected persons from New England, since wee about three months past had the news here from Boston that several libells ware disperst there to the same effect, and although the same is sufficiently contradicted and is proved to be a mere falsehood, yett since itt is so printed in the mindes off those heathens it will be in vaine to be overpressing with them to diswade them thereoff. Wee are off the same opinion with your selfe that it would be most distructive to this gouvernment that by occasion off said jealousies the said five nations should joine with Canida. You have therefore done very well that you have already sent two persons to the Maquaas [i.e., Mohawk] land to endeavor by all possible meanes to remove any such jealousies and doe judge it further most safe that you proceed in like manner by sending alsoo to the rest off the nations as you conveniently can, and to acquaint them either by your selves or by such persons as you shall thinck fitt and know to be most acceptable to the Indians.

Imprimus, that wee have news from beyond the Zeas that the English and the Dutch nations are joined together cheefly to curb the pride of France, and that wee dayly expect orders to be in warr with them.

Secondly, That from Boston wee had about three months agoe intelligence that Sir Edmund Andros had joined with the French, But that it was since contradicted. That he was now seized on att Boston, But thatt wee could not hear any such thing was laid to his charge and thereby concluded to be a falsehood.

Thirdly, That they might be assured off the entire and old friendship off the Inhabitants off this gouvernment. Thatt wee are now fortifying off New Yorcke, although wee doe not feare the French, only to be upon our guard, and to be ready when orders comes from beyond

Zea which we expect will be to fight the French as our and their ennemy to bring them low.

Fourthly, That the persons here [who] made a stop to their late victories against Canida are laid aside and that they need nott to suffer any more abuses from those off Canida. That the five nations therefore must stick together and not suffer any of them to goe to Canida for to be deluded, poisoned or betrayed nor to suffer any French to live amongst them.

Fifthly, That if they shall see cause att their going in warr against any off their ennemies, to leave their old, wives, and children amonghst the Christians near Albany, That care will be taken for their maintenance and protection.

Sixthly, To remove all jealousies which the French or others might have raised against the gouvernment and to assure them of our friendship, you are to present to each of the five nations one barrell of powder to be imployed if need be against our and their ennemy.

Gentlemen this is at presentt what we can thinck may bee convenient to bee of-fered, but since the tempers and the manners of the Indians are best knowne to your selves, We leave to your menagement the wordings off the proposalls and the adding off what you will find to be more needfull, tending for the comon safety of your county in particular as well as the gouvernment in generall. But as for to suffer any to goe and trade in the country, wee thinck it not safe. And by all meanes you must take prudent care that noe cause of offence be given from our side. And although any harme should be done by any Indian (which God forbid) That you be onely in the defensive part for to prevent an open warr. But that you [should] rather endeavour to quell any such offences as criminalls and offenders against any knowne law of the gouvernement. In the meantime wee recomand you to be watchfull with courage and to diswade the people from being allarmed att every idle Indian story. Endeavour cheefly to preserve peace and unity amongst yourselves which is alsoo our cheevest studie here, waiting with patience daily to receive orders from England.

31. Nicholson Recognizes the Source of Sedition, May 15, 1689

["Minutes of the Councell att New Yorke," May 15, 1689, "Documents Relating to the Administration of Jacob Leisler," N.-Y. Hist. Soc., *Collections,* 1 (1868), 259-61]

Wee have received from severall parts most various reports concerning the present state off affaires in Europe and in particular off the unparaleld changes in England. Yett to this very day altogether distitute off any certainty which wee hope to receive ere long. In the meanewhile wee have thougt it our duty by this opportunity for to give your honour [the Secretary of State] some account off the troublesome state and condition off this Province and Gouvernment.

Your Honor will find by the inclosed printed summons and declaration upon what pretence some off the Inhabitants marchants and gentry off Boston and places adjacent have throwne downe all manner of gouvernment there and set up for themselves. They have alsoo seized the gouvernor, Sir Edmund Andros, with several off his Councell officers and gentlemen which still are kept in close custodie and prison, disbanded the standard melitia and in fine (as it is reported) suffer the rabble to comit severall insolences.

The Collonies off Rhoad Island and Connecticott have followed their steps. and as it is reported, have chosen for them selves alsoo new Gouvernours. In soe much that this part off the dominion was onely inclined to rest at peace and quiet till orders doe arrive and would have undoubtedly soe continued unlesse the seed off sedition had been blazed from thence to some outward skirts off this province.

And at first in Suffolck County being the east end off Long Island all majestrates and military officers ware put out by the people and others chosen by them. The same patterne was alsoo followed by Queens County and County of Westchester.

This would not satisfie them, but upon hopes to find the Inhabitants off this citty divided and on a faire pretence to be exceedingly concerned and zealous for the safety off the Citty and fortt against any attack or invasion off the French, greatt part off their melitie have taken up armes and are now come at or neare Jamaica about fourteen miles from this place, in order if they could to make themselves master off this Citty and fortt to plunder as it is feared this Citty or at least such members as they would see cause to expose to the rabble. And to that end severall of them with the assistance off some ill affected and restlesse spiritts amongst us used all imaginable meanes to stirr up the Inhabitants off this Citty to sedition and rebellion, but God be thanked who hath blessed our endeavours that wee have hetherto prevented their dangerous designs, but know not how long wee shall be able to resist their further attempts.

But now wee ware anew allarmed from Albany that some Indians in that County ware jealous off this gouvernment and that some Insolencies had been committed by them occasioned as wee suppose by meanes off some libells and falsehoods lately come from Boston possessing the Indians with feare that Sir Edmund had joined with the French off Canida to cutt them off.

Its most certaine that the Gouvernor off Canida will not slip this opportunity to inflame those jealousies and [by] all faire and plaiesable meanes endeavour to unite our Indians to himselfe which would tend to the utter ruine off all the English settlements on this Continent.

Wherefore wee shall not be wanting to use our utmost endeavors for the removing off said jealousies and the securing off our five Cantons and warlike Indian nations to our selves. In the midst off all the troubles within our selves wee ware dayly allarmed with rumors off warr with France, which occasioned a resolve to be made for new fortifying off this Citty since all the former (for what reason wee know not) are suffered to fall to ruine, if not for some part demolished, but how to raise money for the accomplishing of any such fortifications noe way could be found to resolve us there in as our condition is now.

Att this very conjuncture off time began severall off the marchants to dispute the paying off any customes and other duties as illegally established and seeing thatt it was not possible to put a stop to their currant or to uphold the revenue on the same foot wee conveaned all the civell and military officers off this Citty and with their consent and advise did order that the said revenue arrizing by the customs, excise and weigh being from the first day off this instant month off May should be applyed towards the paying and defraying off the charges off said fortifications by which meanes wee hope in some manner to preserve the said revenue. . . .

In all these Revolutions and troubles wee have been deprived off all advice and assistance off any other off the members off the Councell soe thatt all the burthen in this present conjuncture has onely laine on those few members residing in New Yorcke.

32. Nicholson's Government Repudiated

A. Two Councilors Beg to be Excused, May 22, 1689

["Minutes of the Councell att New Yorke," May 22, 1689, "Documents Relating to the Administration of Jacob Leisler," N.-Y. Hist. Soc., *Collections*, 1 (1868), 265-66]

Colonel [Andrew] Hamilton and Colonel [William (Tangier)] Smith being sent for . . . came to New Yorcke and declared their readinesse to serve the king and country and appeared before the Gouvernor and Councell.

Colonel Hamilton first speaking said That he is always ready to serve Sir Edmund Andros and the Country, but finds him selfe obliged by a Commission off Sir Edmund Andros to be judge off the inferior Courts off Comon pleas in East Jersey, which are to be kept the first, second and third Wednesday in June and alsoo that the people there is still in quiett and [he] feares that his absence from those Courts might throw the people in mutiny or rebellion. And since he came in New Yorcke finding the people all in an uprore and disaffected to his Excellency by reason off the rumors they had from people coming from Boston, did think it not advisable in these dangerous times to act any further for fear it would bring the place in actual rebellion.

Colonel Smith alsoo shewed and declared his willingnesse to serve his Excellency Sir Edmund Andros, The Lieutenant Gouvernor having spoken to him in that behalfe. Butt hee living att Setaucket the middle off Long Island ware the people already shoocke off this gouvernment and taking him to be a papist or a frind off them, fears if hee should goe to Boston that the people in his towne would rise and plunder his house, if not offer violence to his family, and for the rest is off the same opinion as Colonel Hamilton.

The Lieutenant Governor and Councell, taking the matter in mature deliberation seeing the uprores in all parts off the Gouvernment, the people incensed against his Excellency by the libells and other reports from Boston, and alsoo having received a letter from Simon Bradstreet and Wait Winthrop, Esq., att Boston wherein they refuse to sett his Excellency att liberty, and alsoo having heard that Major Brockholst, Major MacGregory and George Lockhart are taken att Pemaquid, the Lieutenant Gouvernor and Councell thinck it most safe to for bear acting in the premises till they see the minds off the people better satisfied and quieted.

B. Nicholson Rejects Albany's Offer to Fight, May 24, 1689

["Minutes of the Councell att New Yorke," May 24, 1689, "Documents Relating to the Administration of Jacob Leisler," N.-Y. Hist. Soc., *Collections*, 1 (1868), 266-67]

The [Lieutenant] Governor havinge received a letter from the Majestrates att Albany acquainting his honor that the affaires with the Indians is in a pretty good state and noe feare off any trouble with them, but that to the contrary between sixty and seaventy young men thatt ware two years agoe taken and plundered by the French and kept in prison by them are gott together and demand comission or letter off martt to goe to Canida and take off [from] the French subjects their estates so much as will pay them for their goods taken with all damages, etc.

The Gouvernor and Councell taking the same into consideration did think it necessary to send them the following letter, vizt.

New Yorcke, 1689. May the 24th.
Gentlemen,

Wee have received yours . . . and have communicated the same to all the magistrates off this Citty, who are all off one unanimous opinion that it is not safe for this gouvernment to suffer or to give any commission or letter off mart to the Young men that ware at Ottawa To goe towards Canida or elsewheare, Because wee dayly expect orders out off England and doe not know wether it is warr or peace between England and France. But [we] recommend their readinesse if occasion should bee, and therefore you must in noe manner suffer their proceedings. If att any time you have letters or messingers from any part off New England you are to send them to us, to prevent the stirring off division amongst you and us.

C. Nicholson Repudiated by the New York City Militia, May 31, 1689

["Minutes of the Councell att New Yorke," May 31, 1689, "Documents Relating to the Administration of Jacob Leisler," N.-Y. Hist. Soc., Collections, 1 (1868), 268]

The Councell being mett the Lieutenant Gouvernor acquainted the board that most part off the Citty's melitia where in rebellion, That noe comands, either from him selfe or their Colonel [Nicholas Bayard] ware in any ways regarded nor obeyed. That he was credibly informed some off the officers ware the Instigators and Inflamers off it, and therefore desired the Mayor to conveane this afternoone att the City hall the Court of Mayor Aldermen Comon Councell and all the military officers of this Citty for to advise with them off this matter off great moment, which accordingly was ordered.

The Insurrection Accomplished

33. The Nature of the Uprising

A. The Inhabitants of New York City Rise, May 31, 1689

[Minutes of the General Meeting of the Lt. Gov., Council, Aldermen, and Common Council of New York City, and Military Officers, May 31, 1689, "Documents Relating to the Administration of Jacob Leisler," N.-Y. Hist. Soc., Collections, 1 (1868), 288]

The Inhabitants of New Yorke ryseing this afternoone have taken possession of the Fortt, disarmed the souldiers, and came with a squadron armed in Courtt demanding the keys of the Garrison and with force would and will have them. They forced Captain Lodwick to come into the Town hall and came there armed demanding the keys againe and would have them delivered to Captain Lodwick. The Lieutenant Governor seeing himself forced asked the advice of this Board what to doe in this confused businesse.

This Board for to hinder and prevent bloodshed and further mischiefe and for endeavouring to quiett the minds of the people think it best considering they being forced to itt to let them have the keys.

His Honor proposeing to this Board what way or whether any meanes may be found to reduce this people from their riseing or what other method may bee taken to bring them to their former obedience, This Board are of opinion that there is noe way to reduce them by force but their advice is, since they are rise on their owne heads without any aid that they be lett alone for some time.

B. THE NEW YORK CITY MILITIA EXPLAINS ITS ACTIONS, JUNE 1689

[Address of the Militia to King William III and Queen Mary, June 1689, O'Callaghan, ed., *Documents Relative to Colonial New York*, III, 583-84]

Although wee your Majesties dutiful loyall and obedient subjects have not yet Received the honor to have your Majesties proclaimed amongst us . . . yet wee haveing by way of Barbadoes, received the joyful news and undoubted satisfaction, that your Majestys being proclaimed King of England France and Ireland, wee cannot forbear to prostrate ourselves with all submission at your Royall feet, and to expresse our exceeding joy. . . . Blessing the great God of heaven and earth who has pleased to make your Majesty so happy an instrument in our deliverance from Tyranny, popery and slavery, and to put it into your Royall breasts to undertake so glorious a work towards the reestablishment and preservation of the true protestant Religion, liberty and property. . . . We having also long groaned under the same oppression, having been governed of late, most part, by papists who had in a most arbitrary way subverted our ancient priviledges, making us in effect slaves to their will contrary to the laws of England. And this was chiefly effected by those who are known ennemies to our Religion and liberty. Yet we have with all humbleness submitted ourselves thereto, not doubting but the great God would in his own time send us deliver-

ance. . . . Now we your Majesties most loyall subjects being not only encouraged but invited by your Royall declaration at your first arrivall in England, as alsoe since by the unanimous declaration of the Lords spiritual and temporal assembled at Westminster, thought it our bounden duty to do our endevour to preserve and secure ourselves, and to preserve our being betrayed to any forraigne Ennemy, which we have done without any lett or hindrance or any molestation to any person by taking possession in your Majesty's names of the fort of this citty—disarming some few papists therein—and do keep and guard said fort against all your Majesties ennemies whatsoever until such time [as] your Majesty's Royall will shall be further known, wholly submitting ourselves to your Majestyes pleasure herein. Yet we had not presumed to have done this before we had your Majestyes Royal order, but that we were under most just fears and jealousyes to have been betrayed to our ennemy. Our late Governour Sir Edmund Andros executing a most arbitrary commission procured from the late King, most in command over us being bitter papists; our Lieutenant Governor Captain Nicholson, altho a pretended protestant, yet, contrary both to his promises and pretences, countenancing the Popish party, denying to exclude both Officers in the custom house and Souldiers in the fort, being most Papists, contrary to the known laws of England, altho he was often thereto solicited, and the Companies of our train bands keeping guard in the said fort being threatened by the said Lieutenant Governor Captain Nicholson for acting nothing beyond their duty ... placing a sentinnell at a certain sally port in the said fort where we might justly suspect an ennemy to enter, and at some other convenient places which required the same, which he refuseing, entertaining secretly at the same time severall souldiers wholly strangers to the Towne being some Irish into the Garrison and threatning our serjeants and [one] of the officers . . . to pistol them with unreasonable expressions to fire the town about our ears or words to that effect, and of the rash hasty and furious expressions and threats against us for so acting our duty civilly and with submission. . . . We have been fain to do, and now do with all submission lay ourselves at the feet of your sacred Majestyes, humbly imploring your Majestyes favor and protection assuring your Majestyes our only design and intentions was to secure ourselves and country to be wholly devoted to your Majestyes will and pleasure in the disposeing of our Government.

C. COLONEL BAYARD'S VERSION OF THE UPRISING, JUNE 4, 1689

["Minutes of the Councell att New Yorke," June 4, 1689, "Documents Relating to the Administration of Jacob Leisler," N.-Y. Hist. Soc., *Collections*, 1 (1868), 269-70]

Colonel Bayard gave an account to the Councell in what manner most part of the soldiers of Captain Minviele, Captain de Peyster, Captain Lodwick, and Captain de Bruyn on yesterday being in armes att the place off Parade before the fortt, had been disobedient to the comands off their said officers and in a rebellious manner left their said officers, went to the fortt to side with Captain Leisler and committed insufferable insolences.

That Mr. Dischington was arrived with his sloope from Barbados, was att his landing not suffered to speake to any person being forced by a file off musqueteers to goe into the fortt, and his gasetts, etc. taken from him.

That Nicholas Gerrits arriving alsoe from Barbados (bringing the first certaine news that the most illustrious prince William off Orange and princess Mary ware proclaimed att Barbados King and Queen of England, etc., which alsoo was confirmed by a gasette off their being proclaimed in London) was served in like manner.

That they having intelligence thatt Philip French a marchant who lately arrived from England to Boston, would be here this night by land. A file of musquetteirs was sent by the Captain off the fortt about a mile out of the towne to seize and bring him into the fortt, which accordingly was done.

That Nicholas de la Plyne arriving from Boston in his vessel was served in like manner, all the letters he brought demanded, and two letters directed to the Major [Stephanus Van] Cortlandt broke open and read in the fort and soe sent [to] him.

Colonel Bayard made his complaint that being about some business att the custome house, Captain Leisler came in, and by filthy and scurrilous expressions called him over and over You a Colonel off a tirannicall power, with several other threatning words, that he would see him hanged etc.

The said Colonel Bayard acquainted the Councell alsoo that by the instigation off said Leisler the rabble was sett on and so invetteritt against him because he would not take the peoples part against the Lieutenant Gouvernour, That by very credible hands he was informed that he was in great danger to be devoured and his house pulled downe, etc.

D. Captain Leisler's Version of the Uprising, June 4, 1689

[Leisler to Simon Bradstreet, June 4, 1689, Edmund B. O'Callaghan, ed., *The Documentary History of the State of New York*, 4 vols. (Albany, 1849-51), II, 3-4]

I make bold to acquaint you [the governor of Massachusetts Bay Colony] of the securing of the fort by the traine bonds of New york. . . . In two dayes after the Governor and his Counsell with severall of their creatures had gained so much upon the people that they were afraied and halfe of myne company . . . they worked most upon had left me, but the second of this instant, being my watch in the fort I came with 49 men and entered in the fort . . . whereupon I resolved not to leave till I had brought all the traine bound fully to joine with me. The 3d wee had newes of three ships in sight upon which I tooke occasione to alarume the towne and gott five captanes besides me and 400 men to signe the enclosed . . . which discouraged the adverse party, and since they have been indifferent still. The Lieut. Governor Nicholls[on] is departed last night without taking leave, It is beleeved he intends to goe with Collonell Dongan who has layen in the bay this sixteen dayes. . . . the most part of the country have invited the rest to appeare as a counsell of safty two men out of one [i.e., each] County, the 26th of this instant. In the mean tyme the fort is guarded by five companies[,] two watches[,] 1½ company per night, and the Capt whose watch it is is for that tyme Captain of the fort, the Collector in the Custome house is a rank papist, I cannot gett the other Captanes to resolve to turne him out, but acts still as before. The Mayer medles with no civill affaires and discourages constables to keep the peace expecting some seditione for to make the Inhabitants odious, There is non[e] acts other then in quality of a single Capt. Sir Edmond Andross and his wicked crew have carried all the Records out of this country to Boston, I hope by the prudent care in the late expeditione at Boston have taken care to preserve it, and I request you take a speciall care for it.

34. Nicholson Leaves the Colony, June 6, 1689

["Minutes of the Councell att New Yorke," June 6, 1689, "Documents Relating to the Administration of Jacob Leisler," N.-Y. Hist. Soc., *Collections*, 1 (1868), 270]

The Lieutenant Gouvernor and Councell being mett itt was the advice of the Councill that it was most safe for the Lieutenant Governour to depart for England by the first ship, for to give an account of the desperate and deplorable state of the government, and to pray for some immediate releese.

35. Divergent Views of Leisler's Rule

A. THE LEISLERIAN VIEW, DECEMBER 1689

[Benjamin Blagge's Memorial, O'Callaghan, ed., *Documentary History of New York*, II, 55-58]

A memoriall of what has occurred in . . . New York since the news of Their Majesties happy Arrivall in England. Setting forth the necessity of removing Capt. Francis Nicholson (late Lieutenant Governor of the said Province) and putting the command thereof into [the] hands of such persons, of whose fidelity and good Inclination to their present Majesties the aforesaid Province is well assured.

The said Capt. Nicholson (in imitation of his Predecessor, Collonel Dongan) wholly neglected to repair the Fort and Fortifications of the city, and that not without a vehement suspicion, thereby the more easily to betray the same into the enemies hands, of which he gave the said Province sufficient grounds of apprehensions by discovering both by words and actions, his disaffection to the happy Revolution in England, and also to the inhabitants of the City by threatening to fire the same about their ears.

Whereupon the Inhabitants in order to secure the said Fort and City for their Majesties use and to repair and fortify the same and to place the government of the Province in the hands of some of undoubted loyalty and affection to their present Majesties Did remove the said Capt. Nicholson, and made choice of Capt. Jacob Leisler with a Committee (who were also chosen by the people) to take into their hands the Care and Charge of the Government untill Their Majesties Pleasure should be further known.

Shortly after arrived their Majesties Proclamation to Proclaim them King and Queen of England, France and Ireland, notice whereof was given to those of the former Councill and to the Mayor and Aldrmen of the City to assist in proclaiming thereof with the proper ceremonies for that solemnity, who desired an hours time to consider of it, which time being expired and no complyance yielded, but on the contrary an aversion discovered thereto, The said Capt. Leisler accompanyed with the Committee and most part of the Inhabitants, did with all the Demonstrations of Joy and affection they were capable of celebrate the same.

Whereupon the Mayor and Aldermen were suspended and some persons confined, who were the most eminent in opposing Their Majesties Interest and this Revolution, and some short time after this Their Majesties Letter arrived, Directed to Capt. Francis Nicholson Esq, Lieutenant Governor of Their Majesties Province of New York and in his absence, to such as for the time being do take care for the preservation of their Majesties Peace, and Administring the Laws in that Their Majesties Province, Ordering such to take upon them the Place of Lieutenant Governor and Commander in Chief of the said Province, and to proclaim King William and Queen Mary King and Queen of England Scotland France and Ireland and Supreme Lord and Lady of the Province of New York, if not already done, which was accordingly performed.

The Inhabitants of the said City and Province, conceiving that by vertue of Their Majesties said Letter, the said Capt. Leisler was sufficiently Impowered to Receive the same and to act accordingly It gave them a generall satisfaction, whereupon the said Committee were immediately dismissed and a Councill chosen by whose assistance Capt. Leisler acts in the said Government pursuant to His Majestys Order.

The members of the former Government notwithstanding gave all the opposition they could to this Reformation and have created a Faction in the said Province to the [point of] endangering the loss thereof, since it happens at a time that we are under continuall alarms from the frequent attacks the French make upon our Frontiers. So that without the care and precaution aforesaid this Their Majesties Province was in apparent hazard of being delivered up to the Canada Forces belonging to the French King, whereby Their present Majesties most loyall protestant subjects of this Province would have been rendered miserable, equall to their fears, and this Province become a Colony of the French. . . .

The Fort and City are therefore now in a good posture wanting only Ammunition.

The Commissions are called in from those of the former Militia who acted under Colonel Dongan and Sir Edmond Andros, and other Commissions granted in the name of their present Majesties to such as are well affected to their Majesties Interest.

Upon these our actings for the Securing Their Majesties Interest in this Province and conserving the publick Peace our enemys have endeavoured all they can to misrepresent us and load us with Reproach, by terming our aforesaid proceedings a *Dutch Plott,* because indeed three quarter parts of the Inhabitants are descended from the Dutch and speak that language, and they also threaten our ruine if ever the Government come into their hands again.

Which that it may not doe, and Their Majesties most loyal and dutifull subjects in this province may reap the benefit and blessing of this most happy Revolution, and not be made a Prey to most implacable and Insulting enemies on our Borders, who are ready to enter and devour us—humbly Submitting ourselves to your Majesties most Royal Will and Pleasure.

B. THE VIEW OF THE DISPLACED COUNCILORS, APRIL 27, 1691

[The Answer of Bayard and Nicolls to Benjamin Blagge's Memorial, O'Callaghan, ed., *Documentary History of New York*, II, 388-90]

For the greater quiet and satisfacon of the people, the said Capt. Nicholson admitted Detachments of the Citty Militia and desired the assistance of the severall Countyes of the Province as well for their Councill and advice as the comon defence to Watch and ward in the Fort which gave occasion to Captain Leisler and others . . . all men of meane birth sordid Education and desperate Fortunes by inflaming the people with idle and improbable stories and false suggestions whilst Capt. Nicholson and the others of the Council assisted with the Mayor and Aldermen of the City and Militia Officers of the province all Protestants and principall Freeholders were Consulting att the City Hall for the peace and preservation of the Country to expell the garrison force the keys from Capt. Nicholson and assumed this military power over their Majesties subjects of this province[.] which poynt being so far gayned the lesser and meaner part of the people being overawed by the strength of the Fort were easily induced to choose such a Committe as they were directed for the Confirmacon of the actions of the said Leisler and others his followers.

The Gentlemen of the former Councill Mayor and aldermen of the Citty were not made acquainted with any order or proclamation For proclaiming their Majesties in this province but on the Contrary upon Rumor of such orders being come to the Towne, they sent to Leysler and others to enquire of the truth but could have no certaine intelligence from them. And what aversion possibly could be discovered in those persons to their Majesties prosperity and accession to the throne their letter to the Secretary of State upon the first newes of the Revolution their Education and constancy in the profession of the protestant Religion and Continuall affection to the English Crowne may sufficiently evince and the Journalls of their proceedings in those times apparently declare.

The Mayor and Aldermen were not suspended but remayned untill the usuall time of [their] election, nor did any of the persons confined in any manner oppose their Majesties interest or the revolution but were all of them of the protestant Religion well affected to their Majesties persons and Government and the Empire of the English Crowne in these parts.

The Inhabitants of the Province werre farr from understanding his Majesties letter to be directed for Capt. Leisler or that any powers or authorityes therein Contained were given to him. The Letters was not openly communicated but when diverse of their Majesties good and faithful protestant Leige Subjects principall Freeholders of the province desired of Capt. Leysler who had surreptitiously got the same into his own hands that they might either have a Coppy or heare the same read that they might pay all duty and obedience to their Majesties Orders accordingly, they were not only denyed the same but dismissed with menaces contempt and rude language.

Noe Reluctance or Resistance in the least was ever shewne or offered to their Majesties Government in the province but it was received with a hearty and Unanimous Consent and general joy and gladness and the only Opposition that ever was made was against the manifest irraconal and intollerable violence and oppression of Jacob Leisler and his faction, whose Religion before those times was as unaccomptable and obscure as their birth and fortunes by whose occasion the Ruines of Scanechtadae [Schenectady] and other depradations of the French and Indians happened and unto whom the same is wholly attributed. . . .

The notion of a Dutch Plott cannot be applicable to Leysler and his adherents. The much greater part of Albany which wholly Consists of dutch people and all the men of best repute for Religion Estates and Integrity of the dutch Nation throughout the whole Province having alwayes been manifestly against Leysler and his Society in all their illegall and Irregular proceeedings.

CHAPTER SIX

THE CONSEQUENCES OF REBELLION

As the year 1691 opened, the old aristocracy of the colony, either imprisoned, exiled, or in hiding, eagerly awaited the arrival of Governor Henry Sloughter, and they joyously greeted the entrance of three
vessels into the harbor on January 28. Their initial enthusiasm was
somewhat dampened when they realized that the Governor was not
aboard—his ship had separated from the others near Bermuda. Only
Captain Richard Ingoldesby of the company of foot soldiers and several
councilors-designate arrived, and they had no authority until the Governor proclaimed his commission.

Leisler faced a delicate question of protocol, for Ingoldesby, although legally powerless, was the vanguard of the new government. It
was politic to treat him well. Leisler offered accomodations to the new
royal troops, but Ingoldesby insisted that he would only accept the fort
itself as befitting the king's soldiers. This Leisler refused; he had
strong doubts as to Ingoldesby's real intentions, and rumors of a Catholic plot to seize the colony still persisted. Neither side would give in,
and the growing tension culminated in a minor battle on March 17, a
fight which would shortly assume tragic proportions.

When Sloughter's vessel finally arrived on March 19, he sent Ingoldesby three times to demand the fort's surrender. Each time, Leisler
returned an emissary to make certain that the Governor had really arrived and carried a commission from William and Mary, not James II.
The emissaries were cast into jail, as were Leisler and his aides when
they finally capitulated after the third demand.

Governor Sloughter surrounded himself with the leaders of the old
entrenched party of privilege, men who had suffered most at Leisler's
hands. These men were determined to make of that misguided zealot
an example that would deter all future upstarts from following in his
footsteps. Preparations were therefore quickly completed for the trial

of the rebel leaders on charges of treason and murder for their opposition to Ingoldesby by force of arms two days before Sloughter landed in
the colony.

Aside from the surprising acquittal of two of the defendants, the
results of the trial were a foregone conclusion. Leisler refused to recognize the court's right to sit in judgment on his actions as Lieutenant Governor, claiming that only the Crown itself could do so, and he was tried
as a mute along with his son-in-law, Jacob Milborne. The eight other
defendants pleaded innocent. Leisler, Milborne, and six others were
convicted of the crimes charged to them and sentenced to be executed
(No. 36 A). While reprieves were granted to the six lesser figures, there
was a sharp division of opinion as to the fate of the two leaders. Many
supported a reprieve pending the King's pleasure (No. 36 B), but
Sloughter's advisers bitterly opposed such a move (No. 36 C-D). Buffeted
by contrary views, Sloughter left the decision in the hands of the Council, composed of Leisler's bitterest enemies, and they quickly resolved
to make an example of Leisler and Milborne. Two days later, the leaders were taken to the gallows where Leisler made a moving speech (No.
36 E). He and his son-in-law were then hanged and their heads separated
from their bodies.

Although the rebellion was over, two martyrs had been created, and
the aftermath of the executions reverberated throughout the colony for
a quarter of a century. Successive governors aligned themselves with the
old privileged order in the colony and did nothing to alleviate the problems which originally prompted the rebellion. Even the Assembly,
which was re-established and promptly adopted an impressive bill of
rights (No. 37), quickly fell prey to factionalism. Thus those discontented for any reason constantly evoked the memories of the martyrs,
and the bloody standard was frequently unfurled. The bitterness of
New York politics was accentuated, the issues confused, and the real
problems ignored under the camouflage of intense partisanship.

In the years following, the Leislerian versus anti-Leislerian hostility
extended to every field of endeavor, and even spread beyond the bounds
of the colony—Governor Sir William Phips of Massachusetts became
involved in a running argument with Governor Fletcher over the fate
of Abraham Gouverneur, who escaped from New York while under
sentence. Governors Sloughter, Ingoldesby, and Fletcher were either
weak, corrupt, or both, and they severely repressed the Leislerians while
utilizing the conflict for their own ends (No. 38). By allying themselves
with the anti-Leislerians, they frequently found their administrations
easy and sometimes personally profitable.

Although unable to bring about a change within New York, the
Leislerians were busy in England. With the help of the Massachusetts

agents and other friends in London, they secured an order to stop all further prosecutions of the Leislerians, a pardon for those still under sentence, and eventually a parliamentary reversal of the attainder against Leisler and Milborne. Most important, they finally secured the recall of the hated Benjamin Fletcher and his replacement by the Earl of Bellomont.

Of all these governors, Bellomont alone sought to create an equilibrium in order to break the vicious pattern that dominated the colony's politics, and for a time he seemed to succeed. But he, too, finally bent under the pressure, although he fell in with the Leislerians rather than their enemies. During the latter part of his administration, Leisler's followers began to exact the vengeance of which they had long dreamed—Leisler's and Milborne's bodies were exhumed and reburied with the pomp due a royal governor, their estates were restored to their families, and their followers first tasted the fruit of power and high office (No. 39 A, C). In a private lament, Robert Livingston, a leading anti-Leislerian, expressed his resentment in verse (No. 39 B).

Bellomont's sudden death left the government in the hands of his cousin, John Nanfan, a weak and ineffectual administrator, who became a tool of the Leislerians. Now the old aristocracy felt the bitter lash of persecution (No. 40). Nicholas Bayard was convicted of treason under the statute he had helped write to suppress the Leislerians, Robert Livingston's estate was confiscated, and James Graham and Stephanus Van Cortlandt became prime targets but cheated the Leislerians by dying too soon.

With the appointment of Edward Hyde, Lord Cornbury, perhaps the most venal governor in New York's history, the vindictiveness indulged in by the Leislerians came to an end and the reverse situation developed. Better than any predecessor or successor, Cornbury learned how to utilize the split within the colony to his own advantage, and he eventually became repugnant to those on both sides who were not totally immoral (No. 41). As soon as his commission expired, he was cast into a debtor's prison in New York City where he remained until his father's death transferred to him the title and wealth of the earldom of Clarendon.

Not until the arrival of Robert Hunter did the colony have a governor both strong enough and shrewd enough to break with the ingrained pattern of violent hatred. He realized the failings of the previous administrations, and he sought to compose the differences instead of inflaming them. Certain natural factors came to his help—the staleness of the old battle cries, development of new problems to which the old factional scheme was irrelevant, the death of many of the original participants—and he used these to the utmost. By the end of his tenure, the old wounds were finally healed and the Assembly for the first time lauded a governor (No. 42). The Old Testament approach of an eye for an eye and a tooth for a tooth gave way to a more sophisticated view, a realization that the power of public office could be more effectively and profitably used to enhance one's own fortune instead of dissipating it in the fruitless pursuit of vengeance.

The Collapse of the Leislerian Movement

36. The Creation of Martyrs

A. Sentences Against Leisler and Milborne, April 8, 1691

[Lawrence H. Leder, ed., "Records of the Trials of Jacob Leisler and His Associates," N.-Y. Hist. Soc., *Quarterly*, 36 (1952), 454]

Therefore it is Considered by the said Justices of our said Lord and Lady the King and Queen Now here that the said Jacob Leisler Jacob Milbourne and Gerrardus Beekman be Carryed to the place from Whence they Came and from thence to the place of Execution that there they shall be severall[y] hanged by the Neck and being Alive their bodys be Cutt Downe to the Earth that their Bowells be taken out and they being Alive burnt before their faces that their heads shall be struck off and their Bodys Cutt in four parts and which shall be Desposed of as their Majesties Shall Assigne.

B. A Bostonian Expects Clemency, April 16, 1691

[Francis Foxcroft to William Blathwayt, Apr. 16, 1691, Blathwayt Papers, V, Colonial Williamsburg, Inc.]

I feare ere long I with many more may be glad of an oppertunity of takeing Sanctuary under your protection. We harden our Selves in our Rebellions by every Instance cautionary to us of our own case, and I thinke I am safe, when I conclude our Seers drawe Incourragements from every report of ill designes, upon the present State in England, and some say openly that a 2d Revolution is of absolute necessity there. The mock Governor (Quondum) at New Yorke, the proceedings against him occasions different discourse, but the Sume of all is that it would recomend Governor Sloughter to the wise and good men of the world to reserve him for an Instance of the King's vaunted Clemency. The complications of this crime it seemes hath lessened the guilt, being soe like our own pattern we canot but love our own Bratt from Yorke.

C. Anti-Leislerians Demand Blood Vengeance, May 6, 1691

[Nicholas Bayard to Francis Nicholson, May 6, 1691, Blathwayt Papers, VII, Colonial Williamsburg, Inc.]

I suppose that all of them will be reprieved till the Kings Pleasure be knowne except the two first [Leisler and Milborne], who have been the greatest Rogues and do still remaine obstinate! Tho 'tis feared and dreaded by many (that wish well to his Excellency and the Safety of the Government) that the Instruments that saved P[eter] D[e] L[anoy] and S[amuel] Edsall will prevaile to procure a reprieve for them alsoo; which if it should soo happen, it will soo distress all honest men that it will be the occasione that many will be forced to remove themselves to some safer parts, since itts to be expected that in case no exemplar punishment of such heinous crimes be made, that the Cry of the Innocent blood which they have soo barbarously Spilt will not only remaine as a curse uppon us, but if those villaines be winkt at and soo past by, wee must expect to be free from like wicked attempts no longer.

D. The Failure to Secure Complete Retribution, May 7, 1691

[William Nicolls to William Blathwayt, May 7, 1691, Blathwayt Papers, XV, Pt. II, Colonial Williamsburg, Inc.]

The circomstances wee now are in renders every one very uneasy, and arises from this cause: Edsall, Delanoy, Williams, Corten [Coerteen], Beekman, Brasier, Vermelie, Milborn, and Leisler being the chiefest actors in our late disturbances have been arrained for high treason, and all except the two last pleaded and past their tryalls, *Edsall and Delanoy By the strange favourable charge given by Mr. Dudley* and the ignorance of the jury, were (to the wonder as well as regrett of all honest men who had known what active firebrands they had both been) *cleared by verdict,* the other five and one Abraham Gouverneur for murder were convicted, but Leisler and Milborne with their wonted impudence were pleased to stand mutes and refused to plead, upon which the usual sentence for treason was pronounced against them and all men were in a generall Expectation that the same would have been executed to the terror of others for the future, . . . but hitherto they are all safe and well, and the fear of a reprieve till further Order from the King, gives so universall discontent, and the hopes of itt raises Leislers faction to that heighth of confidence, that many of them have had the boldness to affirm the Governor durst not touch their lives. . . . *The source of all these and other our evils is attributed to the President [of the Council, Joseph] Dudley, whose actions demonstrate on all Occasions, his affection and assiduous care for those of Leislers Faction, which tho he has not the Courage to own bare fact, yet itts manifest and apparent to all that are not very dimsighted, and all hopes of any good from him or his Councils to this Government have already taken their flight.*

E. Leisler's Last Words on the Gallows, May 16, 1691

[O'Callaghan, ed., *Documentary History of New York*, II, 376-78]

Gentlemen and fellow brethren . . . we are not at present unsensible of our dying State and Condition. . . . we Submit our lives and all that unto us appertaineth into the hands of divine protection. . . . As to our State in this world among the rest of our hard fortunes in this seat of tears it is true we have lately on the important request of a Committee choose [chosen] by the Major Part of the Inhabitants of this province . . . taken (to the present griefe and vexation of our poore afflicted relations left behind) great and weighty matters of State affairs requiring at Such an helme more wise and Cunning powerfull pilotts than either of us ever was. But considering that in the time of this distracted Countrey's [greatest] necessity amongst us no such Persons could be found . . . [capable] of Uniting us against a Common enemy [or] would not undertake [it], we conceive for the Glory of the protestant interest[,] the Establishment of the present Government under our Sovereign Lord and Lady King William and Queen Mary etc., and the Strengthening against all foreign attempts, of this confused City and Province . . . it a very serviceable Act that our poore endeavours should not be wanting in any thing that was needful for the Support of ourselves and posterity hereafter. Whereby we must confess, and often times against our will, several enormities have been committed from the day of our first undertakings until the arrival of his excellency, the Honorable Colonel Henry Sloughter, who now for his Majesty's Sake, we love and Honor. And often times, during our unhappy abode in power, longed to see that a periode thereby might be put to such distracted orders, as then were raging, . . . of which some we must Confess on our side hath been committed through Ignorance, some through a Jealous fear that disaffected persons would not be true to the present interest of the Crowne of England[,] some peradventure through misinformation and misconstruction of People's intent and meaning, some through rashness by want of Consideration, and then through passion haste and anger, which . . . to declare would take up more time than present can be afforded. . . . Seeing there is no recalling of the same, or possibility of giv[ing] further Satisfaction, first of the great god of heaven and then afterwards of the several offended persons, we humbly begg pardon and forgiveness, desiring them every one with a Christian Charity in our graves with us to bury all malice, hatred, and Envy that therein might be incurred. And further before God and the World here we do declare and protest as Dying Sinners that we do not only forgive the greatest and most inveterate of our enemies, but According to that most Excellent patron of our dying Saviour, we say to the God of Justice: father, forgive them for they Know not what they do. And so farre from revenge[ful] we do depart this world, that we require and make it our dying supplication to every[one] of our relations and friends and acquaintences, that they should in time to come for ever be forgetfull of any injury done to us or either of us, so that on both Side, that discord and [dissension] (which by the devil in the beginning was created) might with our dying sides be buried in oblivion, never more to rise up to the inflamation of future posterity. The Lord grant that the offering up of our blood might be a full satisfaction for all disorders to this present day committed, and that forever after the Spiritt of unity might remain among our felow brethren continuing upon earth. Knowing that in a Strange land it is the divine providence of heaven, not our desarts, that have so well protected our unhappy province, this day all that for our dying comfort we can say, as concerning the point for which we were condemned, is to declare as our last words before that God whom we hope before long to see[,] that our maine end, totall Intent, and endeavors to the fullness of that understanding with which we were endowed . . . had no other than to maintaine against popery or any Schism or heresy whatever the interest of our Sovereign Lord and Lady that now is, and the reformed protestant Churches in those parts. . . . [The appearance of] misconstructed and Scandalous reports (we at present must confess by divers are thrown upon us) as tho we intended to Support the dying, intrest of the late King James . . . [for] the Contradiction of which we need not trouble [with] many arguments, being persuaded that every good protestant of this Country who have been for any time acquainted with our transactions can from his conscience averre the falsehoods and maliciousness of such aspersions. As concerning Major Ingoldesby's coming to demand the Garrison after his arrival, [had] he but in the least produced any Satisfaction of his power to receive the same and discharge us, we would as readily have delivered the fort, as he could demand the same, all which seeing [it is] past and gone is Scarce worth nothing.

The Lord of his infinite Mercy preserve the King and Queen from all their traytors and deceitfull Enemies. God be merciful unto and bless with peace and unity these their Kingdoms unto which we belong. God preserve this province from greedy outragious Enemies abroad and Spite full, inveterate wretches at home. God bless the Govenor of this place, God Bless the council Assembly and Government now Established that they all may be united to propagate their Majesties' interest, the Country's good and the Establishment of Piety. The Lord of Heaven, of his infinite mercy bless all that wish well to Zion and Convert those that are out of the way.

37. The Rights and Privileges of New Yorkers, May 13, 1691

[The Colonial Laws of New York, I, 244-48]

Forasmuch as the Representatives of this their Majesties Province of New York now Convened in Generall Assembly are deeply sensible of their Majesties most gratious favour in restoring to them the undoubted Rights and Priviledges of Englishemen by declareing their Royall will and pleasure in their Letters Pattents to his Excellency . . . that he should with the advice and consent of their Councill from time to time as need shall require to summon and call generall Assemblys of the Inhabitants being freeholders according to the usage of their Majesties other Plantations in America. And that this most excellent constitution soe necessary and soe much Esteemed by our Ancestors may ever continue unto their Majesties Subjects within this Province of New York; the Representatives . . . humbly pray that the rights Priviledges Libertyes and francheses according to the Lawes and statutes of their Majesties Realm of England may be confirmed unto their Majesties most dutyfull and loyall Subjects . . . of New York by Authority of this generall assembly. . . . And it is hereby enacted and declared by the Authority of the same, That the supreame Legislative power and authorite under their Majesties . . . shall forever be and reside in A Governour in Chief and Councill appointed by their Majesties . . . And the people by their Representatives mett and Convened in generall Assembly;

that the exercice and administration of the government over the said Province shall, persuant to their Majesties Letters Pattents be in the said Governour in Chief, and Councill with whose advice and Consent or with att least five of them, he is to rule and Govern the same, according to the Lawes thereof, and for any defect therein according to the Laws of England and not otherwise. That in Case the Governour in Chief shall Dye or be Absent out of the Province; and that there be noe person within the said Province Commissionated by their Majesties . . . to be governour or Commander in Chief that then the Councill for the time being or soe many of them as are in the said Province doe take upon them the administration of the government and the Execution of the Lawes thereof and powers and authorities belonging to the Governour in Chief and Councill, the first in nomination in which Councill is to preside untill the said Governour shall return and arrive in the said Province againe or the pleasure of their Majesties . . . be further known. That for the good government and rule of their Majestys Subjects a session of a generall Assembly be held in this Province once in every yeare. That every freeholder within this province and freeman in any Corporation shall have his free Choice and voat in the electing, of the Representatives without any manner of Constraint or Imposition; And that in all elections the Majority of votes shall carry itt, and by freeholders is to be understood every one who shall have fourty shillings per Annum in freehold. That the persons to be elected to Sitt as Representatives in the Generall Assembly from time to time . . . shall be according to the proportion and number hereafter expressed . . . and as many more as their Majesties . . . shall think fitt to establish. That all persons Chosen and Assembled in manner aforesaid or the Major part of them **shall be deemed and accounted the representatives of this Province in gen-**

erall assembly, that the Representatives . . . may appoint their own times of meeting during their sessions and may adjourn their house from time to time as to them shall seem meet and convenient. That the said representatives as aforesaid Conven'd are the sole Judges of the Qualifications of their own Members, and likewise of all undue Ellections, and may from time to time purg the house As they shall see occation That noe member of the generall assembly or their Servants dureing the Time of their Sessions and whilst they shall be going to and returning from the said Assembly shall be arrested, sued, Imprisoned or any wayes molested or troubled or be Compelled to make answer to any suite, bill, plaint Declaration or otherwise, Cases of high Treason and fellony onely Excepted. That all Bills agreed upon by the Representatives or the Major part of them shall be presented unto the Governour and the Councill for their approbation and Consent all and every which said Bills soe approved of and consented to by the Governor and the Councill shall be Esteemed and accounted the Laws of this Province which said Lawes shall continue and remaine in force untill they be disallowed by their Majesties . . . or expire by their own limitation. That in All Cases of death or Absence of any of the said Representatives the Governour for the time being, shall Issue out A Writt of Summons . . . willing and requireing the freeholders . . . to Elect others in their places and stead. That noe freeman shall be taken and Imprisoned or be desiezed of his freehold, or liberty or free Custom's, or out Law'd or Exiled or any other wayes destroyed, nor shall be passed upon, adjudged or Condemned but by the Lawfull Judgment of his peers and by the Law of this Province, Justice nor right shall be neither sold denied or delayed to any person within this Province. That noe Aid, tax, tollage, assessment, Custome Loan, Benevolence gift, Excise duty or Imposition whatsoever shall be laid assessed Imposed, Levyed or required of or on any of their Majesties Subjects within this Province etc. or their estates upon any manor of Colour or Pretence whatsoever but by the Act and Consent of the governor and Councill and Representatives of the people in generall Assembly mett and Convened; That noe man of what estate or Condition soever shall be put out of his Lands, tenements, nor taken nor Imprisoned nor disinherited nor banished nor any wayes destroyed or molested without first being brought to Answer by due Course of Law. That A freeman shall not be Amerced for A small fault but after the maner of his fault, And for A great fault after the greatness thereof, saveing to him his freehold and A husbandman saveing to him his wainage; and A merchant saveing to him his Merchandize; and none of the said Amercements shall be Assessed but by the Oath of twelve honest and Lawfull men of the Vicinage provided the faults and Misdemeaners be not in Contempt of Courts of Judicature. All tryalls shall be by the verdict of Twelve men and as nere as may be Peares or equalls of the neighbourhood of the place where the fact shall arise or grow; whether the same be by Indictment declaracon or Information or otherwise against the person or defendant. That in all cases capitall or criminall there shall be a grand Inquest who shall first present the offence; and then twelve good men of the neighbourhood, to try the offendor, who after his plea to the Indictment shall be allowed his reasonable challenges. That in all Cases whatsoever bayle by sufficient suretyes shall be allowed and taken unless for Treason or fellony plainely and specially expressed and mentioned in the Warrant of Committment; and that the Fellony be such as is restrained from bayle by the Law of England. That noe freeman shall be Compelled to receive any souldiers or Marrinors; Except Inholders and other houses of Publique entertainment; who are to Quarter for Ready money into his house and there Suffer them to Sojorne against their Wills, Provided it be not in time of actuall warr within this Province. That noe Commission for proceeding by Martiall Law against any of his Majesties Subjects within this Province etc. shall Issue forth to any person or persons whatsoever least by Colour of them any of his Majesties Subjects be destroyed or put to death. Except all such officers and souldiers that are in Garrison and pay dureing the time of actuall Warr. That all the Lands within this Province shall be esteemed and accounted Land of Freehold and Inheritance in free and Common soccage according to the tenure of East Greenwich in their Majesties Realm of England. . . That noe person or persons which profess faith in God by Jesus Christ his onely sonn shall at any time be any wayes molested punished disturbed disquieted or called in question for any difference in opinion, or matter of Conscience in Religeous Concernment who doe not under that pretence disturb the Civill peace of the Province and that all and every such Person or persons may from time to time and at all times hereafter freely and fully Enjoy his or their opinion persuasions Judgements in matters of conscience and Religion throughout all this Province and freely meet at Convenient places within this Province, and there worshipp according to their respective perswasions without being hindred or molested, they behaveing themselves peaceably Quietly, modestly and religiously, and not useing this Liberty to Licentiousness nor to the Civill Injury or outward disturbance of others. Allwayes provided that noething herein mentioned or Contained shall extend to give Liberty for any persons of the Romish Religion to exercise their manor of worshipp contrary to the Laws and Statutes of their Majesties Kingdom of England.

The Politics of Revenge

38. The Anti-Leislerians Retaliate

A. LEGAL OSTRACISM, MAY 16, 1691

[Colonial Laws of New York, I, 255-57]

The Governor Councill and representatives convened in generall Assembly takeing into their serious Considerations the many great troubles and disorders that have been lately within this Province and that by occasion thereof and otherwise many of their Majesties Subjects are fallen in danger of and lie open to great penaltyes and forfeitures. And with all Considering the Ignorance of many and the dutyfull affections of others of their Majesties Loyall subjects, out of an earnest desire to deliver them from the penaltyes and forfeitures aforesaid and to the intent that their offences may not hereafter be brought in Judgment Question or Remembrance to the least Endamagement of them either in their lives Libertyes Estates or reputations but that they haveing an entire confidence in their Majesties and perfect union among themselves may be encouraged in their duty to their Majesties government and more fully and securely Enjoy the benefitt of it. It is therefore necessary that there be extended unto them A generall and free pardon. That all their Majesties subjects by this Clemencie and Indulgence may be the better Induced henceforth more Carefully to observe the Lawes and performe their Loyall and due Obedience to their Majesties. Be it therefore Enacted . . . that all and every the said Subjects Inhabiting within this Province . . . shall be and are by the Authoritie of this present Assembly Acquitted pardoned released and discharged against their Majesties . . . from all manner of Trea-sons fellonies Misprisions of Treason Treasonable or seditious words and libell, Misprisions of Felony Seditious and Unlawful meetings and of all offences whereby any person may be charged with the penalty and danger of premunire. And also of and from all riotts routs offences, Contempts Trespasses and enteries wrongs deceits misdemeaners forfeitures penaltys paines of death paines Corporall and paines precuniary; And generally of and from all other things Causes Quarrells suites Judgements and Executions in this present Act not hereafter Excepted which may be or Can by their Majesties in any ways or by any meanes pardoned before the Nineteenth day of March last past to any of the Subjects aforesaid; And be it further Enacted . . . that this pardon shall be as good and effectuall in Law to every of their Majesties said Subjects in for and against all things which be not hereafter in this present Act Excepted. . . . Excepted and allwayes foreprised out of this generall pardon all and every the persons hereafter named and expressed Jacob Leisler, Jacob Milborne, Gerrardus Beekman, Abraham Gouverneur, Abraham Brazier, Thomas Williams, Mindert Coerteen, Johannes Vermilye, Already attainted of Treason and murther, And Nicholas Blank, Gerrit Duyckinck, Hendrick Jansen, John Coe, William Lawrence in East Jersey, Cornelius Pluvier, William Churchill, Joost Stoll, Samuel Staats, Jacob Mauritz, Robert Leacock, Michael Hansen, Richard Ponton of the County of West-Chester, Joseph Smith, John Baily, Roeloff Swartwout, Anthony Swartwout, Johannes Provoost, Jacob Melyn, Benjamin Blagge, Joachim Staats, and Richard Pretty.

B. Jacob Leisler, Jr.'s Summary View of Events, 1696

[Memorial of Messrs. Jacob Leisler and Abraham Governeur to the Privy Council, Sept. 25, 1696, O'Callaghan, ed., *Documents Relative to Colonial New York*, IV, 213-16]

In Aprill 1689 those of New England who were well affected to the Protestant interest seized Sir Edmund Andross their Governor and then declared in favour of the Revolution. Upon the arrivall of this newes in New Yorke in May following the Protestant party perceiving that Mr. Nicholson, Sir Edmund Andross his Lieutenant, would not declare for his now Majesty the people seized the Fort, and the Captains of the Militia by turnes commanded. And soon after, those Captains and the people in generall proclaimed the King and Queene (soone after which Mr. Nicholson left New Yorke) and then sent Circular letters to 'all parts of this Province to choose their Representatives for a Generall Assembly; which was done accordingly. And in June following this Assembly mett and constituted Captain Leisler, Captain of the Fort for their Majesties' service, till their Majesties pleasure were knowne. In August then following the same Assembly appointed the said Captain Leisler Comander in Cheif of this Province.

In December then following there came to New York a messenger with a letter from his Majesty thus directed (vizt.) To our trusty and Well beloved Francis Nicholson Esqr. our Lieutenant Governor and Comander in Cheife of our Province of New Yorke in America and in his absence to such as for the time being take care for preserveing the peace and administring the lawes in our said Province. . . . This letter was delivered to Captain Leisler (Nicholson having been gone some months before)

by which letter such as then comanded in Cheife were impowered to take upon them the government till further Order. Under this Authority the said Captain Leisler continued Governor about 13 months. Soone after Captain Leisler had thus received authority, he gave . . . assistance and encouragement to the Indians then in arms against the French. . . .

In January 1690[91] Captain Ingoldesby arrived at New Yorke with a Comission to obey the Comander in Cheife for the time being but upon his arrivall he sent Mr. Chidley Brooke (now Collector of New Yorke) and his Lieutenant into the Fort to Captain Leisler and Mr. Brooke demanded the Fort to be delivered up to Captain Ingoldesby, which Captain Leisler refuseing, Ingoldesby with his owne Company and severall others waged warre against the Fort. And this Mr. Brooke threatened many that unless they would assist Captain Ingoldesby against Captain Leisler they should be declared rebells and treated as such.

Captain Ingoldesby continued thus for 6 weekes calling to his assistance such as before opposed the revolution and were of Andross . . . Councell, which were afterwards of Colonel Sloughters Councell and still are of the present Councell.

About 6 weeks after Captain Ingoldesby's arrivall Colonel Sloughter, who was made Governor of New Yorke, came to New Yorke vizt. 19 March 1690 [91] in the evening. As soon as Captain Leisler was thereof informed, he sent two persons to congratulate his arrivall, but Colonel Sloughter imprisoned them. Notwithstanding which Captain Leisler tooke imediate care for the delivery of the Fort the next morning to Colonel Sloughter which was done accordingly.

But Colonel Sloughter at the instigation of one Mr. Dudley, President of his Councell, this Mr. Brooke and severall others, treated Captain Leisler and many more as traitors, for not delivering the Fort to Captain Ingoldesby (whose Comission by expresse words was to obey the Comander in Cheife, which Captain Leisler had beene by virtue of his Majesty's letter above 12 months before Captain Ingoldesby arrived). Many of this Province upon Captain Leisler's being thus treated fledd from New Yorke, others that remained were imprisoned as ryoters for acting under Captain Leisler, and Captain Leisler with severall others [were] indicted for high Treason and murder, in holding out the Fort against Captain Ingoldesby, and tryed before Mr. Dudley as President, Captain Ingoldesby Mr. Brooke and others.

Captain Leisler and Mr. Milborne insisted upon his Majesty's authority, by vertue of the before mentioned letter, and desired the Court (before they pleaded) to declare whether the said letter had not given Captain Leisler an authority to take upon him the Government. To this the Court would give noe answer, unless Captain Leisler would plead, which Captain Leisler and Mr. Milborne refused to doe till that question was answered by the Court. Whereupon the Court gave judgment against them both as traiters and they were accordingly executed. This whole matter being proved before the Parliament in 1694 the Attainders of Captain Leisler, Mr. Milborne, and Mr. Gouverneur were by Act of Parliament reversed.

Whilest Captain Leisler and severall of his party were, as before, in custody, Colonel Sloughter called an Assembly, but such as were chosen and had beene well affected to Captain Leisler's interest, were refused to be admitted into the Assembly. Which Assembly thus partially chose[n] gave Captain Ingoldesby £100 for what he did against Captain Leisler, and to another [Captain William Kidd] for the same reason £150, both summes out of the publick money and this Assembly declared what Captain Leisler did was illegall and desired his execution, which was granted.

Colonel Sloughter then continued about 5 months in the government and then dyed. Upon whose death the then Councell att New Yorke appointed Captain Ingoldesby to be their Governor, and dureing his administration severall were proceeded against as ryoters for what they did under Captain Leisler, and some of these pretended ryoters haveing some time before given baile in £50 for their appearance came to England to informe the King and Councell, with the beforementioned proceedings, and dureing their absence their estates were seized and their securityes proceeded against and foure times as much levyed as the baile amounted unto.

Others were threatned that unless they pleaded guilty to the indictment for a ryott they should be proceeded against as traytors, which they refuseing to doe, were kept about eleaven months in custody, but were then discharged by his Majesty's generall order, which comanded the Governor of New Yorke, not only to discharge their persons but likewise to vacate the said recognizances and all proceedings thereon. But notwithstanding neither the money or goods seized upon those recognizances were restored. For Colonel Fletcher who was by their Majesties appointed to succeed Colonel Sloughter was served with the said Order of his Majesty and his Councell, but refused to obey the same unles those prisoners would petition him for their discharge, threatning them that unless they did petition him and his Councell he would hang them. Whereupon they petitioned for their liberty and were discharged, but notwithstanding Colonel Fletcher had beene often petitioned for a restitution of what had been seized by vertue of the before mentioned recognizances, noe restitution could ever be had of any part thereof.

Colonel Fletcher soone after his arrivall called a General Assembly, but finding that most of those chosen had beene well affected to Captain Leislers interest, he did refuse them and comanded the Electors to goe to a new election. Upon which second election the same being again chosen, the Governor would not admitt them, but packed an Assembly of whom he pleased.

In the latter end of 1694 the then Assembly perceiveing that the publick taxes and revenue in about 3 yeares had beene neare £40000 and that the same was generally misapplyed, they desired the Governor that an Account might be given them how the publick moneys had beene disbursed; but the Governor (notwithstanding at the first meeting of this Assembly he promised the same) refused to doe itt, saying itt was the Assemblyes business to raise the money and the Governour and Councells to lay it out, and that he would give an account thereof to none but his Majesty, with which answer the Assembly not being satisfyed but still insisting upon an account, Colonel Fletcher dissolved them.

In 1695 Colonel Fletcher called a new Assembly, but threatned those of the last, that if they came to any elections, he would shoot them, and thereupon imposed upon the freeholders seamen and soldiers armed with clubbs and bayonetts, as electors, and by those electors packed an Assembly, who appointed Mr. Brooke and Mr. Nicolls to come for England as their Agents to represent to his Majesty the state of the Province. . . .

Besides the before mentioned miscarriages, there have beene many more particular abuses comitted too tedious here to be related. And the present Governor to prevent any discoveries of his male administration, forceth such as he hath cause to suspect may come for England to give any information of his mismanagement to enter into bonds not to depart that government.

C. Peter Delanoy's View of Governor Fletcher, June 13, 1695

[O'Callaghan, ed., *Documents Relative to Colonial New York*, IV, 221-24]

We are under the common calamity of war, as you are, but want the blessing of a free government and our ancient libertyes which you so eminently enjoy in England and make the war easie to you. I remember the remark you made when our present Governor was sent hither, vizt., that he was a necessitous man who you fear'd would therefore more consider the advancement of his own private fortunes than the publick benefit of the Province; and I can now assure you we found you a true prophet, and wish you could foretell our deliverance as well as you did our oppressions from this arbitrary man.

At his first arrivall here he insinuated into the inhabitants the great interest and credit he had at Whitehall, which would baffle any complaints that could be made against his administration. And this back'd with the grandeur of a Coach and six horses (a pomp this place had never seen in any former Governor no more than himself [had] been us'd to it in his own Country,) struck such a terror into the people, as easily prepard 'em for the pack-saddles he has laid upon 'em. To recount all his arts of squeezing money both out of the publick and private purses would make a volume instead of a letter, and therefore I shall only mention some few of the stratagems that from thence you may guesse of this Hercules by his foot. The Assembly as is usuall to new Governors, made him a complement, and gave him a penny in the pound of the inhabitants estates. The Assessors observ'd the method formerly practised in such cases, but his Excellency thinking the some not sufficient (though it amounted to above £600) accus'd 'em of partiallity and threatned to commit 'em to goal for not assessing the inhabitants high enough. He takes a particular delight in having presents made to him, declaring he looks upon 'em as marks of their esteem of him, and he keeps a catalogue of the persons who show that good manners, as men most worthy of his favor. This knack has found employment for our silversmiths and furnish'd his Excellency with more plate (besides variety of other things) then all our former Governors ever received. Such clowns as dont practise this good breeding, fall under his frowns, or a haughty glance of his eye at least, if they dont feel the weight of his hands. The Souldiers one would think were but a poor game for so great a man to prey upon, but yet they feel their share of his hungry avarice. I was lately informed by one of the Council at Albany that his Excellency takes 10 shillings per annum out of every one of their subsistence money, and if the furnishers of that money cannot by reason of the rise of provisions subsist 'em for 5 pence per day, they are order'd to raise it 5½ pence of purpose that his 10 shillings may be secur'd. Some Officers he makes his favorites who are his tools and pimp to his frauds upon the publick. . . . He very often takes his progress to Connecticut, Pennsylvania, and other places, and all that tyme lives suitable to his character, but his table is maintained at the charge of the province without any abatement of the salary the King allows him for that purpose. His pride and arrogance to all the neighbouring Governors has been a great detriment to this Province and frequently the occasion of retarding that relief which was necessary, and would otherwise have been afforded us in time of extreamity. Instead of that fair understanding and correspondency which became men in their posts, Sir William Phips and he maintained a paper war betwixt themselves and constantly exchang'd scurrilous letters, which upon a strict enquiry I find wholly owing to the haughtinesse of our Governor. His vanity is as remarkable as his other qualities I have mention'd. . . . Poverty you know Sir is but a poor protection against power, and this the Albany men experienced the next time his Excellency visited that place. For when he found that he could not wheedle a present out of 'em, he made use of his authority to get one in this manner. He ordered two of the principall gates of the Citty where the Indians used to enter, to be shut up, cautiously alledging the danger of keeping open so many gates during the war. Severall poor traders who had built their houses near those gates purposely for the Indian trade would have been ruin'd if these gates had continued shut, and therefore rais'd a contribution of fifty or sixty of their best furs which they presented to his Excellency and thereby removed his Excellencys apprehensions of the danger those gates exposed the Citty to. . . .

These things though bad enough in any officer and more particularly in the Governor of a Province, yet me thinks are of much less malignity than what I am now going to add, and that is the base and insolent behavior of our Governor towards a Generall Assembly. This we account the barriere and guard of our libertys and propertys, but it signifies very little since his arrivall. If any act for the benefit of the people be desired to passe, he sells it [to] 'em as dear as he can, and if they will not rise to his price they must goe without it. . . .

In short Sir no body lives tolerably

under him but those who submit themselves to be his creatures and in his interests, such as the Judges and other officers who are dependant of him. His accounts indeed are pass'd by the Councill, but when such jobbs are to be done, his creatures only are summoned such as I mentioned before, who dare not oppose him, but are forced to approve what he requires. After this all you will perhaps wonder when I tell you that this man's bell ring[s] twice a day for prayers and that he appears with a great affectation of piety. But this is true, and it is as true that it makes him only more ridiculous, not more respected. For we are a sort of downright blundering people that measure mens piety more by their practice than by their pretence to it, or ostentation of it. . . .

And now Sir that I have told you [of] our distemper you will easily guesse at the cure we desire. It is the removall of this man, and we are not sollicitous whether he is gently recall'd or falls into disgrace, so we are rid of him.

39. Governor Bellomont and the Leislerians

A. GOVERNOR BELLOMONT DESCRIBES FACTIONALISM, 1698

[Excerpts from Letters of Bellomont, May 8— Oct. 27, 1698, O'Callaghan, ed., *Documents Relative to Colonial New York,* IV, 303-4, 315, 325-26, 327, 379-80, 400-401, 415-16]

[May 8, 1698] I issued out writts for the calling a new Assembly . . . and then I hope methods will be found for the quieting and uniting the minds of the people, who have been divided with great heats for these several years, occasioned at first by the execution of those men who were most forward in the happy Revolution, and ever since kept up and aggrevated with great industrie, even so far that the presumption that I shall be equal in my administrations (or their own guilt) hath so prevailed on most of the Gentlemen of the Councill to [make them] forget their oaths and duty to His Majesty. So that none of them have yet applyed to me to informe me of the State of the Province, or offered to me any assistance in the Government, although they know I am come a stranger amongst them, and unbyassed as to their animosity's. But instead thereof constant Cabals and clubbs of them are held dayly at Colonel Fletcher's lodgings (from whence I have as great reason to believe) false reports and rumors are spread about the City and province, whereby mens minds are disturbed, and an odium cast upon the Government, and thus these Gentlemen of the Councill by drawing back endeavour to make this Government uneasy to me. . . .

I shall take the best and most speedy methods I can for the Just observance of the acts of Trade, by suspending of careless or corrupt Officers, but I shall have but small assistance from the Gentlemen of His Majesty's Councill, because they are most of them Merchants, and several of themselves the persons concerned in the breach of these laws. And I perceive by their carriage and resentment of my making the forementioned small seizure [of the ship *Fortune* for illegal trading], that they are surprized that my discharge of my oath and duty gives them so unacustomed a disturbance. However, I shall not be discouraged but instead thereof shall forthwith for His Majesty's service, suspend several of them, from being of His Majesty's Councill, and try to find fitter person to supply their places, who will be more ready to assist me in matters of Government and due observance of the laws. . . .

[May 25, 1698] I have been so moderate towards Colonel Fletcher and his friends that I have turned out none of them, not so much as his Sheriffs, who are complained against for very foul practices in the elections and returns of Members to serve in the present Assembly, notwithstanding my proclamation strictly forbidding any such practices, by which means great discontents arise among those who are precluded by foul play from their right of sitting in the House. And such irregularities are dayly committed in the House in the point of order, that I begin to despair of their doing any good for His Majesty's service or their Countrie's.

What I have last writt leads me naturally to observe to your Lordships the great pains Colonel Fletcher took to divide the people here and to foment the fewd between Leisler's party and the opposite party, and went so far in it as to publish a book (and took the advice of Councill in doing it) to revive the old story of Leisler. . . . You will . . . judge whether this book was not calculated for putting this Town and Countrey into a combustion. . . .

[June 27, 1698] Your Lordships will likewise find, that as the two Gentlemen removed from the Councill by me viz: Mr. Brooke and Mr. Pinhorne, were two of Captain Leisler's Judges who, I find, was most barbarously murthered for his forwardnesse in the Revolution here, so the late Governor made advantage to divide the people by supposing a Dutch and English interest to be different here, and therefore under the notion of a Church of England, to be put in opposition to the Dutch and French churches established here, he supported a few rascally English who are a scandall to their nation and the Protestant Religion, and here great opposers to the Protestant Religion, and who joyned with him in the worst methods of gaine and severely

used the Dutch, except some few Merchants, whose trade he favored, who ought to have an equal benefit of the English Government who are most hearty for his present Majesty, and are a sober industrious people and obedient to Government. . . .

[July 7, 1698] I do not think it fit for me to call another Assembly, or leave this Province till I receive some new orders from England which shall put a censure upon the late Governor's Administration which is the source of all the difficulties I meet with, and supports the insolence of his party. But if Colonel Fletcher's Administration here meets with that discountenance and punishment in England which in my poor judgement it deserves, the people here will be as tame as Lambs, and all their ill humour will vanish, and then I need not doubt but an Assembly will be tractable in continuing the Revenue to His Majesty, which is the thing I cheiftly stickle for. I desire you would urge two or three things to their Lordships above all others, that I might have a power to vacate all Fletcher's [land] grants, which are so extravagant, that the province can never be peopled. There are half a dozen of his grants that come not much short of Yorkshire, for extent of land, and the persons that are the grantees have no merit. . . . He has granted away and sold all the conveniencies of a Governor here (vizt.) a Farm called the King's Farme, he has given to the Church here, but 'tis observable, his devotion did not carry him to do it till he heard I was certainly to superseed him; part of that Farm, which is meadow ground and a scarce thing here, he sold to Captain Evans commander of the Richmond Frigatt; . . . part of the King's garden too he has granted and sold to one Heathcote a Merchant. . . . I shall think Fletcher has the best luck with his insolence and corruption that ever any Governor had. I have given all the discountenance to Piracy that I am capable of doing, and that is one article which raises their clamour against me in this town; they say I have ruined the Town by hindering the Privateers (for so they call pirates) from bringing in a £100,000 since my coming. . . .

[September 21, 1698] I have yet made noe one step in the change of officers in the Militia or of persons in the Commission of the peace or officers in civill imployments (except the displacing of Willson the Sheriff of this towne) but I find it absolutely necessary for the King's service that I should make an alteration in the three classes above mentioned, the persons that are at present in Office being generally men of an ill character and disaffected to his Majesty's Government. If I am not to[o] late in this reforme I now write of, I fancy I shall be able with a little management, which shall be fair and upon the square, to compasse the continuing the revenue for five years longer, which was the time it was granted for under Colonel Fletcher's government. When that is once done I shall make it my businesse to bring the parties to a ballance. I can see no reason that the English and Dutch that are called Leisler's party should be any longer excluded from a share in the government. They are reputed to be two thirds of the people of this Province, and why they should be crushed and oppressed soe long as they are obedient to the laws and government of England, I see no reason in the world. And that they are a more sober and virtuous people and better affected to His Majesty's government then the other party, I averr it for a truth which I am able to justifie.

The Jacobite party in this towne have a clubb commonly every Saturday (which was Colonel Fletcher's clubb day). Last Saturday was seaven night there mett twenty seaven of them, their ringleaders are Colonel Bayard, Colonel Minviele both of the Councill, Mr. Nicolls late of the Councill, and Willson late Sheriff of this towne; there is

so great a rancor and inveteracy in these people that I think it by noe means proper for me to leave this province till I have your Lordships' orders . . . for I do verily believe if I should goe from hence the people would fall together by the ears. . . .

[October 21, 1698] About three weeks since the relations of Mr. Leisler and Mr. Milborne desired leave to take up the bodies that had been buried near the gallows and give them Christian burial in the Dutch Church here. I thought their request so reasonable that I consented to it, partly out of a principall of compassion, but cheifly out of a respect to the Act of Parliament for reversing the attainder of those two men; which Act does also legitimate Captain Leisler's assuming the government of this Province and putts a censure upon the illegality of his execution, as your Lordships will see by the Act for Reversing the attainder of these men. . . . I may add to these a third motive, that prevailed with me, which is, that Colonel Fletcher refused to obey that Act of Parliament by restoring the heirs of those two men to their father's estate; which treatment of his, gave his party the boldness to villifie it, by calling it a libell, a forgery, an Act surreptitiously obtained in the Parliament of England. And I have been told that the rage and malice of some of that party have transported them to the burning it. I that am a hearty lover of English laws and that value no Englishman that is not so, thought it proper to assert the Act of Parliament which had been treated with infamy. My design is cheifly to give the people here a just idea of English laws, that they bear the stamp of the highest authority of the King and Nation of England, and ought to be respected as sacred. There was great opposition made to the burying of those two men by the contrary party, but I was resolved, for the reasons I have already mentioned, to give that satisfaction to the relations of those unfortunate men. I had no reason to apprehend any disorder from a meeting of Leisler's friends or such as think that the proceeding against him was arbitrary and cruell; for I formerly told your Lordships that I have found those people more obedient to Government then the contrary party. There was a great concourse of people at the funerall (1200 'tis said) and would 'tis thought have been as many more, but that it blew a rank storm for two or three days together, that hindered people from coming down or crossing the rivers. . . .

[October 27, 1698] I send with this my proclamation for a Fast and Humiliation, thinking it a proper means to remove the heats and differences among the parties here. Last Wednesday was the day, and as a proof of the wickedness of the people who indeavour to give me disturbance in my government, few of them came to Church, and not one of the ringleaders, neither Bayard, Nicolls, Wilson, nor severall others that are not worth my naming to you. . . .

Mr. Brooke the late Collector carried over a Bill prepared [by] the last Assembly to reconcile parties here. Tho' it has a specious name, there is for all that a snake in the grass, which is this: Mr. Nicolls, whom I suspended from the Councill and who is of all others the most active inverate enemy I have here, drew that Bill, and calculated it for his own advantage. For he has made the indemnity in the Bill to extend no further than to Colonel Fletcher's arrivall here at New York, and all the extravagent processes at Law, Decrees and Judgments were obtained during his government, and among the rest Nicolls obtained a judgment for five hundred pound[s] against a very honest Dutchman here, upon pretence of false imprisonment in Leisler's government. The truth of the case is, Nicolls opposed the Revolution, and this Dutchman by order of the then Governour Leisler seized him, and for his contumacy he was put in prison, and 'tis well known Nicolls was not worth half £500 when that judgment was given. But this is not all; the factious merchants and people in this town to the number of twenty-eight raised a hundred pound[s] by subscription . . . to bribe some officer about the Court and obtain the King's peremptory order to me to passe that reconciling Bill.

B. AN ANTI-LEISLERIAN EXPRESSES HIMSELF IN VERSE, 1702

[[Robert Livingston], "A Satyr Upon the Times," 1702, Livingston-Redmond MSS., Franklin D. Roosevelt Library, Hyde Park, N. Y.]

Unhappy York doom'd by Eternal fate
To curst divisions in affares of State.
Happy in being under the Brittish Sway
But curs'd in being ruled another way
When Boors and butterboxes doe pertake
Of Favors which an English man must Lack
When Trade (the brittish Darling) is Supprest
And Merchants (under form of law) opprest

When Justice in the hands of Poverty
Shall Sacrifice the honest Property
When English Laws by Dutchmen shall be made
To Ease themselves and English Subjects Lade,
When to Complain of greevances is thought
A Crime and to addresse the king a fault
When those aggreev'd (instead of a Redresse)

are forc'd to find a gaole for their recess
When aldermen returne themselves and are
Proov'd Perjured yet it does no crime appear
Bless my kind heaven and send me farr from hence
Where Villaines Triumph under a pretence
of Loyalty and make the Laws their tools
To Serve their wicked ends and Cherish fools
But tell me Satyr whence these ills proceed
And bite the author till thou make him bleed
Twas gold (that curst Tempter) that did bribe
The grand Ringleader of this hellish Tribe
great by his Title Vile in his every action
He's gon but has entailed a Curse on's faction
A fawning Sycophant he's left behind
Cunning and Rogue enough to embroyle mankind
Devout he Seems as tho Religion was
His aim, but gold would make him goe to mass
But ere I Leave him let him have my curse
May he to Nevis Pack with Empty Purse
And there receive the just rewards of Some
He has wrong'd, then be ship'd off to hang at home
And now (Dear Satyr) keener whet thy Pen
Vennom'd as adders Teeth and bite agen
A Crafty knave delivered from a jayle
To be a Statesman here, who'll never fail
The Laws to turn and wind, wher's Interest Sways
And overrule the barrmen as he please

He's Proud as Lucifer tho poor as job
greedy as Cibernis mercilesse as the mob
Feirce as a Lyon in's Judiciall Chair
But when he's out as Timerous as a hare
And Cowardly he vents his Venom'd gall
garded (by King's authority) from's fall
me thinks I see this haughty wight assend
The Bench of Justice where his Looks portend
Certain Destruction as a Sacrifice
To his malice hatred or his avarice
Without he's Scarlet, Black as hell within
His Eyes all fire kindled by his Sinn
Have you not Seen the horse Leech Suck and Swell
gorg'd with unwholsome blood he burst and fell
May this Viperous monster thus be curst
Swoln up with rank ambition may he burst
And if ther's Such a Place as authors tell
Lett him be damn'd to domineer in hell
There are Some other Villans on the Stage
That Scarce are worthy of Poetick rage
a gogle Eyd Serpent from Batavia Sprung
Who if he had his right had long time hung
Thers Hickins Doctins too, but let him passe
A Low Dutch quack no better than an asse
There is a meager Long backt hell hound too
To name no more of the vile sordid crew
Black and Malitious blood runns throu his Veins
And Shaking nodle shews his want of brains
As for the rest o the Scoundrells let em wait
The approaching Change and then Lament their fate.

C. The Leislerians Recapitulate Their Grievances, May 15, 1699

[MSS. New York Assembly Journal, 1698-1705, 62-64, N.-Y. Hist. Soc.]

We the Representatives of this, his Majesty's Province Conven'd in General Assembly, do with all due Respect and Humility, approach your Lordship [the Earl of Bellomont], to Assure you that the same inviolable Loyalty which has hitherto affected and inflamed our hearts towards the Crown and Government of England, will ever preserve us in a most Religious and steady Perseverence therein, being thoroughly sensible how great a Blessing it is to be subject to the best and greatest of Kings, and under so noble a Constitution of Laws as makes ENGLAND this day the Envy of all its Neighbour Nations. Yet we Cannot but with great greif of heart represent to your Lordship, that we have not of late yeares enjoyed the felicity of those Excellent Laws, which in their own nature and designment are to Extent to all the Subjects of the Crown, how remote soever, at least Virtually, and wherein the Lives, Libertyes and properties of the subjects are Concerned.

We were very uneasy under an Arbitrary Comission in the late King James's Reigne, which gave the Governor of this Province, among other Arbitrary powers, that of Levying mony without calling an Assembly, whereby we reckoned that our Lives, as well as Estates, were subject to the Arbitrary will of a Governor contrary to the known Laws of England; and mony was actually Levyed on us, pursuant to the illegal powers of the said Commission. The exercise whereof and the dreadfull violence we also apprehended would be done to our Consciences, in respect of our Holy Protestant Religion, from a Popish Arbitrary King, made us Unanimously and heartily throw off the Yoke of Popish Tyranny, and declare for his then Highnesse the Prince of ORANGE, upon the first News we had of his Glorious and Unparalleled Expedition into England.

We acted then, as we conceived, on a Right Principle, and we were the more Confirmed in that Belief, because we acted in Concert and Conformity with the Glorious People of England. But to our great amazement and sorrow we have suffered severely for our early service to King William and the Crown of England, most of us in our Libertyes and Estates, and two of our Friends (who had the Honesty and Courage to stand in the Gap when others shamefully drew back and deserted the Protestant Cause, and were therefore by Universal Consent of the People thought most worthy to be cheif in Comand, till orders should come from England) who fell a Sacrifice to the Rage and Malice of the Jacobite Party in this Province, who tho' few in Number at that time, had Nevertheless the Power and influence to prevaile on the weakest of men, Colonel Henry Sloughter, Governor of this Province, to order a Tryal for those brave Men, and appoint such a sett of Judges, as by principle and prejudice, would not faile to gratifie the Malice of their Party, as they did under a forme of Law, which made it the more Cruel and Arbitrary, the said Tryal being ordered by the Governor, and mannaged by the Bench Contrary to all the Rules of Justice and Humanity; for we are able to make appear, if thereunto Required, that never a Revolution was carried on and mannaged with more moderation in any part of the Christian World.

And further to instance the weakness as well as the Cruelty of the said Governor in appointing Nicholas Bayard,

William Nicolls (lately Suspended by your Lordship from his Majesty's Council) and several others to mannage the tryal against Captain Leisler, Mr. Milborne, and the other six Prisoners who were all their a Vowed Enemies, and bore a Mortal Grudge to the said Captain Leisler, for their haveing been by him imprisoned in the Fort for opposeing the late happy Revolution and endeavoring to raise a Tumult among the People, and disturb the peace of the Government, and for telling Captain Leisler to his face, That the Parliament of England Voting and enacting the Throne's being Vacant, was non sence, that there was no Such thing possible in Nature, nor could be by the Laws of England. Governor Sloughter too by Lodging in Nicholas Bayard's house was the more pressed, and sooner prevailed on by Bayards Importunity to sign the Warrant of Execution. And as an Infallible token of the share he had in that Council, there was a Flag hung out of a Window of his House for two days together, before the day of Execution, as a Trophy and signal of the Point gained by him on the said Governor and of the Victory over the Lives, not only of Innocent, but most deserving men. In those days it was, when the Protestant subjects were disarmed, and Papists armed; Nay the Publick faith of Government was Violated, for a Reprieve had been sealed to respit the Execution of those Gentlemen, untill his Majesty's pleasure should be known, yet before this could be known [to] his Majesty they were Executed. And notwithstanding the Governors Proclamation, to invite such as fled to shun the hard fate, several whereof were nevertheless fined and Imprisoned; and certainely more had undergone the hard fate of Captain Leisler and Mr. Milborne, had it Not been for Governor Sloughter's suddain Death, and the reflection he had, tho to late, of this Barbarous and unwarrantable Strange Execution. This was the end of Captain Leisler and Mr. Milborne,

the former whereof has Expended £2700 out of his own proper Estate for the service of his Majesty, as was made appear to a Comittee of this House. These were the Days of Wrath and utter Darkness, so that we must say with the Apostles, Wo unto them, for they have gone in the way of Cain.

Then, Contrary to his Majesty's Letters Patents, Richard Ingoldesby, a hotheaded inconsiderable person, and a simple Captain of foot, is made Comander in Cheif; and in all the time of his administration, oppression is still continued. Nor could the change of Governors remedy the same, by the coming of Colonel Fletcher, who altho no blood [was] Spilt, yet bruised the Bone of the Remnant left, and made his Government an Entire Mass of Corruption, by Encourageing Pyracy and Unlawful Trade, and giveing away almost all the Vacant Lands in the Province to a few disaffected and undeserving men, neglecting the frontieers of this Province and packing Representatives to serve in General Assembly, Imbezilling and squandering away the Revenue and other publick monys, setting atheistical Persons in places of greatest Trust in the Government. All which, and many more Instances of his male administration, as we are informed, have been already transmitted to England by your Lordship.

The Representatives Conven'd in General Assembly, takeing notice of what was done herein, for releif, by that most Senate, the Parliament of England, in Reversing of the attainders of Jacob Leisler, Mr. Milborne, and others, cannot but with the greatest of Zeal, and fervency of affection, send up their Prayers to the great majesty of Heaven and Earth, for the Preservation of his Majestys Royal Person, and of that most Excellent Constitution, and for the Ministers of State, the influence of whose wise and honest Council, is felt even at this vast Distance from England. And in humble Confidence of his Majestys goodness, we humbly pray your Excellency to lay before his Majesty this, our humble Petition, hoping that the same good angel who led your Excellency to attend his Majesty, when Prince of Orange, in his Glorious Expedition for England, and brought your Excellency safe amongst us, to put a stop to the oppressions we groaned under, will now move your Lordship in our behalf, to interceed with his Majesty for our Releif (although as Christians we would forgive our Enemies and oppressors) That he would be graciously pleased to Extend of his Royal Bounty and Favour on the Families of the said Leisler and Milborne, and also order the Sum of Two thousand seaven hundred Pounds to be paid unto her (and that care be taken to pay such Debts as are owing for what was Expended in the late happy Revolution in this Province) in Con-

sideration of their suffering and services for his Majestys Interest and this Province.

That for the better administration of Justice two able judges be sent from England (and two or three able Council, who have acquired to that noble profession by study, and not by usurpation) for the maintenance whereof we shall not be wanting.

That Colonel Fletcher's Coat of Arms may be pulled down from the Kings Chapell in the Fort, and Trinity Church in this Citty; that since he left no monuments of Virtue and a Just Administration, those of his Nautious and Insupportable Pride and Vanity, may not remain to Posterity, especially since his Birth was so mean and obscure as that he was not entituled to bear a Coat of Arms.

40. An Anti-Leislerian Analysis, 1701

[Caleb Heathcote to Gilbert Heathcote, 1701, Blathwayt Papers, BL 218-24, Huntington Library]

I cannot omit giveing you a Narrative of the unhappy circumstances of this poor province, the foundation of whose nursery was laid (saving what his fellow Laboror Captain Leisler did in order thereunto) by the late Earl of Bellomont, who haveing conceivd an Irreconcilable hatred against those his unbounded Maleice and Injustice had made his enemies that he omitted nothing he could devise to harass and make them uneasie. To give a full rehearsal of his Barbarities would not only be needless but swell to a Vollume, and blessed be God for removing that scurge from us whose memory will stink in the nostrills of all good men for severall ages. For were I deposed uppon oath I could scarcely name one man in the province but which I believe to be either a knave or a fool that joyned with that nasty faction. And were it possible to

give you a lively description of those in whose hands the Powers of government now are, and by him it was [so] settled, I would submit my head to the blok, if the like was ever seene or heard of since the foundation of the earth. The whole boddy of them consisting chiefly of a herd of tools and Creatures who observed no other Lawes and rules but his Will and pleasure, and haveing as an addition to our Misery taken care to furnish himselfe with skilful hands the better to ruine us by rules. I am confident that of two thirds of the Province of which full that number of the People are against Leisler's Crew, one halfe must have left the Country had the Earl lived, and the other must have submitted to an unheard of Tyranny and oppression. When I consider of the plotte of Villany that was laid by that vile Lord it amazes me to think how it should be possible for soo much Wikedness to be in one man. When the main spring of their designes was by his death happily broke wee flatterd ourselves with the hopes of peace, but the leavin of their mallice still remaining and his favoritts haveing the power of government in their hands [they] omit no oppertunity of a Revenge, and use all means tho never soo Illegal and Indirect to perpetuate their dominion over us of which because I wont be troublesome will only give you two instances and by those you may Judge of the reste. . . . I could besides Instance a thousand passages of the Like nature done by this barbarous Crew, but as I said before It will be to tedious soo shall spare you and my selfe that trouble. When I looke bak and consider with what temper and [?] the English have undergone all their oppressions affronts and hardships, It amazes mee as well as to think that amongst mankind professing the Christian religion there should be soo wicked a herd as in soo Cruel and unheard of a manner to persecute those of the same profession. Were it papist against Protestant, or the reverse, or Jacobin against Williamists, nay were it Churchmen against dissipators or Common Wealth party against the Church, this might carry some face with it, but it is soo farr from that, that both partyes, that is to say the Dutch are all of one Church and religion and soo are the English, and all of em verry zealous for the present Government, being not 20 papists and Jacobins in the whole Province. And as for the English party they have given sufficient proofe of their Loyalties, haveing the government almost wholy in their possession in Colonel Sloughters Ingoldesby and Fletchers time, and it is Visible that they defended the Province and maintained their ground during the late Warr with as much honor as any government in America. Soo that tis Verry plain our quarrels are not gounded on the Intrest of the King and the Protestant Religion as those beasts pretend, but tis the trash and refuse of the people of the province, against all the best and most substantiall of the Dutch all the honest protestants and 7/8 of the English. . . . The Province being now growne to soo great a heat, that tis verry dangerous breaking forth into flames, and I beleave itt would have come to mischief ere now were not the Soldjers and Saylers verry firm to the English party, the Rable Dutch talking much after that rate, but God be thankt wee are able to keepe them in order unless they have a mind to have their throats Cutt. . . . Wee are free from all plotts tricks designs and Contrivaments and Want nothing but to be at peace and union with our Enemys and that they would be soo good-naturd as to forgive, and accept of their forgiveness whom they have soo greatly Injured by Plundring Imprisonment etc. And since wee cannot agree in settling their disorders amongst ourselves, Wee pray the King and Parliament would do it for us.

41. Cornbury's Use of Factionalism

A. Lewis Morris' Description, February 9, 1707

[Lewis Morris, by order of the Assembly of New Jersey, to Secretary of State Boyle, Feb. 9, 1707, O'Callaghan, ed., *Documents Relative to Colonial New York*, V, 37-38]

As to the raieseing a revenue for a certain time, especially so long a time 'tis what they are utterly averse to, for the instances of the misaplication of the revenue in the neighbouring government of New Yorke are so many and the extravagance of its aplication in New Jersie soe great, that it is in my opinion impracticable to perswade an Assembly in this part of America to trust a Governour after my Lord Cornbury. When I spoke of the extravagant application of the Revenue of New Jersie, I forgot to add the difficulty of knowing how 'tis applyed; for though her Majesty directs that the Assembly examine the Accounts of the disposall of money raised by them, yet the Governour eludes the ends of that instruction and protects one Peter Fauconier a French man Receiver Generall in that Province [New York], from giving the Assembly the satisfaction they ought to have. The fact is thus;—the Assembly ordered Fauconier to lay the Accounts before them; he did, and severall articles there were, which they thought very extravagant; they directed him to bring his vouchers; the answer he returns is (if I remember) he is accountable to the Auditor Generall, and with out my Lord's direction he cannot do it, which he has not had nor is not like to get; and there it sticks.

If this, and what's inclosed lets your honor see the state of New Jersie, I have my end; I ad that its the impudent conduct of the Governours, to call it no worse, that has been the great prejudice of her Majesties service in America, the various kinds of injustice and oppression, the sordid and mercenary measures they have taken, the mean things they have stoopt to, the trash of mankind that has been their favorites and tooles and by them raised to posts of honor and proffit as rewards for accomplishing the worst ends, has stunted the growth of these otherwise thriving plantations, and you may easily judge what effects are the unavoidable consequences of such causes, except mankind can be brought to love such things as by the principalls of human nature they must necesarly hate.

Tis this has filled the Charter governments with people and makes them fond of suporting an administration in which they can call their Governour to an account and punish them for male administration with out the uncertaine and tedious success of application to courts; and were it not for the stingeness and narrowness of their principles (pardon this disagreeable truth) the governments under her Majesties more imediate administration had long ere this been thin'd of inhabitants, and when a way is found that Governours may not do acts of injustice with impunity the Charter governments wont long subsist.

All the apologie I shall make for the lenth of this is, that I mean it for her Majesties service and hope the goodness of the intent will induce a pardon for the meanesse of the performance, and did I not feare tyring your Honor would enter into the state of the Province of New York; but I hope some abler hand has done this Province and my Lord Cornbury so much justice as to lay before you an administration no where so exactly parralel'd as in that of Gessius Florus, Governour of Judea [who practised every species of iniquity], and has told you that her Majesties revenue here is nigh expiring and will certainly fall, if some elce ben't sent in my Lord's stead.

We are told Sir Gilbert Heathcote has made some intrest for his brother Colonel Caleb Heathcote: he will be a man to the generall sattisfaction of the people, and at this juncture to obteine a resetlement of her Majesties revenue, no man fitter. I know no man understands the Province or People better, or is more capable of doeing her Majestie reall service. He is an honest man and the reverse of my Lord Cornbury; of whom I must say something which perhaps no boddy will think worth their while to tell, and that is, his dressing publicly in woman's cloaths every day, and putting a stop to all publique business while he is pleaseing himself with that peculiar but detestable magot.

B. ROBERT LIVINGSTON'S DESCRIPTION, JUNE 2, 1707

[Livingston to William Lowndes, June 2, 1707, Treasury Papers, 1/102, 134-35, Public Record Office, London]

When I landed [in New York] I found most people very uneasy under this gentlemans administration, and heard such unaccountable actions, that I durst not attempt to give your honor an account of them as not being possible to be believ'd. The assembly who have hitherto been at Variance with him being allow'd by an order from home, to have their own Treasurer, have pass'd some acts, for the Levying of money to defray the Charges of fortifying the Citty of New York and the Charge of the Indians at Albany. But as for the money formerly given its alledg'd no just account is yet Rendred, the Province much in debt, no body paid, the Revenue Swallowd up, insomuch as tis credibly Reported when the Revenue expires by its own limitation next May come twelve-month, the Assembly will not Raise it. Tis said he is wholly addicted to his pleasure, and enriching himself with strange and unheard of methods, having some few Creatures about him, whose Councils he pursues to the mischief of the Principal Inhabitants. His dressing himself in womens Cloths Commonly

every morning is so unaccountable that if hundred[s] of Spectators did not dayly see him, it would be incredible. After dinner till 12 a Clok at night, is spent at the Botle. The debts of the Province are so much augmented that ten years Revenue if setled will not clear them, and I have heard his personall Debts here computed to Six thousand four hundred pounds. . . .

In fine our Trade decays, our house Rents fall, our Vessels are taken [by the French], and everything goes behind hand, and a visible Judgement appears since this gentleman came among us. We have a poor dispirited people, a mixture of English, Dutch, and French that Live in the Province, and if they be never so much oppressed, dare not Complain, because they are not unanimous, and doe not stick to one another. So that a governor if he be not a man of honor and Probity can oppresse the people when he pleases—its but Striking in with one Party and they assist him to destroy the other. And this is our case, by which we are under such discouragements that many desert the province.

The End of Vindictiveness

42. The Assembly Lauds a Governor for the First Time, June 25, 1719

[Journal of the Votes and Proceedings of the General Assembly of the Colony of New York, 2 vols. (New York, 1764-66), I, 438-39]

When we reflect upon your [i.e., Robert Hunter's] past Conduct, your just, mild and tender Administration, it heightens the Concern we have for your Departure, and makes our Grief such, as Words cannot truly express.

You have governed well and wisely, like a prudent Magistrate, like an affectionate Parent, and wherever you go, and to whatever Station the divine Providence shall please to assign you, our sincere Desires and Prayers for the Happiness of you and yours, shall always attend you.

We have seen many Governors, and may see more; and as none of those, who had the Honour to serve in your Station, were ever so justly fixt in the Affections of the Governed, so those to come will acquire no mean Reputation, when it can be truly said of them, their Conduct has been like yours.

We thankfully accept the Honour you do us, in calling yourself our Countryman; give us Leave then, to desire, that you will not forget, this is your Country, and (if you can) make haste to return to it.

But if the Service of our Sovereign will not admit of what we so earnestly Desire, and his Commands, deny us that Happiness, permit us to Address you, as our Friend, and give us your Assistance, when we are oppressed with an Administration the Reverse of yours.

PART III

THE GLORIOUS REVOLUTION
IN MARYLAND

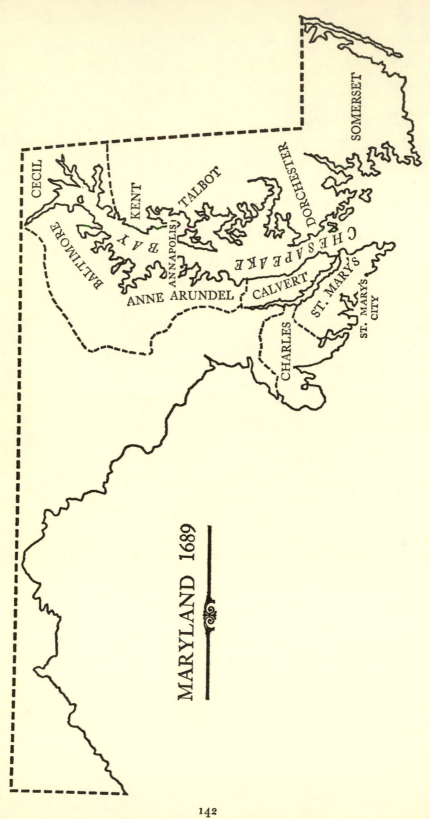

MARYLAND 1689

CECIL

BALTIMORE

KENT

ANNE ARUNDEL

ANNAPOLIS

TALBOT

BAY

CHESAPEAKE

DORCHESTER

SOMERSET

CALVERT

CHARLES

ST. MARY'S

ST. MARY'S CITY

CHAPTER SEVEN

SEEDS OF DISCONTENT

A CENTURY ago John Pendleton Kennedy, a distinguished Maryland man of letters, wrote that the period "from 1688 to 1692 is one of our darkest intervals. . . . It begins with a domestic revolution and ends with the appointment of a Royal Governor and that is pretty nearly all we know about it." Although many documents illuminating this dark interval have come to light since 1860, the history of the revolution in Maryland continues to contain many mysterious gaps. During the rebellion and for two years following, the records were either kept poorly or not at all. And when the capital was shifted from St. Mary's to Annapolis in 1695 many documents were damaged. Others that survived were consumed by the fire which destroyed the state house in 1704.

In the face of insufficient information historians have continually conflicted in assessing causes, evaluating effects, and interpreting the meaning of the revolution. One scholar recently wrote that the uprising led by the Protestant Association was "one of the first great American experiences with Democracy." Others have disputed the validity of this verdict, viewing the opposing factions as engaged in a struggle for irresponsible control of the sources of political power, with the interests of the people a mask disguising their provincial pretensions.

Most students of Maryland's seventeenth-century history agree, however, that this community of 25,000 persons (in 1688) was periodically wrenched by unrest. There were insurrections in 1659, 1676, and 1681, when Lord Culpeper wrote to the Lords of Trade from Virginia that "Maryland is now in torment, and not only troubled with our disease, poverty, but in very great danger of falling in pieces; whether it be that old Lord Baltimore's politic maxims are not pursued or that they are unsuited to this age" (Nos. 43 and 48).

Those "politic maxims" were predicated upon the Proprietor's charter, the constitution of the province granted by Charles I half-a-century earlier. This archaic document was cut from a medieval pattern and seemed an anachronism to the freeholders and their representatives in the lower house of the General Assembly. But what this body disputed as arbitrary or inflexible exercise of the Proprietor's prerogative, the Council, or upper house, upheld according to the letter of his Lordship's charter. Thus the frictions frequently arising from conflicting views of the nature of the highest public authority reached an impasse: the proprietary party, represented by the Governor and Council, claimed privileges based on a fourteenth-century grant, while the lower house and opponents of the Calverts countered with demands based upon rights wrested from the Crown by the seventeenth-century House of Commons. Two such problems over which recriminations were frequently exchanged were the number of delegates each county might elect to the General Assembly (No. 44) and the use of the executive veto power (No. 45).

In addition the Proprietor was accused by the opposition of nepotism and favoritism in granting provincial offices and lands. Until 1680 all business relating to land grants, patents, and escheats was managed by the Governor and his Council, or the Secretary of the colony. When a land office was established in 1680, it was presided over by a council comprising three cousins of the Proprietor and his stepson. In 1681 the English Privy Council called on Charles Calvert, Lord Baltimore, to exonerate himself against charges of partiality to his coreligionists, the Roman Catholics. Several months later, however, a group including men who led the Protestant Association in 1689 vindicated the Proprietor of partisanship (No. 46).

The Protestants outnumbered the Catholics in Maryland at this time by better than 20 to one, and the general coincidence of Catholicism with the Calvert party and Protestantism with the anti-proprietary party compounded political tensions and provided a dimension of bitter bigotry (No. 47).

Many of the grievances which those hostile to the Proprietor complained of were economic. Some objected to rising tax rates (No. 48), while others resented their exclusion from the Indian trade, which required licenses obtained only with difficulty. Planters and merchants disagreed with the proprietary view of the best way to stimulate the provincial economy, which was notably depressed during the decade preceding 1689 (No. 49). (Note in reading the documents that tobacco was worth a penny a pound.) Finally, much hard feeling followed alterations made in the pattern of land distribution—the abolition of the headright system (No. 50).

Among the leaders of the 1689 insurgency John Coode, Kenelm

Cheseldyne, Nehemiah Blakiston, and Henry Jowles were most prominent. The first three were brothers-in-law, all having married daughters
of Thomas Gerard who helped lead the 1659 revolt against the second
Lord Baltimore. Coode, caricatured by a contemporary as "being of
a middle Stature, a deformed person, his face resembling that of a
Baboon or munckeys, Club-footed, his feet standing inwards one to the
other and a notorious coward," had a considerable career as an agitator
and had consistently been a focus of controversy in Maryland. He was
anathema to Lord Baltimore, who saw him as a source of disaffection
and linked him with Maryland's revolutionary tradition (No. 43).
Both Cheseldyne and Jowles had been party to litigation which set them
in opposition to the Calverts, and Blakiston's alienation from the Proprietor became manifest in the 1680's (No. 51).

In addition to the experience of personal, political, and legal conflicts with the Calverts, these rebel leaders shared another resentment
with many of their fellows and supporters—frustrated ambition. They
had achieved the highest offices in their respective counties and many
positions of middling importance on the provincial level. But the highest stratum of authority and concomitant social prestige were just out
of reach in the grasp of the proprietary party. Only revolution might
make them room at the top.

Because his province was an integral part of an imperial system, Lord
Baltimore's problems included several outside the internal intricacies
of his bailiwick. Uneasy relations between the Proprietor's party and
Crown officials in the colony heightened his difficulties in dealing with
factious individuals in opposition, many of whom were allied with the
royal civil servants in the struggle against the ruling elite (No. 51).
Feeling ran high a few years before the revolution when Lord Baltimore's deputy governor killed a royal customs collector who was also
a member of the anti-proprietary party.

Moreover the settlement of Pennsylvania after 1681 led to boundary
disputes and competition for settlers, ultimately forcing Lord Baltimore to return to London after 1684. The Quaker William Penn—no
friend to the Calverts—was not above arousing the freemen of northern
Maryland against their government. Tensions such as these combined
with a series of untoward events in 1688-89 were sufficient to produce
politics of upheaval.

In Lord Baltimore's absence his subordinates were unequal to the
task of quieting these problems and protagonists. In 1688 the Crown,
through the proprietary government, sought a prohibition against the
export of bulk tobacco from the Chesapeake area. Hence it became
necessary to convene the General Assembly, whose lower house strongly
opposed the proposal (No. 52). When Lord Baltimore's surrogate, Wil-

liam Joseph, opened the crucial session in November he antagonized the Assembly with a diatribe they found didactic and authoritarian (No. 53). A contentious sequence of squabbles ensued which resulted in the lower house's being prorogued several times, but not without their first presenting a statement of grievances (No. 54).

In January 1689, Lord Baltimore's deputies wrote him an account of the proceedings of the General Assembly just past, and concluded by remarking that "all things are peaceable and quiet" (No. 55). Perhaps they wished to reassure his Lordship, knowing that he faced the loss of his charter in London, owing to infringements of the Navigation Acts and the desire of the Crown to centralize colonial administration. But if the Proprietor's subordinates felt domestic conditions were secure, they were apparently less confident about dangers from without. The very day they wrote Lord Baltimore that all was quiet they also proclaimed that all public weapons should be submitted to the county sheriffs for repair and readiness. Whether or not this was a pretext for disarming the opposition, it nevertheless soon proved prophetic. In March there was rumor of a conspiracy among the provincial Indians and Catholics which set the Protestants in an uproar. Following an investigation a bipartisan group promptly labeled the scare a "slevelesse fear and imagination" (No. 56). But the people refused to be set at ease. With her thin and scattered population spread over an area divided by a wide bay and broken by many creeks and rivers, such rumors had been endemic in Maryland for years. But, as a Virginian wrote in 1681, if Indians "should attack we [in Virginia] are in an ill condition for defence, and Maryland in a worse by reason of her intestine distractions."

A Legacy of Unrest

43. John Coode and the Rebellion of 1681

[Philip Calvert, Chancellor of Maryland, to Henry Meese, a merchant in London, Dec. 29, 1681, Maryland Historical Society]

I find by the Masters of the Ships, that the Imprisonment of Captain Josias Fendal, and Captain John Coode, hath made so great a noise at London; and therefore I thought it necessary to give you an account of it, as having been formerly an Inhabitant of Mary-land, and an Eye-witness of the carriage of Captain Fendel, in the years 1659 and 1660 when he Perfidiously broke his Oath and Trust, being Governour of this Province; cancell'd his Commission from the then Lord Proprietor, and took a new one from the Assembly. For that offence he was only Fin'd, and declar'd uncapable of ever bearing any Office in this Province, as you may remember, and that hath gaul'd him ever since. And to get into Office, he now sets all his Wits to work, inciting the People in Charles's County to Mutiny and Sedition; and Tampering with some of the Justices of Peace in St. Maries County: First, telling the People they were Fools to pay any Taxes, (though laid by Act of Assembly;) that there was Wars in England between the King and the Parliament; and that now [that] nothing was Treason a man might say anything: And then to the Justices, hinting how easie a matter it was to overturn the Government here, by seizing the Lord Proprietor, the Chancellor, Secretary, and Colonel Darnal, all the rest (as he said) signifying nothing. The Justice of Peace told him, he had no Commission, and that it would be downright Rebellion. He went from him, and revealed this discourse to another Justice, who discovered this whole matter to my Lord. Shortly after this, Captain John Coode falls upon a time, at a Feast, into discourse with a Papist, who was Suing a Friend of his for a piece of Land, for that no Papist in Mary-land should be Owner of any Land at all in this Province within three Months; for that he had ten thousand Men at his Command; and he could make it High-Water, or Low-Water, when he pleased.

After this, Coode was observed to make Visits to Fendal, which he never used to do before, and they both went over into Virginia; and within few days after their return from thence a Boat designed for Carolina from Maryland, was forced in by bad weather to a House in Virginia, where the Owner of the Boat heard that Fendal and Coode had been thereabouts; and that the whole discourse there was, that Fendal intended to raise Mutiny in Maryland, and that he and Coode would carry their Families into Virginia. This being Sworn to, and at that very instant Information being given, that one of Captain Coode's Servants reported, that his Master intended to remove his Family on the Thursday following into Virginia; made my Lord think it high time to look to the Security and Peace of the Province, and therefore sent Colonel Darnal with about ten Men, to bring Coode and Fendal before him and the Council; Colonel Darnal came to Coodes when it was light, and the Servants using to go to work opened the door, at which Colonel Darnal entered alone, leaving his Men without, and coming into Mr. Coode's Chamber, told him he was his Prisoner; Coode at first laid his hand upon his Sword, but at last yielded; after which Colonel Darnal went over the River, and took Captain Fendal also, and brought them before my Lord and Council. And the next day after, Mrs. Coode did Hector my Lord at a rate I never heard from a Woman before; by which you may conclude she was not run mad with the fright of her Husbands being pull'd out of his Bed, as we are told her Son Slye falsly reports at London.

Three or four days after, I saw her at St. Maries, and then I did suspect she would not continue long in her Wits, knowing she had been Mad a while upon the death of her eldest Son, about the year 1659, and had heard she sometimes fell into the like Fits since.

After this, my Lord took Bail for Coode within five days, but Fendal was kept untill my Lord had secured Lieutenant George Godfrey, who laid a Plot to unhorse his Captain, and carry the Troop to the rescue of Fendal, instead of searching for the Indians, that had Murther'd some of our Planters, and were daily expected to fall into Charles County, in great numbers; as they afterwards did in less than three Weeks.

My Lord intends to send over their Tryals, that the World may see with how much Favour the Court proceeded, and to stop the Mouth of Calumny.

Politics and Religion

44. A Controversy Over Burgesses

A. AN ORDINANCE OF THE PROPRIETOR TOUCHING ASSEMBLIES, SEPTEMBER 6, 1681

[W. H. Browne, ed., *Archives of Maryland* (Baltimore, 1883——), XVII, 15-17]

Charles Absolute Lord and Proprietary . . . To our two houses of Assembly and to all the Freemen of our said Province of Maryland greeteing in our Lord God Everlasting. . . . Prince Charles the First . . . by his Letters Pattents gave unto our said Father, his heyres and Successors . . . absolute power to ordeine, make, Enact, and under his and their Seale to publish any Lawes whatsoever of and with the advice and Assent of the Freemen of the said Province or of their Delegates or Deputyes to be by him the said Lord Proprietary or his heyres Assembled in such sort or forme as to him or them . . . should seeme best. And Forasmuch as the forme of Assembling the said Freemen[,] their Delegates and Deputyes hath hitherto been altogether uncertain from the very beginning of the Seateing of this Province

For the settleing therefore of the mindes of the Freemen, and Establishing a certainty for the future wherein our peace may rest as upon a sure foundation. By the advice of our Councill, Wee doe hereby publish ordeine and Declare that from and after the dissolution of this present generall Assembly whensoever Wee . . . shall think fitt to call an Assembly for the Establishing any Lawes or otherwise to consult of the arduous and urgent affaires of this our Province, Writts shall issue out of our Chancery under the greate Seale . . . , Impowering the Sheriff of every County . . . and the Mayor Alderman and Common Councill or other Officer . . . , requireing them respectively to Elect two Delegates or Deputyes and noe more for every County City Burrough or Towne Corporate then in being.

B. THE ADDRESS OF THE DELEGATES OF THE LOWER HOUSE TO THE PROPRIETOR, NOVEMBER 2, 1682

[Browne, ed., *Archives of Maryland*, VII, 345-46]

We Begg and hope that We may with Your Lordships favour and Good liking Discharge Ourselves faithfully in that Trust reposed in us by the freemen of this Province, who Notwithstanding they have Complyed with Your Lordships Writts for Election in Chooseing Two Deputies or Delegates for each County, thereby Sufficiently Empowering us to Advise and Consent to and with Your

Lordship upon the Urgent Affairs of this Province, yet they have given Instruction to their severall Delegates to pray and make Provision that they may be restored to their former freedom of Chooseing and electing the accustomed Number of Delegates for each County to be the representative Body of this Province. . . . We have Studyed by avoiding all Obstinacy to your Lordships Design to find out an Expedient that may as well fully Comply with your Lordships good intentions and Satisfie the Minds and Desire of the People, and this by a Bill Directing that all Writts for the future, may go out for the Electing of Two three or four Delegates for each County at the Choice of the Freemen thereof; And this may it Please Your Lordship We most Humbly Advise to be the most Honourable and safest way as well for your Lordship as Ourselves. And We doubt not that when it shall thereby Appear without all Contradiction to the Freemen of this Province, that Your Lordship designs Nothing therein but the Ease and welfare of the Inhabitants, they will readily Consent and Agree to Elect such and So Many as they find agreeable to your Lordships Desires for that End.

45. Lord Baltimore's Veto Power as an Issue

A. A Petition of the Lower House to Lord Baltimore, September 17, 1681

[Browne, ed., *Archives of Maryland*, VII, 181-82]

That having taken into Consideration the Inconveniencies that may happen in Case of Your Lordships Departure at any time out of this Province, and not sufficiently Empowering in your Absence Your Lordships Governor or Lieutenant Generall to give a full and Absolute Consent to Such Laws as may then be Enacted, for remedy of which this house having prepared one Good and Equitable Bill which is herewith all presented to your Lordship Entituled an Act for the Confirmation of the Laws of the Province in this and future Assemblies, and Sent the same unto the Upper house of Assembly, afterwards Seconded with Severall Good and Unanswerable reasons, to induce their Honours Assent to the Same, which to Our great Grief and Dissatisfaction after some Considerable Delay was returned Disassented to, whereby We have been Left frustrated (so far) of Our Innocent and Equitable desires of getting their Honours Assent to the said Bill, So much to the Advantage and Content of the Inhabitants of this Province—

Wherefore Your Lordships most Humble Petitioners the Delegates of this General Assembly, Do make this their further Address and Application to your Lordship Desiring Your Lordship to take the Premises into your Consideration, and to Signifie your Lordships Willingness to the Upper house of Assembly for the Passing the said Bill that there may be no longer hindrance of the Same; which will be ever taken and acknowledged as a Signal kindness and favour.

B. Lord Baltimore's Declaration in the Upper House, April 23, 1684

[Browne, ed., *Archives of Maryland*, XIII, 40]

To the bill for Assertaineing the true force and validity of the Lawes of this province, I give this Answere, that though I owne my promise and engagement to both my houses of Assembly made in September 1681: *vizt.*, that in my absence out of this Province, I would signifie my assent or dissassent to any lawes within Eighteen months. Yett doe I not think it convenient to obleige my heires and Successores by an Act to those inconveniences and mischeifes that may happen by their assenting or disassenting to any lawes within Twenty monthes, that shalbe made perpetuall dureing such their absence.

C. THE PROPRIETOR'S PROCLAMATION VETOING THE LAWS OF 1678, MAY 5, 1684

[Browne, ed., *Archives of Maryland*, XVII, 261]

Whereas severall doubts and disputes have been made concerning the uncertainty of the Lawes of this our Province for want of our Assent or dissent thereunto publickly declared and made knowne: And wee being now (upon urgent occasions relateing to Our Self, and the publick State and wellfare of this our Province us thereunto mooveing) suddenly designed on a voyage for England; Wee have thought fitt and convenient (upon peruseall and due consideration had of the Lawes aforesaid) to proclaime publish and make knowne ... our Dissent to all and Every the Act and Acts of Assembly of this our Province made (dureing our absence out of this Province) in the yeare of our Lord God [1678], which are hereby invalidated, adnulled, made void, and to stand for nought to all intents and purposes, except onely such of the said Acts as we have (since our arrivall here) by our Assent in a generall Assembly continued, confirmed, or revived, which are also to stand continued, confirmed or revived to all Intents and purposes.

46. Lord Baltimore Accused of Favoritism

A. A LETTER FROM THE PRIVY COUNCIL TO LORD BALTIMORE, OCTOBER 12, 1681

[Browne, ed., *Archives of Maryland*, V, 300-301]

After Our hearty Commendation to your Lordship, Information having been given unto Us, That there are very few of his Majesties Protestant Subjects admitted to be of the Councill of the Colony of Maryland, and that there is partiallity and favour shewed on all occasions towards those of the Popish Religion to the discouragement of his Majesties Protestant Subjects which We hope may proceed from misrepresentation, yett Wee cannot but take notice thereof unto your Lordship praying and requiring you to cause the same if true to be speedily redressed, and that in the distribution of the Armes and Ammunition ... your Lordship do express your trust and confidence in His Majesties Protestant Subjects by putting the said Armes into their hands.

B. THE COUNCIL OF MARYLAND VINDICATES LORD BALTIMORE'S POLICY, MAY 13, 1682

[Browne, ed., *Archives of Maryland*, V, 353-55]

Whereas through the envy, malice and hatred of some particular, turbulent, factious spirits, not only disaffected to this, but also dissatisfied with, uneasie under, and averse to all manner of rule and Government, severall ill reports and foul aspersions have of late been cast upon the Government of this Province under the right honourable Charles Lord Baltimore . . . representing his Lordshipp as violent against the Protestants here inhabiting; conceiving and entertaining groundless Jealousies against them, and upon all occasions showing partiality and favour to those of the Popish persuasion to the great discouragement and oppression of others His Majestie's Protestant subjects, who are said meerly upon the account of their religion, to be kept under and at a distance from all possibility of advancement to any place of honour or profitt within the Province, and to render the same more odious and contemptible to the world, such reports have not only been scattered abroad amongst several persons from one to another, but (as we have seen and heard) through the instigation, means, and procurement . . . of the authors themselves, have for the more general contagion been exposed to public view in print, thereby to take the deeper impression on the minds of the vulgar, not only to the derogation of his Lordshipps honor, but also of very ill consequence to the whole Province in General, by terrifying and preventing thereby others His Majestie's loving subjects from resorting hither to cohabitt with us as formerly for our greater strength and fortification against the Indians, and also for the better cultivating and improveing of this Country, to the great damage, detriment and prejudice of such . . . Subjects as are here already resident both as to their lives and estates by that means.

We therefore the Subscribers professing the Gospell of Jesus Christ according to the Litturgy of the Church of England and Protestants against the doctrine and practice of the Church of rome . . . hold ourselves in conscience and duty obliged by this our impartial,

true and sincere remonstrance or Declaration to unfold the naked truth . . . and to purge his Lordship and this Government, whereof we are, from all those false, scandalous and malicious aspersions, which the venomous blasts of such inveterate, malignant, turbulent spirits have cast thereon.

And therefore in the first place we doe hereby unanimously acknowledge and publish to the world the general freedom and priviledge which we and all persons whatsoever Inhabitants of this Province, of what condition soever, doe enjoy in our lives, liberties and estates under this His Lordship's Government . . . as effectually and in as full and ample manner to all intents and purposes as any of His Majestie's Subjects within any part of His Majestie's dominions whatsoever with the free and public exercise and enjoyment of our religion whatsoever it be, whether Protestant or other professing the name of Jesus. . . . We doe also declare and make known that besides our owne experience we have observed his Lordshipp's favours impartially distributed, and Places of Honor, trust and profit conferred on the most qualified for that purpose and service without any respect or regard had to the religion of the participants, of which generally and for the most part it hath so happened that the Protestants have been the greatest number, the halfe of His Lordshipp's Council nearest to his person are Protestants, his late Governor Thomas Notely, Esquire, and Benjamin Rozer, Esquire, of his Council, also lately deceased, both Protestants, the major part of his Lordshipp's Commissioners or Justices of the peace . . . Protestants; those likewise that have the charge of the Militia of this Province generally or [are] for the most part Protestants, . . . nine Colonels or principal Officers of the Militia all Protestants, and . . . only three of the romish persuasion Colonels or principal Officers of the Militia. . . . In like manner all other Officers and places of Honor or profitt within this Province, civill or military, impartially and equally (if not for the most part on Protestants) conferred. This not only in vindication of his Lordships honor, and this his Government, but also for the publick interest of the Province therein concerned.

[Signatures include WILLIAM DIGGES, KENELM CHESELDYNE, JOHN ROUSBY and 22 others]

47. Religious Differences in Maryland

A. A Letter to the Archbishop of Canterbury from John Yeo, Minister in Maryland, May 25, 1676

[Browne, ed., *Archives of Maryland*, V, 130-32]

These Rude and indigested lines . . . are to acquaint Your Grace with the Deplorable estate and condition of the Province of Maryland for want of an established Ministry. Here are in this Province tenn or twelve Countys and in them at least twenty thousand Soules and but three Protestant ministers of us that are Conformable to the Doctrine and Discipline of the Church of England. Others there are (I must confess) that Runn before they are Sent and Pretend they are Ministers of the Gospell that never have a Legall call or Ordination to such an holy office. Neither (indeed) are they qualified for it, being for the most part such as never understood any thing of learning and yet take upon them to be Dispencers of the word and to Administer Sacrament of Baptisme and sow seeds of Divission amongst the People and noe law Provided for the Suppression of such in this Province. Soe that here is a great Necesstie of able and learned men to confut the gaine sayer, espetially having soe many Profest enemies as the Popish Priests and Jesuits are, who are incoraged and Provided for and the Quaker takes care and provides for those that are Speakers in their conventicles, but noe care is taken or Provision made for the building up Christians in the Protestant Religion by means whereof not only many Dayly fall away either to Popery, Quakerism or Phanaticisme, but alsoe the lords day is prophaned, Religion despised, and all notorious vices committed soe that it is become a Sodom of uncleaness and a Pest house of iniquity. I doubt not but Your Grace will take it into Consideration and do Your utmost for our Eternall welfare, and now is the time that Your Grace may be an instrument of a universall reformation amongst us with greatest facillity, Cacillius Lord barron Baltimore, and absolut Proprietor of Maryland being dead and Charles lord Barron of Baltimore and our Governour being bound for England this Year (as I am informed) to Receive a farther confirmation of that Province from his Majestie, at which time I Doubt but Your Grace may soe prevaile with him as that a maintenance for a Protestant ministry may be established as well in this Province as in Virginia, Barbados and all other his Majesties Plantations in west indies and then there will be incoragement for able men to come amongst us, and that some Person may have power to examine all such Ministers as shall be admitted into any County or parish.

B. Lord Baltimore's Paper Setting Forth the Present State of Religion in Maryland, 1676

[Browne, ed., *Archives of Maryland*, V, 133-34]

That for the encouragement of all such persons as were desirous and willing to adventure and transport themselves and families into the Province of Maryland a law there made by the advice and consent of the Delegates of the Freemen concerning Religion, wherein a toleration is given to all persons beleeving in Jesus Christ freely to exercise their Religion and that no person of what judgment soever, beleeving as aforesaid should at any time be molested or discountenanced for or in Respect of his Religion or in the free exercise thereof and that noe one should be compelled to the beliefe or exercise of any other against his consent. Upon this Act the greatest part of the people and Inhabitants now in Maryland have setled themselves and families there and for these many years this toleration and liberty has been known and continued in the Government of that Province.

That those Persons of the Church of England there who at any time have encouraged any Ministers to come over into that Province have had several sent unto them as at this time there are residing there foure that the Lord Baltemore knows of who have Plantations and settled beings of their owne and those that have not any such beings are maintained by a voluntary contribution of those of their own persuasion, as others of the Presbiterians, Independents, Anabaptists, Quakers and Romish Church are.

That in every Country in the Province of Maryland there are a sufficient number of Churches and Houses called Meeting Houses for the people there and these have been built and are still kept in good repair by a free and voluntary contribution of all such as frequent the said Churches and Meeting Houses. . . .

The greatest part of the Inhabitants of that Province (three of four at least) doe consist of Praesbiterians, Independents, Anabaptists and Quakers, those of the Church of England as well as those of the Romish being the fewest, so that it will be a most difficult task to draw such persons to consent unto a Law which shall compel them to maintain Ministers of a contrary persuasion to themselves, they having already an assurance by that Act for Religion that they have all freedom in point of Religion and Divine Worship and noe penalties or payments imposed upon them in that particular.

The Economics of Discontent

48. A Dispute Over Taxes, 1676

[A Remonstrance of the Upper House Regarding the Causes of the Public Taxes, 1676, Browne, ed., *Archives of Maryland*, XV, 137-40]

The Governor and Councell . . . cannot but with wonder and Amazement reflect upon the Levity not to say Ingratitude of the People, who have bin so farre blinded by the Spetious pretences of some desperate and ill Affected persons as to runn out into an Actuall Rebellion against his Lordshipps Government. . . . The great Clamour is against the greatnes of the Taxes; the debarring of some Freemen who have nothing to Entitle themselves to a being in this Province, from voting in the Choice of the Delegates for makeing of the Lawes, and lastly that those poore Freemen are Obliged to pay taxes equall with the rich. As to the first we Appeale to the whole world to Judge whether the Lord Proprietary were not forced to the Expensive warre against the Sasquehannoughs last yeare. . . . What reason then have the People to repine att their being protected? unlesse they value not their owne lives att the rate the Proprietary himselfe Values the meanest of the People. If the Taxe continue this yeare tis the same necessity of defending the People that causes itt, and the paying for the building of the State house three yeares since ordered and begun by consent of an Assembly in a tyme of our greatest peace. . . .

As to the votes of Freemen who have neither lands nor visible personall Estate, in the Election of Delegates for the Assembly wee doe say, that as the Lord Proprietary can call Assemblys by his Patent whensoever and in what manner to him shall seeme most fitt and convenient, Itt is no wonder that he should chuse this as the fittest and most convenient manner, and most agreeable to the Lawe and Custome of England, For what man in England can be admitted to the Election of Parliament, men that hath not a visible Estate in land or

Goods? nay are there not infinite numbers concluded in Parliament without vote in the Elections, though they have great Estates both in land and Goods? . . . Wee doe promise to propound the case of the indigent Freemen to his Lordshipp att his returne, and to offer him such reasons and motives as may incline him to permitt the next Election to be made by the Votes of all the Freemen indifferently. This is all that lyes in our powers to doe in this case. . . .

The last part which concernes the poore Freemans paying equall Taxe with the rich, we must needs looke upon as a peice of Sophistry, imposed upon the credulous Freemen by some malignant Spiritt, who Repines that he cannot as well Cheate the publique of the Freemans Leavy, as he hath beguiled the Freeman out of his Crop. What Freeman is itt that ever paid for more than his own head? and what rich man is itt that hath not paid for every Servant and Slave he hath? but put the case itt be hard the poore Freeman should pay as much for his head, as the Rich man doth for his owne head, why must my Lord or his Governour and Councell beare the blame of this which my Lord himselfe cannot helpe without the consent of an Assembly? . . .

Looke, we Intreate you, upon the distressed and miserable Condition of our Neighbour Colony [Virginia] torne in peeces under the maske of publique Reformation and ease from taxes. . . .

49. The Condition of the Provincial Economy, 1682

[An Act to Improve Commerce, Apr. 1682, Browne, ed., *Archives of Maryland*, VII, 321-22]

Whereas by reason of the present Low and inconsiderable rate of tobacco occasioned by the usuall great Cropps planted and made of the same, which hath been the Chiefe and principall Comoditie within this Province, the Inhabitants are Reduced to very great

necessities and want if without some sudden remidy will soone Involve them in a most deplorable and Calamitous Condition. And whereas the planting and sowing of graine and Raising Provision and Exportation thereof out of this Province will in some measure Redress this sore and grievous Evill by encouragement of Navigation and bringing in some supply to the People, which duering the present failure of the price of tobacco Cannot be had or expected, Bee it Enacted by the Right Honorable the Lord Proprietary by and with the Advice and Consent of the Upper and Lower houses of this present Generall Assembly and the Authority of the same, that from and after the end of this present Session of Assembly Indian Corne, Wheate, Oates, Barley, Rye, Peas, Porke, Beefe, Baccon be deemed, Reputed, accepted and taken for Lawfull and Currant payment and payments of money to Tobacco Debt or Debts, whatsoever from or to any person or persons whatsoever, Debtor or Creditor Inhabiting or tradeing into this Province his Lordshipps Rents and Publique Leavys onely excepted, att such Rates and Prises and in such manner as hereafter in this present act is mentioned and Contained (that is to say) Indian Corne, shelled shall be rated at Eighteen pence mony Sterling, or Eighteen pounds of tobacco the Bushell, Wheate at foure shillings or forty Eight pounds of tobacco per bushell. . . .

It shall and may be Lawfull to and for all manner of persons whatsoever, Inhabitants or traders into this Province to buy, export, or Carry away any quantity or quantitys of Corne, Porcke, Beefe, or Baccon as aforesaid into any Dominion or Country out of this Province without any manner of Restraint, Prohibition, or any other imposition other then is already by the Laws of this Province imposed and allowed of any Law, useage, or Ordinance to the Contrary in any wise notwithstanding. Provided and be it enacted by the authority aforesaid that this act nor any thing therein Conteyned shall not be Construed, deemed, or taken to have any respect looking back or relation to any tobacco or money debt or debts made or Contracted before the end of this present session of Assembly. . . . Provided and be it enacted by the authority aforesaid that if any debt or debts shall or may be payable or due from or to any person or persons, Debtor or Creditor liveing or tradeing into this Province under thirty three shillings and four pence or foure hundred pounds of tobacco, that then and in such Case it shall be tendered and paid in any one particular Comoditie or kinde of Corne and Provision that is made Currant and rated as aforesaid and not in divers the said particular kinde or Comoditie to be at the Ellection of the payer or debtor, this act to endure for three yeares or to the end of the next sessions of Assembly, which shall first happen.

50. The Abolition of the Headright System, 1683

[Lord Baltimore's Certificate of the Manner of Selling Out Land, 1683, Browne, ed., *Archives of Maryland*, V, 390-91]

Whereas formerly by my Fathers Conditions of Plantations there was fifty acres of Land allowed for every Servant or other person transported into his Provinces here to reside and dwell, of which the transporter was to make Oath as also that for such persons so by him transported hither he never had the benefit of the Conditions of Plantations which were usually termed Rights to Land in Maryland; and whereas those Rights of late years have been most of them brought up of the Merchants and Commanders, transporters of Servants into this Province by the Collectors . . . and the Deputy Surveyors of this Province who often disposed of the same to the poor inhabitants at excessive Rates, and by the dishonesty of some dealers many denies such Rights have been twice sworne to and sold to the great abuse of the said conditions of Plantation for the ease therefore of the said Inhabitants; as also to prevent the like abuses for the future I thought good to alter My Fathers Conditions of Plantation and instead of a Right due upon the transportation of a servant, for which the poor Planter often payd to the Deputy Surveyors and the several Collectors four hundred weight of tobacco and some times more, I declared I would accept of one hundred weight of tobacco for every fifty acres hereafter should be taken up with which the Inhabitants, not only the small ones, but also the great ones, are much better satisfyed; and whereas on the sea board side on the back of Somerset and Dorchester Counties and also at the Whore Kills there was many years ago but half Rent sett upon such Lands as should be taken up there, so there is but fifty weight of tobacco for every fifty acres that shall be taken up in those parts. This it seems is taken in ill part by Mr Penn, and for this he accuseth mee of breach of faith, a violater of the amicable treaty. . . . I have been ill used by my Neighbor (I conceive), having not by any action of mine deserved to be termed a faithless person and one not fit to bee treated with.

51. Lord Baltimore's Difficulty Over the Royal Customs

A. Nehemiah Blakiston's Letter to the Customs Commissioners, April 20, 1685

[Browne, ed., *Archives of Maryland*, XVII, 451-54]

The most horrid Murder of his Majesties Collector here, hath been and is daily seconded, with very apparent tokens of approvement both from Talbott the bloody malefactor and all his adherents, who are busie in extenuateing his crime, and have conspired and procured his Escape from prison in Virginia, and from thence transported him into Maryland, where he remaines publickly knowne at his owne house; There's little hopes of his being brought to Justice, that he may receive condign punishment[,] there being a litterall Intercourse and correspondence betweene him and some principall Magistrates of this Province, and noe effectuall course taken for his apprehension, which I humbly conceive may be a strong argument, and signall token to your Honors of the ill and wicked carriage of things here, ever since Mr Rousbys murder; I have been continually discountenanced and obstructed in my proceedings in his Majesties Service by the chiefe persons left and Deputed for the Government of this Province; they have conteained and disowned my Commission, to me and burnt my Certificates to Masters of Shipps, and have diverted and disswaded Masters of Shipps from applying themselves any waies to me, and soe have Entred cleared and dispatched Shipps without my notice or privity, By which meanes I am certain severall Transgressors have escaped, and many frauds past undetected. My Lord Baltemores Councill have also assumed a power to themselves to Depute another to be Collector in Severall Rivers; to leavy and receive all his Majesties rates duties and Impositions . . . , and for my disowneing and not complyeing with those appointed . . . Collectors and for my dissenting from their proceedings, I have been served with warrants to appeare before some of them, and then threatned me with bringing me to the Provinciall

Court, and with infliction of severall punishments banishment, and utter ruine of me and my family[.] One of them especially[,]by name Coll. William Digges[,] Domineeres and tells me I shall not maintaine my Commission here, unless by great gunns. . . . But notwithstanding all threatnings and difficulties I shall proceed to the best of my knowledge and endeavours to execute the Dutyes of my place and Commission. . . . I hope your Honors will approve me and make it knowne, that his Majesties Officer shall be owned and supported in that legall and indubitable authority derived from your Honors against all opposers and adversaries of his Majesties Soveraignty. . . . I am confident his Majestie is prejudiced severall thousand pounds by the obstruction and confusion that's caused in his Majesties affaires and concernes here. . . . there was some prohibited goods putt on shoare neere St. Maries from on board of a shipp that fled from me out of Pottuxent River. The said goods with all speed were seized by the said Major Sewall and Coll. Darnall, who appointed a tryall for the same, In which Business they might have had witnesses enough, besides there was the Depositions of some persons, who are still resident in the Province, whose proofe could have effected the condemnation of the said goods, notwithstanding all this which they well knew, were cleared and acquitted, and those materiall witnesses never sommoned in the business.

B. Lord Baltimore's Rejoinder, April 20, 1685

[Browne, ed., *Archives of Maryland*, XVII, 455-57]

It plainely appeareth by a Letter from the Governor of Virginia to the Deputies of Maryland, that the escape made by George Talbott out of prison was occasioned by the corruption of the guard, and not procured by any Persons of Maryland, as is falsely suggested in the Letter of the said Blackiston. And that as soone as the Governor of Virginia had given notice to the Deputies of Maryland of the said Talbotts escape, especiall care was taken immediately by them for his apprehension. . . .

His Lordship is very confident, Mr Blackiston has noe just cause to complain of his being discountenanced in the execution of his place, for that he very well knowes his Officers dare not presume to offer any contempt, nor shew the least disrespect either to his person or commission[.] Nor would they presume to disswade Masters of vessells from presenting themselves and their certificates to his Majesties officers, His Lordship haveing long since ordered that they should apply themselves to the Kings Collector as well as to his owne, and such was the practice whilest Mr Christopher Rousby was liveing, and the truth of this may be easily knowne, from severall Masters of ships, and others now in Towne[.] After Mr Christopher Rousby was soe unfortunately killed by George Talbott, the Deputies of Maryland did presume to appoint Coll. William Digges, and Major Nicholas Sewall, (both of them persons of good repute and Estates) to Officiate as Collector of his Majesties Dues, untill another person could be appointed by the Commissioners of his Majesties Customs. . . .

Tis not possible for any person that understands the trade of Maryland to beleive his Majestie should be prejudiced Severall thousand pounds, if his Lordships Officers should be as malicious and as wicked as the said Blackiston doth endeavour by his Letter to represent them, For whilest Mr Christopher Rousby lived, who understood the Office well, and knew as much as any person how to make the most of it, there never was much above one hundred pounds in one yeare received by him, for soe he often declared to his Lordship. . . .

But Mr Blakiston takes care to signifie that he doubts he shall receive little Tobacco this yeare, and gives this as a reason that his Lordships Officers threaten the Masters of vessells that in case they pay not the penny per pound duty to them, they shall be sued and their vessells seized[.] And yett notwithstanding this Complaint his Lordship is ready to make it appeare, that the said Blackiston had received severall thousand pounds of Tobacco, even afore he had writt that Letter and the same had paid away to his Creditors who never had any hopes of being satisfied by him untill he had obteined his Majesties Commission[.] This will be proved if required[.] Soe that Mr Blakiston had noeother way, this yeare to make up his accompts with the Commissioners of his Majesties customs but by pretending greate obstructions from his Lordships Officers.

What Mr Blakiston has mentioned concerning Major Sewall is as untrue as the rest of his Letter, for when the said Sewall had given him notice of Severall Irish Vessells he intended to seize, the said Blakiston neglected to assist him in it, and soe the said Sewall was forced to proceed without him. . . . his Lordship does not doubt but it will in the end appeare some prejudice and ill will the said Blakiston beares toward his officers, for their haveing detected some late abuses which the said Blakiston has been guilty off in his Office.

Incitements on the Eve of Rebellion

52. The Assembly Protests a Proposal About Bulk Tobacco, November 28, 1688

[Browne, ed., *Archives of Maryland*, XIII, 198-99]

Having received from your honours in the Upper house of Assembly a Letter which was from the Lords of his Majesties most honourable privy Council to the . . . Lord Proprietary of this Province . . . whereby his Majestys Royal pleasure is Signified, That his said Lordship in Conjunction with the Governor and Councill of his Majestys Colony and Dominion of Virginia take care a Law be passed in the Respective Assemblies of Virginia and Maryland against the Exportation of Bulk Tobacco from these Plantations Together with a Message from your honours thereunto relating

This house in Answer to the same with all Loyalty to the Kings most Excellent Majesty, Duty to his Lordship, the Lord Proprietary, . . . Do say that the Prohibition of the Exporation of Bulk Tobacco would in the first place prove very Prejudiciall to his Majestys Interest and his Royall Revenue and Income if that (most part if not all) the Bulk Tobacco that is Exported out of Virginia and Maryland for the Kingdom of England is there sold and Consequently pays the full Duty of five pence a pound to his Majesty. Whereas otherwise, if in Cask, a great part of the said Tobacco is usually Exported into Holland and Elsewhere and pays but one half penny per pound Custom; That the Tobacco of that Quality which is more fitt for Bulk and altogether unfitt for Cask to be therein Exported again out of England would by that Meanes be Lessened in that a great if not most part of the same would be left behind in this Countrey and his Majesty by that means prevented of having any Duty att all for the Same.

2d To Prohibit the Exportation of Bulk Tobacco is highly Disadvantagious and Prejudiciall to his Lordship the Lord Proprietary of this Province for that since the said prohibition will Occasion a farr lesser Quantity of Tobacco to be Exported as aforesaid, his Lordship will by that means be a great looser not only in the Revenue of two Shillings per hogshead due by Act of Assembly but also in the Imposition of 14d per Ton. . . .

3dly To Prohibit the Exportation of Bulk Tobacco is Injurious and Ruinous to his Majesties Subjects in this Province, in Virginia and in his Majesties more Immediate Dominions at home; In this Province it would hinder and Deprive the good People of the Sale of all their Tobacco Except such as is Extraordinary bright and Dry Tobacco fitt for the London Merchants who buy it with intent to Transport the Same for Holland, and break off the Trade of those Small Ships that come from the West and North Country who bring in great Quantitys of Severall Serviceable Goods and Supply this Province therewith. And not only so but with those Goods at better prices Purchase their Dark Tobacco which is that, that's Generally Bulkt, And is such that the Londoners will not buy nor carry out, And so all that Tobacco which is not very bright and dry of which the greatest part Consist would lye and rott upon the Owners hands and they thereby perish for want of such of those Goods these small West and North Country Ships bring.

And it would be prejudiciall to his Majesties Subjects of those West and North parts of England by breaking off their Trade to those places whereby their Ships and Men are Employed, their Commoditys Vended and themselves Supplyed plentifully with Tobaccos all which would certainly follow such a Prohibition.

The Premisses being had into due Consideration of this house it is . . . Resolved in this house that such a Prohibition would tend very much to the prejudice of his Majesty and his Lordship and Injurious to the good People of this Province who they Represent for the reasons aforesaid and therefore this house cannot proceed to drawing the same.

53. William Joseph's Address to the Assembly, November 14, 1688

[Browne, ed., *Archives of Maryland*, XIII, 148-53]

There is no power but of God and the Power by which we are Assembled here is undoubtedly Derived from God, to the King, and from the King to his Excellency the Lord Proprietary and from his said Lordship to Us . . . so the End and duty of, and for which this Assembly is now Called and met is that from these four heads. . . .

I Commend to your Care the Utter Suppressing and Abolishing of the several hainous and habitual Crimes now most in Mode and use amongst the People as Drunkeness, Adultry, Swearing, Sabboth breaking, etc.

Drunkeness, Gentlemen, that beastly Sin . . . is but too Common among the People of this Province to the utter Ruin not only of their souls . . . But also of them, their Children and families. . . .

Kings, Gentlemen, are the Lords Anointed and are by God appointed over us to Rule and (next under God) the King we are bound to fear and honour. . . . And the Kings Commands

We are by the Laws of God bound to keep, for that it is said keep the Kings Commandment and that in regard of the Oath of God, for whoso keepeth the Commandment of the king shall feel no evill thing. The King (Gentlemen) by his Order in Council bearing Date the fourth Day of November 1687 hath required of Us that We with Virginia pass an Act prohibiting Bulk Tobacco to be Exported out of this Province etc. . . . Some perhaps will presume to question the Advantage or Disadvantage that may arise by passing of such an Act which is indeed unbecoming Subjects to call in Question the proceedings of the King. . . . But such is the Leven of Some, as always to treate with dislike the best of things even proceeding from the best of Kings, and best of Governments, and that for no other reason but because it Came from the King. . . .

There is one thing yet remains upon which I will (before I conclude this Our Second part of Duty) move the Gentlemen of this honourable Assembly, which is that an Anniversary Act may Unanimously pass of General Thanksgiving to Almighty God for the Infinite Blessing which God of his Goodness has been pleased to bestow on their Sacred Majesties, their Subjects and Dominions, in the Birth of so Noble and glorious a Prince, to be held and kept holy throughout this Province on every Tenth Day of June during the whole Life of the Prince. . . .

Gentlemen, I hope there are not any (in this present Generall Assembly) so Wicked as (by Machiavilian Principles)

shall go about to divide the Interests of my Lord and his People which indeed are not two Interests but one. For that whatsoever shall be for the Good and welfare of his People is also the undoubted Good and Welfare of my Lord whose Chief care and Study is to Encrease wealth and Ease to the Inhabitants of Maryland. Wherefore who ever shall endeavour to Divide the hearts of the People from my Lord, or my Lord from the People, let him (by this Assembly) be Declared a Traitor to Our God, King, Lord and People. . . .

If his Lordships Interests in America were to be disposed of . . . there's none would give (Considering the Charge of Government) the tenth part of what they cost, wherefore as my Lord of his part never did (as he never will) Burthen the People whereby to be Reimbursed the said Charge, so will it be an Act of the highest Ingratitude in the People if of their part they do not Justly and freely pay what is or of right ought to be my Lord's dues. . . .

Gentlemen, I have one thing more to offer which is: First, by way of Advice, that before you Begin to make Laws, you do not begin to breake Laws and—

Secondly, by way of Demand, That you and every of you (as I for example will) take the Oath of Fidelity to the Right Honourable the Lord Proprietary as the Law Directs which if any refuse to do the Government will according to that Law proceed, for if you Obey not the Laws that are made, who, think you, will obey the Laws that [you] are to make?

54. The Grievances of the Lower House, November 22, 1688

[Browne, ed., Archives of Maryland, XIII, 171-73]

Imprimis: Whereas by an Act of Assembly Entituled an Act for raising and providing a Support for his Lordship, the Lord Proprietary of this Province during his Natural Life etc., Made . . .

the 27th Day of March 1671, and by other Acts since made Confirming the same and now in force, It was thereby Provided that his said Lordship, his Receiver or Receivers Generall for the time being shall receive good sound Merchantable Tobacco for his said Lordships Rents and fines, for Alienations of Lands reserved upon the Severall and Respective Grants of Land in this Province at the rate of Two pence per pound, any thing in his said Lordships Grants to the Contrary Notwithstanding. Nevertheless his said Lordships Receivers and other Officers Appointed Contrary to the said Law have and do under Colour of their said Offices not only refuse to receive Tobacco as by the said Law is Provided, But Exact Money Sterling to the great Agreivance and oppression of the Good People of this Province of which we humbly desire Redress and Relief.

Secondly. Whereas the honourable the Secretary's of this Province do charge the People of this Province with Several fees which are not by Law due, particularly in that for Recording Proceedings, which they do take and Extort by way of Execution, the said fees being due and paid under another Denomination of which We humbly desire redress and Reliefe.

Thirdly. Whereas it is provided in the Act for Advancement of Trade that the Right honourable the Lord Proprietary should before the last day of August 1685, for the quick Dispatch of Shipps etc., Appoint in Wicocomoco, St Maries, Patuxent, and Ann Arundel for the Western side of this Province and in Talbot and Somerset Counties for the Eastern Shore, Some fit Officer or Officers for the Entring and Clearing of Ships in the said Severall and respective places, for want of which Trade has been Discouraged to the great Grievance of the Inhabitants of which they humbly desire redress and Relief.

It being likewise very prejudicial to his Lordships Interest and Income.

Fourthly. Whereas it is not only a great Agreivance to the Present Inhabitants of this Province, But also of fatall Consequence to their Posterity, That Laws made and Assented unto by his

Lordship and the People of Province should be dispenced withall by any other Authority than by which they were first made, which we humbly desire to Know if his Lordship do intend to Annull that Clause of the Act about Bringing Tobacco to Towns without an Act of Repeale.

Fifth. Whereas the Attorney General has often presumed upon his own Authority . . . to send out precepts Directed to the Severall Sheriffs, Commanding them to bring the Bodys of Severall the Inhabitants of this Province to the Provincial Courts to Answer such things as should be Objected against them, by which means severall of his Lordships Good People have been taken into the Custody of the severall Sheriffs and brought to the Provincial Court, being altogether Ignorant of what should be laid to their Charge before they Come upon their Tryall, Contrary to the fundamentall and known Laws and to the great Agreivance and Unsupportable Charge and Damage of his Lordships Good People of which We humbly desire to be relieved.

Sixthly. Whereas it is a great Agreivance to the Inhabitants of this Province that any persons not Lawfully Empowered but only pretending a Power from some of his Lordships Militia Officers in time of Peace should as often they have done press and Violently take from severall of the said Inhabitants the most part, if not all, their Store of Meat and other Provisions which should be for the Support and Relief of their Respective families the remaining part of the Year, to the great Damage and oppression of the said Good People, of which We humbly desire to be relieved.

Seventhly. Whereas the Provincial Court being Adjourned to the last Tuesday in January next, which is the Dead time of the year and the most perilous and incomodious time for the people to give their Attendance, We conceive that it is a great Agreivance of which We humbly desire Redress.

Eighthly. That it is a great Greivance to the People of this Province for the Officers of Towns [to] Exact three pence Sterling or three pounds Tobacco per hogshead for any Tobacco whatsoever which is not Actually brought to the several Towns according to the Letter of the further Additionall Act to Act for Advancement of Trade and to the Supplementary Act to the Same Which we humbly desire your honours to take into your most Serious Consideration and that of the same we may have Redress and relief.

55. An Account of the Meeting of the 1688 General Assembly, January 19, 1689

[A Letter from the Government in Maryland to Lord Baltimore, Browne, ed., *Archives of Maryland*, VIII, 62-65]

Wee herewith (to your Lordship) transmit a perticular of our proceeding in the last sessions of Assembly not onely by this our accompt thereof, but by the journall of each dayes passages which with these your Lordship will wee hope receive. In the beginning whereof your Lordship will find the heates and debates wee had with the Lower House about the oath of fidelity to your Lordship which wee insisted upon the rather and indeed cheifely for that your Lordships last expressions to the Assembly in [16]84 was that for the future your Lordship did expect that every member of Assembly should take the oath of fidelity before they should be Admitted to sit. In pursuance whereof the Government did in the Assembly of 1686 propose the said oath of fidelity to the Lower House who excused it at that time saying that had it been proposed to them, In time they would have taken it, but that then they were Entered upon other business and the like for which and other reasons the Government did not then further presse the same. But at opening this Assembly wee humbly conceived it was our duty to cause complyance to your Lordship's said demands in [16]84, and in order thereunto wee resolved to be early with them in this. And accordingly it was by the presidents speech To both houses given them in charge To which the upper house readily obeyed. But the Lower house would by noe meanes Comply. Upon which hot and high debates did arrise and the more they refused to sweare fidelity to your Lordship the more reason wee had to distrust 'em.

But all mild perswasions failing wee sent for 'em up to the upper house which they refused, saying if his Lordship were there in person they would attend and indeed they endeavoured all they could to lay asside your Lordships upper house. Upon which wee thought of a dissolution, but tried them the second time and they refused and the third time. . . . The president made a short speech wherein he told them that wee were sorry to find such early disturbances; that the occassion wee sent for them was about the oath of fidelity; That fidelity was Allegiance which by the Lawes of England might be proposed even to the house of Comons in parliament sitting; And that the refuseing of Allegiance did Imply Rebellion. . . . Upon which the Lower House was desired to returne to their house to consider of it; For till complyant in that perticular wee neither could nor would Enter upon any business. But all in vaine they still persisted, upon which wee would not in honour to your Lordships authority doe otherwise then mainteyne your Lordships right and lawes in this your Lordships Dominion. For wee were not Ignorant of the fatall Consequences hereof if denyall of fidelity to your Lordship were thus permitted. Rebellion might be the next stepp.

Whereupon wee Resolve to try all Endeavours and accordingly, it being then Saturday in the afternoone, wee sent for the Lower House. And they came. Whereafter a few things said to 'em by the president, the Assembly was prorogued till the munday following. And then the oath was Imediately required of every perticular member which after severall refusalls and debates they every man tooke, except one Thurstone, a Quaker, who desired to be dispensed with and it was granted him. And on Munday both houses met againe to whom the president made a short speech. And soe Entered upon business, which afterwards proceeded very amicably and kind even to the end of the sessions, notwithstanding their grievous paper of pretended Agreivances all which were answered to Content. . . . And then was pressed the business about bulke tobacco. Tho wee desspaire of success considering the violent repulse it met with in Virginia, yet wee Endeavoured it all wee could but to no purpose. For wee would get from 'um in that affair was their answer and reasons to the Contrary. . . .

The advantage proposed to your Lordship by payment of all your Lordship's rents and fines for alienations in money at the Inhansed value will, we are well assured, very much increase your Lordship's income to what they now are. For that your Lordship's rents which are now paid in Tobacco at 2 d. per poll is but losse to your Lordship, and the people thereby have (as it were) your Lordship's whole province for nothing. Whereas if the rents that dayly rise and Encrease might be payd in money, there's noe doubt but in a short time the same will be farr more considerable than the duty of the 2 shillings per hogshead. Besides it is proposed to Enrich and people your Lordship's provinces by bringing in of money and tradesmen of all sorts to follow their callings and inhabit the Townes, as by the proposalls to which we referr, Being for our parts, as wee are sworne to serve your Lordship, satisfied That if money be made currant as it is proposed, That it will infinitely redound to your Lordship's advantage, and in a little time even Increase the duty of 2 shillings per hogshead. For the Encouragement thereby to shipping will induce them abundantly to trade into Maryland rather than to Virginia. Besides, as money becomes plenty, people and labour will Encrease and the Export of Tobacco will follow in proportion. But the difficulty in returning of this money to your Lordship is to be Considered, for tho it doe Advance (as without all doubt it will) your Lordship's dues, yet the payment as now made is farr more Convenient to your Lordship then twice as much in Maryland if not returned to answer your Lordship occassions in England. And this wee conceave may be effected as well then as now. For many, especially the Londoners, will as freely . . . pay their money there as here and with more ease then by procuring of pieces of 8, shipping them, Risque, etc. And for the rest of the Traders, they are for the most part but straglers whose money is more safe then their bills, and for soe much of your Lordship's dues as should be rents here, there's noe doubt but the same may be returned by bills of Exchange more securely than at present. For if money be made currant, the planter Adventurer will have occassion for his money here and will give bills on London, being payd the difference twixt money there and here. For our part we are of opinion that your Lordship's dues will be returned then as well as now, the consideration whereof is humbly submitted to your Lordship. But take as it will with your Lordship, the Lower house would by noe meanes hearing of paying their rents in money, whereupon the whole matter was for the present layd aside, And the Assembly prorogued to the second Tuesday in Aprill next.

What mind they will be of then wee know not. . . .

Your Lordship will herewith also receive two private addresses to which we thought fit to put a stop. Wee doe not meane to Addressing or hindering any from soe doeing, but because the same were obteyned at the request of other separate and private interests and designed to have been presented to the King by others not your Lordship's hands, perhaps intended to your Lordship's prejudices. Wherefore wee thought fit to order soe as that noe addresse should goe hence but thro your Lordship's hands and accordingly both said Addresses are herewith Enclosed to your Lordship wherein [you] may do as . . . shall seeme meete.

Herewith may it please your Lordship wee send the Coppy of a proclamation issued as your Lordship will find by which wee have thought fit to call in all the publick Armes whereby to fix and make them fit for service, And upon occassion to distribute the same into such hands as shall faithfully serve the King, your Lordship, and the Country. . . .

And for the Government in Generall . . . all things are peaceable and quiet. All that disturbes us is the noise of those troubles with you in England which doth not altogether dismay us.

56. The Indian-Catholic Conspiracy Rumor

A. A Letter from Lord Baltimore's Deputies to the Government of Virginia, March 26, 1689

[Browne, ed., *Archives of Maryland*, VIII, 83-84]

Wee could not give your honour a more satisfactory answer then by sending herewith the true Coppy of all passages and proceedings that have passed here upon the late noisy Indian afair. In the first place your honour will find the Deposition of one John Atkey, who sweares that he did hear Fyffe say, that he did heare Sharpe say, that he did heare the Easterne shoare Indians when they were drunke say, that they were hired by Coll Darnall to fight against the English. But being asked when they were sober, they would not say any such thing, unto which is annexed the Deposition of Fyffe as also of what Coll Jowles says he will sweare. And next unto these your honour will find the coppy of a paper brought into this province from Virginia bearing date the 15th instant, which is earlier by a day than the first of the information received from your Honour as aforesaid, many Coppies whereof by the Industry of some where imediately dispersed among the people of this province, which being seconded with Rumours of all shapes and Colours soe alarmed the people of Charles and Calvert Counties that many of them tooke Armes. Whereupon Coll Jowles, Major Beale, and others dispatch't expresses to the Council, giving us an Account of the said disturbances, adding that 10,000 Seneca Indians were said to be inforting at the head of patuxen River. . . . Whereupon it was ordered by the Council Imediately to send a sufficient supply of Armes and Amunition to the said Coll Jowles with assurance of further supplyes from time to time as occasion should require. As by the enclosed Coppys of our Letters to the said Coll Jowles and Major Beale it doth and may appeare, sayd Armes and Amunition being sent under the Conduct and care of his honour Coll Digges. And by the Council it was also ordered that Coll Darnall should goe himself in person to the said Coll Jowles and rest of the people in Armes to justify himself, which he accordingly did with that success that upon his arrivall at Colonel Jowles', where were gathered about a hundred men in Armes exercising to whome he gave such satisfacion that they all parted satisfied, every man to his owne home, for that it plainly appeareth they were abused, there being no such thing as any Indians at the head of the River, nor anywhere else, but that all was quiet and well. But such was the buisie spirits of some ill designeing men that when there was noe such thing as any Indians landed at the mouth of the Patuxen River, then it was reported that 9,000 were landed at the mouth of Patuxen River and 900 more landed at Choptico, who it was said had killed severall of the Inhab-

itants, nameing perticularly such and such, all which appearing to be sham by the people who were sayd to be killed appearing in person to the people then in Armes; as also that of the 9,000 and 900 Indians appearing to be false by the assurance of all the neighbourhood hath given that generall satisfaction to the people that blesse God wee are all well and in perfect peace and quiet, there being noe other feares now Remaining But the Comeing over of some Virginians occasion new Disturbances which wee humbly desire may be speedily prevented by the care of the honourable the Government there. And as to the calling home of the Indians wee shall take such Imediate Cource therein as wee doubt not will be satisfactory.

B. A REMONSTRANCE FROM MEMBERS OF THE PROPRIETARY *and* ANTI-PROPRIETARY FACTIONS, MARCH 27, 1689

[Browne, ed., *Archives of Maryland*, VIII, 86-87]

Whereas there has been lately many and great disturbances in this Province, particularly in Calvert and Charles County where the people in several Places of these Counties had gathered themselves together in great parties to defend themselves, as they were persuaded, against a groundless and imaginary plott and designe contrived against them as was rumoured and suspected by the Roman Catholicks inviting the Indians to joyne with them in that detestable and wicked Conspiracy. Wee thought fitt for the better satisfaction of the good people of this Province and that the general peace and quiet thereof may be once again fully and completely setled, to publish and declare under our hand that wee have made an Exact scrutiny and Examination into all circumstances of this pretended design, and have found it to be nothing but a slevelesse fear and imagination fomented by the Artifice of some ill minded persons who are studious and ready to take all

occasions of raising a disturbance for their own private and malitious interest and that by all probable conjectures, which shall be also more dilligently searched into, wee doe find the original of all these mischiefs to arise from Stafford County in Virginia, who have likewise stirred up some more, such like ill minded persons in our Government to continue the same concoctions amongst us and the rather wee are so persuaded and have just cause to believe because that notwithstanding the many and daily rumours of Indians come downe among us and inforted at the head of patu[x]en, and also of another great body of them landed at Mattapany, . . . another party at Cove poynt on the Clifte, another at Choptico and severall more at several other places of this western side of this Province. Wee doe yet find all these reports are notorious, false, and evil. Wee can in noe place trace so much as the footing of any Indians nor heare any truth or certainty of any designes they have to disturb or molest the good people or peace of this Country. Wherefore wee whose Names are here subscribed have thought convenient to signifie the premisses to the Magistrates, officers, and other the good people of this Country as having had the full Examination of the whole matter with the honourable the Deputy Governour and from whom also wee have had as much satisfaction as can be desired of their aversnesse to any such unworthy treacherous practise that soe as many others as shall think fit may signify the same remonstrance for the ample satisfaction of other parts of this Province.

CHAPTER EIGHT

THE PATTERN OF REBELLION

IN January 1689 Maryland received James II's warning of an "Invasion threatened by the Dutch," and Lord Baltimore's Council called in all public arms for repair. In the same month, the Convention Parliament met in London to invite William and Mary to accept the Crown vacated by James. In February, the Privy Council directed Lord Baltimore to draft a proclamation of William and Mary's accession. Although the Proprietor promptly dispatched a proclamation to his Council, the messenger died at Plymouth on the eve of his departure and the crucial documents never reached America. When unofficial word reached Maryland of William and Mary's success, William Joseph's government gave no indication of acknowledging the Protestant monarchs. Paralyzed by the failure to receive orders from the Proprietor, and not wishing nor daring to take the responsibility of upholding new rulers without such instructions, the Catholic-dominated Council procrastinated. While discontent and uncertainty grew, the province was inflamed in March by the Indian-Catholic conspiracy rumor.

When April came, William Joseph and the Council canceled the scheduled meeting of the Assembly, postponing it until October. Although a superficial quiet prevailed in April and May, John Coode and other discontented leaders took advantage of the lull, organizing "An Association in arms for the defence of the Protestant religion, and for asserting the right of King William and Queen Mary to the Province of Maryland and all the English dominions." By June their Majesties had been proclaimed along the Atlantic seaboard, but not in Maryland; there the Protestants, according to a Virginia observer, became "rageingly earnest for the Proclaiming their present Majestys and will not believe but orders have come to that government . . . for Proclaiming their Majestys and that the Government have concealed the commands and are sometimes very positive they will proclaime their Majestys without the order of the Government, which if so will unhinge the whole constitution of that Government and dissolve the whole frame of it." Political insecurity had caused the integration of society to become tenuous; a lawless situation, which social theorists call *anomie,* characterized the colony during the summer months.

On the night of July 16 a messenger informed Henry Darnall, one of Lord Baltimore's deputies, that "John Coode was raising men up Potowmack." The Council was summoned at once, but a messenger sent by them to ascertain the truth of the news was seized by the proleptic Associators as a spy, so that no word came for two days. Then the proprietary party learned that Coode had been joined by men from Charles County to the west. William Digges, another Calvert deputy, organized eighty men and prepared to defend the state house at St. Mary's. The insurgents arrived there on the 27th, and outnumbering Digges' group, forced him to surrender when his men refused to fight. The rebels thus came into possession of the provincial records and the capital. At this time the Protestant Association issued its Declaration, printed and distributed it in the province, and sent it to England (No. 57).

When Digges had gone to defend St. Mary's, his fellow deputies had ascended the Patuxent to gather their forces. They found the militia officers ready to join them, but the freemen were apathetic or pro-Coode. With some difficulty they rounded up several hundred men who were willing to support his Lordship's standard. (Coode by this time had some 750.) When the Council sent a proclamation of pardon to those in arms on condition they return to their homes, Coode countered with a "dyfyance." The insurrectionists then marched on August 1 to Mattapany "fort," Lord Baltimore's plantation eight miles from St. Mary's. The Council and many of their families had gathered there along with William Joseph, who lay sick. It was probably fortified with no more than a log stockade, and the insurgents arrived with two large guns borrowed from a merchantman. Coode's trumpeter summoned the defenders to surrender. Their position being hopeless, they wisely averted bloodshed and capitulated.

The rebels called a convention for August 22, allowing each county four delegates. Coode then directed that all officials except Roman Catholics and those who had declared against the new monarchs should retain their positions. On the appointed election day, many people argued against choosing delegates, and in some counties the number of electors was slim indeed. But all the counties except one were represented at the gathering at St. Mary's City which lasted a fortnight. After a chairman was chosen, Coode and his cohorts relinquished to the assembly "that supreme power which they usurped att first." A committee of secrecy was selected to investigate the Indian-Catholic conspiracy, and the convention circulated a letter to the other colonies, informing them the "conspiracy" had been exposed! On September 4, the convention passed an interim constitution providing for an *ad hoc* steering committee and financial arrangements. Then the assembly adjourned, dispersed, and awaited word from England (No. 58).

But news traveled slowly then and many months would pass before they heard anything definite. The impatient insurgents proclaimed William and Mary King and Queen on September 10 with a great demonstration of joy. Through the autumn of 1689 proponents and opponents of the revolution circulated memorials and counter-memorials for signature among the counties, intending to send these to England. Their fustian substance is uninteresting, but an examination of the signatories reveals that a great many supporters of the Proprietor were petty officeholders appointed by his deputies. Each faction, of course, wrote its own accounts of what had happened and why, and the output of these screeds—justifications and vilifications—amounted to a considerable provincial literature in the months following the revolution (Nos. 57, 58, 59, 61).

The assembly undoubtedly realized that the rebellion had been a closely confined phenomenon, geographically centered in St. Mary's and its neighboring counties, Calvert and Charles. To make a success of their movement the Protestant Associators would have to extend their control to the remoter counties and break the pockets of persons, often Protestant, loyal to his Lordship. The strategy frequently followed was to incarcerate a few leaders of the opposition in each county, hoping the anti-Association inhabitants would acquiesce when deprived of their politically articulate chiefs (No. 59).

Some of the leaders of the proprietary party fled to Virginia where they remained several months. This led to an unsuccessful attempt by Coode to persuade the acting governor of Virginia to extradite the fugitives. When several returned secretly in December 1689, a group of Associators led by customs collector John Payne attempted to seize them. But Payne was killed and the quondam councilors fled again to Virginia. This time Coode's extradition efforts were partially successful, and the trial of the culprits helped keep alive the animosities of the revolution during the months which followed.

Coode's relations with his co-revolutionaries in New York were warmer than those with his neighbors south of the Potomac. In November 1689, he wrote Jacob Leisler, sending a copy of the Association's Declaration (No. 60). Then, late in January 1690, someone in Maryland, perhaps the sheriff of Calvert County, sent Leisler, probably at his request, the fullest account we have of the causes and progress of the revolution in Maryland (No. 61). The Coode-Leisler correspondence began in September 1689 and lasted perhaps eight months.

During these months Lord Baltimore in London learned of his loss and attempted to prod the otherwise occupied Crown officials into hearing his cause. His generous (however expedient) offer of amnesty for the rebels was ignored by the Lords of Trade. Meanwhile, in Maryland, his agent, James Heath, demanded of the Protestant Association that they deliver to him all the bills and bonds remaining in the land office which belonged to his Lordship, as well as other property and funds due the Calverts. After sixteen days Heath received from the committee an answer he considered unsatisfactory, and, his formal protest written, he faded from view (No. 62).

In the spring of 1690 another convention met to establish a new provisional government whereby Coode in conjunction with a committee of 20—two from each county—would rule in the intervals between meetings of the convention. The provisional government met in July to draft charges against Lord Baltimore to be carried to London by Coode and Cheseldyne. They embarked in August, leaving Nehemiah Blakiston in charge. Perhaps Coode felt secure in absenting himself from the colony because he had learned of Chief Justice Holt's recommendation that the Crown legitimize the work of the Protestant Association.

Their own recent usurpation of established authority as well as their Protestant faith inclined the new monarchs to accept the recommendation to recognize the colonial coup and make Maryland a royal province. This was in marked contrast to the situation in 1659 and 1676 when rebellions in Maryland failed because Lord Baltimore had the support of the Crown. Hence the hearings late in 1690 between the agents of the convention and Charles Calvert ended inconclusively. While recriminations were being exchanged, the attorney general initiated proceedings to deprive the Proprietor of his charter. Charles Calvert lost only his political authority in Maryland, however, retaining his financial privileges as provincial landlord. These changes and many others in the constitution of Maryland were embodied in the instructions of the first royal governor of Maryland, Lionel Copley (No. 63).

The Insurrection Accomplished

57. The Declaration of the Protestant Association, July 25, 1689

[Browne, ed., *Archives of Maryland*, VIII, 101-7]

Although the nature and state of Affairs relating to the government of this Province is so well and notoriously known to all persons any way concerned in the same, as to the people Inhabitants here, who are more imediately interested, as might excuse any declaration or apologie for this present inevitable appearance; Yet forasmuch as (by the plotte, contrivances, insinuations, remonstrances, and subscriptions carryed on, suggested, extorted, and obtained, by the Lord Baltemore, his Deputys, Representatives, and officers here) the injustice and tyranny under which we groan, is palliated and most if not all the particulars of our grievances shrowded from the eyes of observation and the hand of redress, Wee thought fitt for general satisfaction, and particularly to undeceive those that may have a sinister account of our proceedings to publish this Declaration of the reasons and motives inducing us thereunto. His Lordships right and title to the Government is by virtue of a Charter to his father Cecilius from King Charles the first. . . . how his present Lordship has managed the power and authority given and granted in the same wee could mourn and lament onely in silence, would our duty to God, our allegiance to his Vicegerent, and the care and welfare of ourselves and posterity permit us.

In the first place in the said Charter is a reservation of the fayth and allegiance due to the Crown of England (the Province and Inhabitants being imediately subject thereunto). But how little that is manifested is too obvious, to all unbyasted persons that ever had anything to do here. The very name and owning of that Sovereign power is some times crime enough to incurr the frownes of our superiors and to render our persons obnoxious and suspected to be ill-affected to the government. The ill usage of and affronts to the Kings Officers belonging to the customes here, were a sufficient argument of this. Wee need but instance the busines of Mr Badcock and Mr Rousby, of whom the former was terribly detained by his Lordshipp from going home to make his just complaints in England upon which he was soon taken sick, and t'was more then probably conjectur'd that the conceit of his confinement was the chief cause of his death which soon after happened. The latter was barbarously murthered upon the execution of his office by one that was an Irish papist and our Cheif Governor.

Allegiance here by those persons under whom wee suffer is little talked of, other then what they would have done and sworn to, to his Lordship the Lord Proprietary, for it was very lately owned by the President himselfe, openly enough in the Upper House of Assembly, that fidelity to his Lordshipp was allegiance and that the denying of the One was the same thing with the refusall or denyall of the other. In that very Oath of Fidelity, that was then imposed under the penalty of banishment there is not so much as the least word or intimation of any duty, fayth or allegiance to be reserved to our Sovereign Lord the King of England.

How the jus regale is improved here, and made the prorogative of his Lordshipp, is so sensibly felt by us all in that absolute authority exercised over us, and by the greatest part of the Inhabitants in the service of their persons, forfeiture and loss of their goods, chatteles, free-holdes and inheritances.

In the next place Churches and Chappels, which by the said Charter should be built and consecrated according to the Ecclesiastical lawes of the Kingdom of England, to our greate regrett and discouragement of our religion, are erected and converted to the use of popish Idolatry and superstition. Jesuits and seminarie preists are the only incumbents; (for which there is a supply provided by sending our popish youth to be educated at St Omers) as also the Chief Advisers and Councellors in affaires of Government, and the richest and most fertile land sett apart for their use and maintenance, while other lands that are piously intended, and given for the maintenance of the Protestant Ministry, become escheats, and are taken as forfeit, the ministers themselves discouraged, and noe care taken for their subsistance.

The power to enact Laws is another branch of his Lordshipp's authority, but how well that has been executed . . . is too notorious. His present Lordshipp, upon the death of his father . . . sent out writts for four (as was [e]ver the usage) for each County to serve as Representatives of the people, but when elected there were two of each respective four pickt out and sumoned to that convention, whereby many Laws were made, and the greatest leavy yet known layd upon the Inhabitants. The next Session the house was filled up, with the remaining two that was left out of the former in which there were many and the best of our Laws enacted to the great benefit and satisfaction of the people. But his Lordship soon after dissolved and declared the best of these Laws, such as he thought fit, null and voyd by Proclamation: Notwithstanding they were assented to in his Lordshipps name, by the Governor in his absence,

and he himselfe some time personally acted and governed by the same; soe that the question in our Courts of Judicature, in any point that relates to many of our Laws, is not so much the relation it has to the said Laws, but whether the Laws themselves be agreable to the pleasure and approbation of his Lordshipp. Whereby our liberty and property is become uncertain and under the arbitrary disposition of the Judge and Commissioners of our Courts of Justice.

The said Assembly being some time after dissolved by proclamation, another was elected and mett consisting only of two members for each County, directly opposite to an Act of Assembly for four . . . but the Execution of that Act was soon after by Proclamation from his Lordshipp out of England suspended the last year, and all officers Military and Civil severely prohibited executing and inflicting the penaltys of the same. Notwithstanding which suspension being in effect a dissolution and abrogateing of the whole Act, the income of three pence per hoggshead to the government (by the said Act payable for every hogshead of tobacco exported) is carefully exacted and collected. How fatall and of what pernicious consequence that unlimited and arbitary pretended authority may be to the Inhabitants, is too apparent, but by considering that by the same reason all the use of the laws whereby our liberties and properties subsiste are subject to the same arbitary disposition, and if timely remedy be not had must stand or fall according to his Lordshipps good will and pleasure.

Nor is this nullyfyeing and suspending power the only grievance that doth perplex and burthen us in relation to Laws, but these laws that are of a certain and unquestioned acceptation are executed and countenanced, as they are more or less agreable to the good liking of our Governor in particular. One very good lawe provides that orphan children should be disposed of to persons of the same religion with that of their dead parents. In direct opposition to which several children of protestants have been committed to the tutlage of papists, and brought up in the Romish Superstition. Wee could instance in a young woman that has been lately forced by order of Council from her husband, committed to the custody of a papist, and brought up in his religion.

T'is endless to enumerate the particulars of this nature, while on the contrary those laws that enhance the grandeur and income of his said Lordshipp are severely imposed and executed, especially one that is against all sense, equity, reason, and law, punishes all speeches, practices and attempts relating to his Lordship and Government that shall be thought mutinous and seditious by the Judge of the provincial Court, with either whipping, branding, boreing through the Tongue, fines, imprisonments, banishment or death, all or either of the said punishments at the discretion of the said Judges, who have given a very recent and remarkable proof of their authority in each particular punishment aforesaid, upon several [of] the good people of this Province, while the rest are in the same danger to have their words and actions lyable to the construction and punishment of the said Judges, and their lives and fortunes to the mercy of their arbitrary fancies, opinions and sentences.

To these Grievances are added Excessive Officers Fees, and that too under Execution directly against the Law made and provided to redress the same, wherein there is no probability of a legall remedy, the Officers themselves that are partys and culpable being Judges. The like Fee being imposed upon and extorted from Masters and Owners of Vessels trading into this Province, without any Law to justifie the same, and directly against the plaine words of the said Charter that say there shall be no imposition or assessment without the consent of the Freemen in the Assembly to the great obstruction of trade and prejudice of the Inhabitants.

The like excessive Fees imposed upon and extorted from the owners of Vessels that are built here or do really belong to the Inhabitants contrary to an Act of Assembly made and provided for the same, wherein moderate and reasonable Fees are ascertained for the promoting and incouragement of Shipping and navigation amongst ourselves.

The frequent pressing of men, horses, boats, provisions and other necessarys in time of peace and often to gratifie private designs and occations, to the great burthen and regrett of the Inhabitants contrary to Law and several Acts of Assembly in that case made and provided.

The seirvice and apprehending of Protestants in their houses with armed force consisting of Papists and that in time of peace, thence hurrying them away to Prisons without Warrant or cause of comittment; these kept and confined with popish guards a long time without tryall.

Not only private but publick outrages, and murthers committed and done by papists upon Protestants without redress, but rather conived at and tolerated by the cheif in authority, and indeed it were in vain to desire or expect any help or other measures from them being papists and guided by the Councills and instigation of the Jesuits, either in these or any other grievances or oppresions. And yet these are the men that are our Cheif Judges at the Comon Law in Chancery, of the Probat of Wills, and the Affairs of Administration in the Upper House of Assembly, and Cheif military Officers and Commanders of our forces, being still the same individuall persons, in all these particular qualifications and places.

These and many more even infinit pressures and Calamitys, wee have hitherto layne with patience under and submitted to, hoping that the same hand of providence that hath sustained us under them would at length in due time release us. And now at length for as much as it hath pleased Almighty God, by meanes of the great prudence and conduct of the best of Princes, our most gracious King William, to putt a check to that great inudation of Slavery and Popery, that had like to overwhelm their Majestys Protestant Subjects in all their Territorys and Dominions . . . Wee hoped and expected in our particular Stations and qualifications, a proportionable shew in soe great a blessing.

But our greatest grief and consternation, upon the first news of the great overture and happy change in England, wee found ourselves surrounded with strong and violent endeavours from our Governors here (being the Lord Baltemores Deputys and Representatives) to defeat us of the same.

Wee still find all the meanes used by these very persons and their Agents, Jesuits, Priests, and lay papists that are of malice can suggest to devise the obedience and loyalty of the inhabitants from their most sacred Majestys, to that height of impudence that solemn masses and prayers·are used . . . in their Chappells and Oratorys for the prosperous success of the popish forces in Ireland, and the French designs against England, whereby they would involve us, in the same crime of disloyalty with themselves and render us obnoxious to the insupportable displeasure of their Majesties. . . .

Wee are every day threatened with the loss of our lives, libertys and Estates, of which wee have great reason to think ourselves in eminent danger by the practises and machinations that are on foot to betray us to the French, Northern and other Indians of which some have been dealt withall, and others invited to assist in our destruction, well remembering the incursion and invade of the said Northern Indians in the year 1681, who were conducted into the heart of this Province by French Jesuits, and lay sore upon us while the Representatives of the Country, then in the Assembly were

severely prest upon by our superiours to yield them an unlimited and tyrannicall power in the Affairs of the Militia. . . .

Wee have considered that all the other branches of their Majesty's Dominions in this part of the world . . . have done their duty in proclaiming and asserting their undoubted right in these and all other their Majesties Territoryes and Countys. . . .

It will not suffer us to be silent in soe great and general a Jubilee, withall considering and looking upon ourselves, discharged, dissolved and free from all manner of duty, obligation or fidelity to the Deputy Governor or Chief Magistrate here, as such they having departed from their Allegiance (upon which alone our said duty and fidelity to them depends) and by their Complices and Agents aforesaid endeavoured the destruction of our religion, lives, libertys, and propertys all which they are bound to protect.

These are the reasons, motives and considerations which wee doe declare have induced us to take up Arms to preserve, vindicate, and assert the sovereign Dominion and right of King William and Queen Mary to this Province; to defend the Protestant Religion among us, and to protect and [s]helter the Inhabitants from all manner of violence, oppression and destruction, that is plotted and designed against them. . . .

For the more effectual Accomplishment of which, wee will take due care that a full and free Assembly be called and conven'd with all possible expedition by whom we may likewise have our condition, circumstances, and our most dutyfull addresses represented and tendered to their Majesties. . . .

Wee will take care, and doe promise that no person now in armes with us, or that shall come to assist us shall committ any outrage or doe any violence to any person whatsoever that shall be found peaceable and quiet and not oppose us in our said just and necessary designes, and that there shall be a just and due satisfaction made for provisions and other necessarys had and received from the Inhabitants and the souldiers punctually and duely payed in such wayes and methodes as have been formerly accustomed or by Law ought to bee.

And wee doe lastly invite and require all manner of persons whatsoever residing or Inhabiting in this Province, as they tender their Allegiance, the Protestant Religion, their Lives, fortunes and Families, to ayd and assist us in this our undertaking.

58. A Good Time for People in Debt, December 31, 1689

[Peter Sayer to Lord Baltimore, Dec. 31, 1689, Browne, ed., *Archives of Maryland*, VIII, 158-62]

Since my last to your Lordship . . . there has not bin a more tragick comedy of rebellion acted, since the royall bounty of King James and King Charles . . . bestowed upon your Ancestors the Charter of this Province . . . ; to lay itt downe in all its acts, and scenes would be too tedious, there being some of the actors (whom God send safely to arrive) will give your Lordship an orall relation of all. I shall onely trouble your Lordship with some few particulars, which they (being forc'd to abscond) may not have notice of. . . .

Last Saturday Jack Llewellin came up to my house, and gives me this brief account of the Assembly. The first thing they did (after they voted themselves a full house, tho' there were ten of the forty two absent, vizt, Anarundell, Somersett, and two of Cecill, but Somersett came over the last day, and excused their delay, saying, they heard all things were done in your Lordship's name, but indeed they intended to own no other power but their Majesties, which excuse was readyly accepted of. . . . They fixed upon the State house Doore a prohibition that no Papist should come into the citty dureing the Assembly. . . . I must tell your Lordship that the Committee of Secrecy appointed for the discovery of Colonel Darnall's and Major Sewall's dealing with the Northern Indians is kept on foot still; It's composed of Blacstone, Jowles, Gilbert Clark, and one or two more I forgott: Upon their report to the House . . . a vote past that letters should be sent to each neighbouring Government, as farr as new England, that the house had found by severall substantiall evidences that your Lordship's deputies have been tampering with the Northern Indians to come in and cut off the Protestants, and therefore desires all of 'em to hold a strict correspondency with this Government and to take up all persons of this Colony that shall seem any way suspicious. . . . The grand Ordinance is not yett come up, which must give the measures to all their actions both civill and millitary. Your Lordship will see in itt all the Officers, and by that know that those that have gott Estates under your Lordship, are as ready to serve Jack Coade as your Lordship, butt there are some entered that I'me sure will never comply with itt. People in debt think itt the bravest time that ever was, no Courts open, nor no law proceedings, which they pray may continue, as long as they live. I asked why Coade and his Councill divested themselves of that supream power which they usurped att first; and t'was tould me that Coade proposed to the House to have a standing Committee to receive all appeals, and be as the Grand Councill of the Countrey; but the house would be all alike in power; that the Officers civill and millitary of each respective County should give definitive sentences in all matters whatsoever, till further Orders out of England, so that Coade and his adherents now have no more power out of their County than we cashiered Officers. They have drawne many impeachments against severall, which are not sent home, and which they keep untill the King sends or orders Commissioners. It's a pleasant thing to see the rascals in their cupps. . . . And now I think I have given your Lordship trouble enough to spoile your next meale; yett, my Lord, this comfort remains still, that the best men and best Protestants such as Colonel Coursey, Colonel Codd, Colonel Wells, and a great many others (men of the best Estates, and real professors of the Protestant Religion) stand stifly up for your Lordship's interests.

59. A Proprietary Account of the Revolution, September 14, 1689

[Nicholas Taney to Madam Barbara Smith, Sept. 14, 1689, Browne, ed., *Archives of Maryland*, VIII, 118-21]

I doubt not but you have heard what pretence those Gentlemen who lately tooke up armes heere in Maryland in their Majestie's names, (to pull down the lawful authority of the Lord Baltemore heere, which he held under theire said Majestys) makes for my confinement in prison along with your husband, the which I hope neither you nor any good Christian or morrall honest man or woman which ever had any acquaintance with my Life and conversation will credit, and that you and all persons to whome this shall come may know what I have done whereby they ground theire pretence. I therefore heere after wright downe the heads of the whole (vizt) at the first of my knowing of their taking up armes, which was sometime in July 1689, I endeavoured with what arguments I could use to persuade all people but chiefly Colonel Jowles (my now chiefe enemy) to lye still and keepe the peace of the Countrey untill their Majestys pleasure should be knowne, for that I looked upon it to be rebellion for persons heere without order from theire Majestys to take up armes against the lawful authority which then rested in the Lord Proprietary under theire Majestys as I did conceive, which arguments with some I presume prevailed so that they lay still, but not with Colonel Jowles. Then afterwards, when they besieged Mattapony, I went first to the Gentlemen's camp and afterwards to Mattapony and as an instrument of peace, soe farr as I could with my weake endeavours, Mr Markham being with me, persuaded both parties to comply without sheading blood and accordingly they did, at which time Mattapony and the Governors being surrounded and the magazines of armes and ammunition all over the Country as soon as possibly they could seized on by those Gentlemen, so that they had the strength and command of most of the Countrey in theire hands, and all Papists in Generall desisting to act any further in Government and Office, but Colonel Jowles and the rest of those Gentlemen not content to rest there or not thinking themselves safe in what they had done, sending out precepts in theire Majestys names requireing the Sherifs of each County to warne the people to meete together and chose delegates and representatives to meete and assemble together under pretence of settling affaires and also a Proclamation that all Officers not being Papists or haveing beene in actual armes nor any ways declared against their Majestie's service, honour and dignity, should continue in theire places and alsoe a declaration of theire owne agreevances to be publiquely read, and Colonel Jowles shewing me some of those papers being directed to me as Sheriff of Calvert County, I not being willing to execute theire Commands, endeavoured to excuse myselfe saying I lookt upon myselfe by the surrender of the Government to be discharged of my Office, whereupon Colonel Jowles tooke some other course to have it done, but afterwards I finding most people of our County, and being informed it was so generally through the Countrey that all people except such as had beene in armes or abettors to theire cause was willing to remaine as they were untill theire Majesty's pleasure should be knowne, and I conceiveing that my consenting to choose delegates and representatives to sitt in such Assembly and they countenancing the thing that was done although they were awed to it would make me guilty as well as they that did it, therefore I resolved not to choose nor consent that any should be chose, however being moddest forebore rayleing or speaking grosly of what was done. And when the time apoynted was come for the Election, Colonel Jowles and divers of his souldiers being at the place and I also and divers of the better sort of the people of our Country, discourse arrose about chooseing representatives and I and many others being much the greater number argued against chooseing any, amongst which discourse Colonel Jowles threatened that if we would not choose representatives freely he would fetch them downe with the long sword and withall required the deputy Clerke to read some papers that he had. Whereupon I askt Colonel Jowles whether those papers were theire Majestys authority and if they were I would read them myselfe; if not they should not be read, but he still bid the Clerke read them. Whereupon I said to him and the rest of the Company, Gentlemen, if the Lord Proprietary have any authority heere I command you, speakeing to the Clerke in the name of the Lord Proprietary, to read no papers heere. Whereupon Colonel Jowles went away in great rage saying he would choose none. Yett afterwards, haveing got some of his souldiers in drinke, hee and they did some what which they called a free choyce, and I and many more of the better sort of the people sett our hands to a paper wrighting that exprest modestly and loyally some reasons why wee were not willing to choose any representatives to sitt in that intended Assembly, for which doeing I was fetched from my house on Sunday the 25th of August 1689 by James Bigger and six other armed men by order of the persons assembled at the command of Coade and his accomplices and kept close prisoner at the house of Philip Lynes under a guard of armed men, and upon the 3d day of September carryed by a Company of souldiers before the said Assembly where Coade accused me of rebellion against theire Majestys King William and Queen Mary for acting as above written and withall told me if I would submit to a tryal they would assigne me Council. Whereto I answered them that I was a free borne and loyall subject to theire Majestyes of England and therefore expected the benefitt of all those laws of England that were made for the preservation of the lives and Estates of all such persons and therefore should not submitt myselfe to any such unlawful authority as I take yours to be. Thereupon they demanded of me who was theire Majestys lawful authority heere. I answered I was, as being an Officer under the Lord Baltemore until theire Majestyes pleasure should be otherwise lawfully made knowne. Then they ordered the souldiers to take me away a while and soone after ordered my bringing againe before them with Mr Smith, and Mr Bother, telling us it was the Order of the House that we must find good and sufficient security to be bound for us to answer before their Majestys' Commissioners lawfull authority what should be objected against us and in the meane time be of good behaviour. To which we answered theire authoritys we lookt upon not lawfull to force us to give any bonds, and that we had Estates in this Countrey sufficient to oblige our staying to answere what any lawful authority could object against us. Then we were againe ordered away to Mr Lyneses with a guard to keepe us prisoners still. And afterwards haveing considered with ourselves, wee informed them by Mr Johns and severall of them themselves speakeing with us, that we would give them what bonds they pleased, for our answering what should be objected against us by any lawfull authority, leaveing out the Clause of good behaviour for that we knew they would make anything they pleased breach of good behaviour, and under pretence of that trouble us againe at theire pleasure, but that would not do so at the adjourning of the Assembly we were all ordered by them to be kept in safe custody of Mr Gilbert Clarke whom they made Sheriff of Charles County, untill we should give bond as above required.

60. Maryland and New York Communicate About Their Revolutions, November 26, 1689

[John Coode to Jacob Leisler, Nov. 26, 1689, O'Callaghan, ed., *Documentary History of New York*, II, 42-44]

Your greate civilitie I have comunicated and represented to all our friends here, who are extremely glad of so neer and convenient a friendship, especially since our circumstances are so alike, and the comon danger so equally threatening: we have still the same reasonable and just aprehensions with yours and the New England government of a great designe that was on foot to betray and ruine their Majesties and the Protestant interest through all these northern parts. The attempts to disarme the Protestants in this Province last spring, the overtures to, and Treaties with our neighbouring and other Indians with other treacherous and inhumane practices, (too tedious for a letter) from the late governor here, gave us just case as to fly to armes at first, so still to persist and stand upon our guard to prevent traiterous interprises and our oune ruine. I thought it convenient herewith to send you our declaration, which is the least part of what we have to say against our Popish politicons, against whom there are dayly more discoverie and informations, of which we have not much before us that in any particular or distinct manner relates to the government unlesse this may be anything significant. We met with a paper to the government from the late King James, relating to a great correspondency and amity we were comanded to keep with our French neighbours in America . . . notwithstanding which, this is remarkable that Colonel Dongan sent to us and Virginia, to contribute our assistance towards a Warr with the French, which was complyed with I understand in Virginia, but disobeyed here, for reasons which I leave to your conjecture—as also what might be meant by settling the bounds and limits of these Collonies unlimited in the said paper. . . . I believe our greate men of this province, some of yours and New England were a Caball and held a great correspondency against the Protestant interest as it was and is the endeavours of the Popish world . . . which observation wee made before our motion here from severall and frequent messages from your parts hither, especially to the Priests who have always the Chief Share in the Management of intrigues against the Protestants: Three of our Popish Governors are fled (to wit) one Darnall, Josephs and Sewall; we have two onely in Custody; one Pye and Hill. With three Priests they had a designe towards your parts [which] feare of discovery hath prevented; they have with them a small yacht and Brigantine. If they be not retaken, having sent after them, we desire you would be pleased to be as kind to us as your circumstances will permit, which shall oblige us to a due requitall, . . . som of opinion that the present circumstances of Albany deserve your greatest considerations. . .

We have written home . . . to his Majesties principall Secretary of State, the present condition and circumstances of us all, wherein we have presumed to intimate the great service you have done his Majesties interest in all these parts, by securing so considerable a member of his dominions.

61. "Mariland's Grevances Wiy The[y] Have Taken Op Arms," January 1690

[Beverly McAnear, ed., "Mariland's Grevances Wiy The[y] Have Taken Op Arms," *Journal of Southern History*, 8 (1942), 392-409]

In answer to your desireinge an account of the Protestants of their first appeareinge and still soe continueinge in Armes in Maryland, take this brief, butt true and unbyassed account, *Vizt*.:

That, in the yeare 1689, after the groath of Popery and Arbitrary power in England had given Encoragement thereunto, the sole management of all affaires in [the] government of the said Province was lodged in the hands of 5 Papists, open declared Enimies to Protestants and their Religeon. And one Protestant, the Lord Baltimore's sonn in Law, whose fortunes as all the rest as the[y] was from Noethinge raised by . . . him [the Proprietor] soe wholly depended on him and all of them of nearest affinitie to him, beinge either brothers or sonns in Law by his Lady and her Children. These men was loaded with the highest places of trust, profitt, and honour in the said Province without any respect had to their fitt Qualifications for the same, unless that be one they soe often boasted of: that they had improved the profitts of their places beyond all that went before them, which indeed canot be deneyed, though most illegally. As for any other [qualifications] they totally wanted them, being skild in neithe[r] Cyvill Law, Common Law, or art of Cyvill goverment further than Conduct by the Councell of the Jessuitts,

their Venerable guides, as the[y] hold them in all affaires. Yett these men was the Governors of the Province, Judges att Common Law and Equitie, and Judges of probat[e] of wills and grantinge administrations, And in the generall assembly Constituted and made a second estate of the Province by the name of An upper house of Assembley without whose Consent noe Lawes Could be Enacted, though att some time they sitt as Deputy Governors and representitives of the Lords Proprietary in the said house, and next, after they have given their assent to the same as an Upper house and second Estate of the Province, Doe then in his Lordship name as Deputie Governors and his representitives in his name declare the same to bee Lawes, in both which Capacyties they are alwayes opposite to the peoples' Interest. Yett Unreasonably Every Assembly [they] Illegally Impose 70 or 80 Thousand pounds of Tobacco by way of Levey upon the People for their Expences and Charge dureinge that time, notwithstandinge the great ann[u]all revenue of 2 shillings per hogshead upon their Tobacco given his Lordshipp by the people for support of the Government, one yeare's profitts of which is thought to bee twice more Value than the said Province ever Cost him in seateinge itt, beinge peopled att first by the Unpeopleinge of his Majesty's Colloney of Virginea, Invited in thither by A more firtile soyl and a bare politique pretence of Libertie of Contience[.] And yett after this threefold assent[,] Contrary to his Lordship's Charter by which the Kinge Constitutes onely two Estates to assent to and make Lawes: To witt, his Lordship and the people by their representitives in an Assembly. These Lawes thus three times assented to still require his Lordship['s] . . . personall assent or disasent out of England or else where his Lordship's residence is whether they shall bee any longer Lawes or Nott, and that assent or disassent is soe privately signified to his Councell without any publique proclamation that the people are as uncertaine what Lawes are in force, as in whom the right of makeing them Consists, and, further, that, assent or disassent soe uncertainely limited as to the time of itt that his Lordship takes the advantage, after he hath experienced the same att his pleasure and as sutes best to his Lordship's Interest, to Nullefie all Lawes advantageous to the peoples' Interest and Confirme all those that make for his own, which the people would never have assented to but upon termes of his Lordship's Consentinge to the other[s], as he lately did all the good and wholesome Lawes madę in the time of the late Governour Nottley for the peoples' benefitt [six] yeare after he had acted by the same by vertue of his pretended prorogative. . . .

Imprimis. The Lawes are soe uncertaine and unknown that the people canot stere their Course with safetie in respect of them, which is a great greevance.

2. The people are burthened every assembley with the summ of 70 or 80 thousand pounds of tobacco for the Charges of his Lordship's Councell and deputie governors under the denomination of an upper house of Assembley, Whereas their maine and onely bussyness there is to advise and Consult his Lordship's Interest and affaires, his Lordship haveinge noe power by the King's Charter to Constitute or make nor they any right or Priviledges Thereby or any of their own distinct from the rest of the people, whereby they should have or require the priviledge of A second Estate of the province to assent to Lawes and therefore ought to have their Charges defrayd by his Lordship.

3. That the often drawinge of Causes before the Councell board and into Chancery determinable onely att Common Law to the Confoundinge of Jurisdictions and makeinge the Common Law, the peoples' best birthright . . . is A greevance.

4. That the Unlifieng [i.e., vetoing] Laws after many yeares actinge by the same under pretence that his Lordship never assented personally to them when his deputies have declared in his name the same to be Laws and that they had power from him on his behalfe to assent to the same . . . is alsoe a grevance.

5. The . . . [erecting any] offices and officers and granting unreasonable fees to the same without Act of Assembley is alsoe A Greiveance, vizt.: Examinor, generall Attorney Generall in provincial Court and the Attorney generall in the County Courts, the Clerk of the Councell's fees and the dorekeeper's fees with maney more.

6. The grantinge Lands as Escheat Lands, before found to be soe by Inquisition is alsoe A greiveance.

7. The granteinge of fines before Conviction or Judgement and to two of the Judges that sitt on the Bench and give their oppinions for fineinge persons is alsoe A great greevance.

8. Fineinge men absent and giveinge them noe day in Court to Answer by scire facias or otherwise and often without Jurys, where the matter of fact ought first to be Inquired of and found is A greevance.

9. That the Exactinge pay . . . of every County for mendinge the Country

Armes, which by Law is to be kept in repaire out of the 2 shillings per hogshead given his Lordship for provideinge and mentaineinge A publique Magazen of armes and Amunition is A greevance.

10. The not keepeinge A sufficient Magazen of Armes and Amunition for defence of the Province accordinge to the afforesaid Law of 2 shillings per hogshead given his Lordship for mentaineinge the same is a greevance.

11. That the Secretaryes takeinge Extroordinary fees in Law bussinesses att both Comon Law and Chancery and in the Land office almost as much more, at least one third more, than the Lawes of the Province allows them is A very great greivance.

12. The Judges for probate of Wills refuseinge to grant probat of wills and administrations att their office but by way of Commission into the Country, by which the fees became double what otherwise they Could be is A greevance.

13. The said Judges not keepinge their Courts Monthly accordinge as the Act of Assembly Enjoynes them is A great damage to Executors and administrators, as alsoe to debtors and Creditors.

14. The Secretaries doe exact such unreasonable yearely rents and sometimes in money from the Clerks of the County Corts that they Canot live of them and pay the same without Exactinge fees of the people Contrary to Law, and by which meanes they are maney of them soe little worth that none but Insufficient persons will accept of them, by which meanes alsoe the records are in maney Counties very ill kept to the prejudice of the present and future ages.

15. That the said Secretaries so Negligently kept the Records of the Common Law and Chancery that 3 or 4 yeares' proceedings of the Proventiall Court lyes in loose minite papers; And the Clark . . . that tooke them in Court for want of payment of his wages refuse to make up the said Records, which none other Can doe, by which all persons their Conserned are subject to be damnified by

writts of Error or otherwise is Alsoe A . . . greiveance.

16. That the said Secretarys imposeinge of 1200 lb. of Tobbacco per annum upon every Attorney that practizes in the Proventiall Court without any Law for the same is alsoe A greivance.

17. That all the Judges att Comon Law and Chancery and Probat of Wills and administrations are soe nere of Kinne that, when any of them are sued as itt often happens, they beinge all of them Dealers, They not thought to bee equall [impartial] Judges (beinge either Uncells or brothers to each other) is A greiveance.

18. That sometimes they have sitt Judges in their own Causes alsoe is A greivance.

19. That noe penall Lawes made against officers Extortinge illegall fees can take any effect against the offenders of them, for . . . the Judges of the proventiall Court and Common Law are either themselves or by their deputies actually possessd of all offices of profit throughout the province. . . .

20. That the said Judges denieinge writts of Error in many Cases Contrary to the statute is a greivance.

21. His Lordship assumeinge to himself the Royall Prerogative of avoiding his grant by pretence of beinge deceived by false suggestions or falss Considerations or in A poynt of Law, . . . whereby many poor Orphans and others had their Pattent of Land [voided] to undoeinge of them, is A greivance.

22. The subtile devise hitherto used and still practized, not onely to stifle but to [in]validate the most Just Complaints made to England of their wrongs and oppressions done to their private persons or the Publique, by frameinge some lyinge, scandalous papers or writeinge of such persons and their Cause and then gettinge subscriptions to the same from their own Creatures and others, Whose Ignorance . . . [timorousness] or expectation of favor drew them to subscrib such papers, and then send itt

away for England to overballance the Creditt of such single complain[an]ts, who might have had 40 subscribers for one to the Contrary . . . . Yea, very Records of Courts of Judicature have beene alttered and made to speake Contrary to the Originall Entery of the Clark. . . .

The Violateinge of the freedome of Elections for Burggases to sitt in the Assembly.

The Imposseinge Exessive fines Contrary to magna Charta. . . .

Maney more of this nature might be added, would itt not swell this paper to too great a Bulk; and thus you see how the Cause hath stood in respect of our Equall rights, by which you may gess how itt hath fared with the religieous while under A bare, politique pretence of Libertie of Contience. Priests and Jessuitts have lived in great wealth and splendor with the favourable asspect of the government . . . whilst the protestants and Clergey wantinge mentainance and liveinge in povertie under the Contemptable lookes of the government, both their persons and doctrine rendered both alike dispiseable in the eyes of the Common people.

The account of A Vigorous prosecutinge . . . [of] An Act against mutinous and seditious speeches, by which Illegal punishments were . . . Inflicted without any declaration therein what words or speech shall be accounted mutinous and tend thereto, but the same is left therein to the discretion of the Judges of the Proventiall Court, which are all his Lordship's relations, and are to be such if they [the judges] shall thinke them soe by the words of the Act, the penalties of which Law are splitinge the Nose, boareinge through the tounge with an hot Iron, fine, Imprisonment, Banishment, death, Confiscation of Lands and goods, all or any the said paines as the Court shall alsoe thinke fitt. . . .

The Imposeinge an oath of fidelitie to be taken to his Lordship by all that beare office or sitt in the generall assembly without any salvo Expressed in the said Oath of Allegance to the Kinge of England. [This is] politiquely Construed to admitt Papists into office and into the generall assembly that refuse . . . to take itt [the oath to the King] and excludes many Protestants from the same that make A scruple of Contience to take the same without that salvo Expressed. . . .

All which, with severall others mentioned in the Protestant Declaration was noe motives to their assumeinge of Armes; but, as they were burdens they had long Endured, soe with patience would have still Continued, Expectinge releife from the all dispossinge hand of Providence uppon the same, had not their Allegence to their Majestys, the Protestant religeon, and the Law of Extreame Necessity (self preservation) enforsed them to that defence as by the Ensueinge relation will fully appeare.

Sometime in October, 1688, here Arived one Mr. Joseps [William Joseph], an Irish popist, with A Commission from the Lord Baltemore to be President here of his Councell, which was noe wayes acceptable to the people for the remembrance they still retained of the Villianies committed by one Talbot, an Irish Papist and then one of the cheif governors here, who A shortt time before most barberously murthered one Mr. Christopher Rousbey, the King's Collector. The said Mr. Josephs published his Commission in october Court with alsoe strict orders from the Lord Baltemore for proclaiminge the then pretended prince of Wal[e]s, which was performed with all Imaginable and exact solemnitie they Could. . . . He alsoe published his Lordship's proclamation for dispenceing with such part of the Law for Townes as his Lordship thought not for his Interest and Continuing the rest that made for itt without assent of his Assembley by virtue of his prerogative, as they told the people, but to noe smale discontent of the said Assembly, Convend the 17th of November next Ensueinge, to see their rights soe Invaded; att which Assembly the said deputiy governors soe highly insisted upon his Lordship's prerogative and their priviledge as an upper house that they tooke upon them[selves], which was never done before, to impose upon the members of the Lower house an oath of fidelitie to his Lordship upon most seveare penalties in which is noe salvo of Allegence to the King of England; The which the said house was willinge to accept, upon that both houses might take the oath of Allegance, which the said upper house refused, giveinge this Answer: that fidelitie to his Lordship was Allegance and denyall of the one was the same thinge with refuseall of the other; and, further, the Lower howse desireinge to know of them if His Lordship by that proclamation att the Court Intended to Annull A part of the Law for Townes without assent of the assembly. It was then Answered that the King had power to dispence with the penall Lawes and soe had his Lordship, and accordingly did the same. Soe that litle bussyness was there effected, only severall Insultinge and threateninge messages was sent from the said upper house to the lower, sometimes as an upper house and sometimes as deputy governors. Att the latter end of the said Assembly Arived The happy news of The Prince of Oringe's Arivall in England with considerable forces Invited thither by the Clergey, Lords, and Comons of the Nation and of his glorious undertakeinge mentioned in his declaration of freeinge the three Kingdoms from Popery and lawless Tyraney, of which news the said Deputy Governors tooke all imaginary Care to Keep the Country Ignorant of, and then peroaged the said Assembly till Apriel next Ensueinge, and in short time after calld in all the Country Armes under pretence of mendinge the same for defence of the Country against the Dutch. But When the certaine and desired News arived of their Majestys, King William and Queen Mary, being Crownd in England and the Dutch was in Amitie and the French att Enmity [with] the English, the said Armes was never mended or ever retorned to the Protestants, but detained from them and thereupon the said Deputy Governors and Jesuites, whose wealthy mindes are ever ready furnished with such politick lyes, did dayly broach Newes (received as they pretended from all parts) of the French King's Invincible Army to Envade England and the late King James' great victories in Ireland and Scotland and his great party in England ready to Joyne in Conqueringe the rebells as they tearmed the protestants, as allsoe the great stringth of the French and Kenada Indians, likely, if occasion served, att the French King's Command to Invade this Province and other their Majestys' protestant Colloneys, drinking their healths and wishinge for their success and the speedy arrivall of that Golden day (as they tearmd itt) likely to vissitt them all, to the terrour of their Majestys' Loyall protestant subjects and encouragement of the papist, their most Professed Enimies. These things, together with the black mouth scandalls And impious Curses dayly and traterously vented against their Majestys' sacred persons and government . . , Created greate jealousies in the minds of the Protestants, which in short time after was much augmented and Confirmed by A generall but true report that all the Indians of the Province was Allarmd and freightened from their townes and that some of them had Cutt up their Corn, A true passage of their makeinge Warr, and, as the Indians themselives related to severall Protestants, the occation of itt was that they was Informed that the English had gotten A Dutch King and that the Protestants Intended to Cut off all the Papists and then to Kill the Indians and that one of the deputy Governors told them they must feight for those people Called Papists[;] the French and Northerine Indians would and then they should overcome the Protestants. This newes soe affrightened the people that some begun to fly into the Colloney of Virginea and others fled to their neighbours' houses and there kept watch Expecting the event, whereupon one Collnell Jowles with about 150 men of Colvert County with such Armes and amunition as they Could gett appeared in A body, demanded their County armes, which was delivered, and that the deputy Governours would take some Course to alley the feares and Jealocies of the people occationed by those matters the Indians as well as the English had reported. With . . . much Intreatie they [the Deputy Governors] promised they would and thereupon they [Jowles' men] laid down their Armes, . . . they expecting the performance of the same, especially the assembly being nigh, which was prorogued to Apriel next Ensueinge. But they Prorogued the same againe to a further time, Notwithstandinge all mens' Earnest desire for the sittinge of the same, and, att A Proventiall Court then held in Apriel as they promised, they Indavoured to Clear themselves, but to soe little purpose that the people was worse satisfied than before, for the said deputy Governors gott A paper subscribed by 8 or 9 persons, most of which was Ignorant of the affaire and not well Informed thereof and soe subscribed itt att their request.

Sometime in July, 1689, Capt. John Cood, with others of their Majestys' Protestant Subjects rose up in armes with such Armes as they had att his house in Ste. Maryes County . . . and Marched down to the Citty of St. Marys to secure the Records, where they [the proprietary faction] weare all in Garrisand in . . . the statehouse. There the guns Ley all out of portholes and windows, but the Protestants, not feareinge anythinge, drew up their men before the said Garison less than within Pistoll shott and sent them in the Protestants' declaration, demandinge that itt may be read [in] publique that all that was therein might heare itt and withall to surrender the Garison with all warlike Provission together with all the records to their Majestys' use, which after 2 or 3 howers' parley was accordinly surrendered. Then Newes came [that] there was in Mattappaney att the Lord Baltimoor's house in Patuxen river 300 men in Garrisond with all warlike provisions, . . . all the deputy Governors and the rest of the papistes except Colonel Digges which had beene in the stathouse, where they were resolved not to surrender, they haveinge there A Jesuite or two to encorage thire designe. But 2 dayes after the surrender of the stathouse, they Marched to the said Matapponey with about six or 7 hundered men which were gathered together by that time[,] assisted with 2 great gunns . . . which said partie of men, marchinge under the Comand and conduct of the said Capt. Cood, Encamped before the said Garrison and sent forth A mesinger to the same with their declaration, demandinge itt to be read to the garrison, which they said they would but never did least the people should thereupon desert itt, and alsoe demanded out of the said fort all their Majesties' protestant subjects which they their against their wills detained, alsoe surrender of the said Garrison with all Warlike provisions there unto their Majestys' use; which some time after they answered by Another Messinger that they desired . . . A Parley, whereupon A second messinger was sent to them demandinge them to sett downe thire termes in writinge, which they sent, but some of them [were] such as the protestants durst not without their Majestys' order Consent unto, but sent them these termes, upon which, if they surrendred not, they must proceed to storm itt. . . .

All which Articles was Inviolably kept with them, though they kept not theirs with the protestants, for Contrary to the same they Conveyed away the greatest part of the Country's armes and amunition to places unknown, and within 5 or 6 dayes after their surrender two of the said deputy governors endeavoured to gett to Nichollson, the Governour att New Yorke. But att New Castle and Dilaware, as they went, they understood that Nicholson, the Governor there, was fled, and that the said fort was taken by the protestants for their present Majestys, and that Coll. Dungon [Governor Thomas Dongan] and other papists was therein hold, and that Andreews [Andros], the governor of New England, was retaken againe Endeavouringe to Escape to New York, and findeing themselves there suspected for holdinge corespondance with them, retorned againe into this Province[.] And, knowinge that the said protestants according to their declaration had in their Majestys' names sent to the severall Counties in the Province, to Elect representives to meett in A generall assembly to setle the Counties in peace till further order from their Majestys, The said two deputys Governors, to witt, [Nicolas] Sewell and [Henry] Darnell, with the rest went from County to County, Inveagleinge some by faire promisses and afraightinge others from their allegence by dayly inventing Newes that the late King James, by Assistance of [the] French had reduced England againe to their obedience and subjectinge [it to] him. Yett this sham would not take, for of tenn Countyes[,] nine of them Elected and sent their representatives. . . . And soe, att the time appointed, the said assembly were first of all persuant to their dutyes, They ordered their present Majestys to be proclaimed and then drew up an Address, 40 of them subscribeinge with all their hands, and then tooke into their Consideration the setlement of the Province in peace and safety till further orders from their Majestys, in doeinge of which they found some dificulty, for, the Province beinge in a place wholely dependinge upon trade, itt was absoelutely necessary to keep up the Courts of Judicature in the severall Countyes for Creditors to receive in their debts, in which, beinge all holden in the Lord

Baltimoor's name and all process Isueinge thereout in the same alsoe, which they were unwilling to Alter without their Majestys' order, had not the present necessity of their Majestys' Interest Inforced them to itt, for the said deputy Governors perswaded the people that, under Colour of that name of Commission, they were safe obayinge the Late Kinge James and renouncinge their Alegence to their present Majesty.

And soe under pretence of mentaineinge the Lord Baltymors interest in the province, they endeavoured totally to destroy that of their Majestys. . . .

And next proceedinge to setle all Civill and military officers pursueant to their Majestys' Declaration . . . [Continuing] all protestants in their places and removeinge all papists out and placeinge protestants in their roomes, and Continued all the temporary Lawes of the Province, and then Laid County levey, which, notwithstandinge all the aforesaid occasions of expence, was the smalest that ever was in the Province and soe caused the same to be drawn up into an ordinance of Assembly by which the matters more fully appear, and soe upon the 4th september, 1689 they adjorned the said Assembly till the first of Apriel next ensueinge. After which, as well as before the said Assembly, the said deputy Governors, by virtue of the said Lord Baltimore's Commission on behalfe of the late King James, used their utmost Indeavours to stir up the people to rebell against their present King William and Queen Mary, which occationed the Militia to the great Charge of the Province [to be placed] constantly upon their gaurd, whereupon the Cheif officer thereof sent to them to repaire to their houses and peaceably there abide and enter into bond to their majestys to answer such things as should be objected against them to their Majestyes' Comissioners or such other authoritie as should Come hither from them, [or] otherwise [he] would force them to it, the which they deneyed, and thereupon Collnel Darnel, one of them, fled for New England. Two others of them was apprehended and remaine under gaurds, and three others of them fled into Virginia entertained there by some popish friends, from whence ever since they have by letters to their Confederates here not failed to forge and invent such lyes and unhappy newes as they thought most fitt to frieghten the people from their Allegance and stir them up to rebellion against their present Majestys, and one of them, to witt, Major Sewell, with about 8 or 9 fugitive papists in A small Yatch came severall times into the province without Enteringe or Cleareinge Accordinge to an act of Parliament, which one Mr. John Pain, their Majestys' Colector, takeinge notice of, pursueant to his duty as the Law required, demanded of him to doe the same, which he Contempttuously deneyed, threateninge him if he offered to Come on Board him, whereupon, the said Sewell Comeinge againe up into the Province [on the third] day of [January], 1689, the said Pain, with 4 men to attend him with A smale boat, thinkinge himself safe under his commission,

in A peaceable way went to goe on board, which they deneyed; and, after half an hower fast argueinge the case with him by the side of the said Yatch, they shott him from off the side of the same in the Breast with two Muskett Bulletts and five high swan shott of which he Imediately dyed, and his Attendants in the boate narrowly Escaped, being persued by them, dischargeinge Gunns att them to the very shoar; and then they retorned again to Virginiea, where, att their Arrivall as is sworn by good Evidence, That Sewell made his Men A great bowll of punch and bid them singe the fight was done, for they had killed John Pain, the King's Collector, which, if soe, indeed itt was done before itt was begune by the Protestants, for they hurt not the least haire of the Papists' head or wronged them one farthing of their Estates, notwithstandinge the Continuall provocations of them. Onely after the aforesaid murder, they disarmed some, finding that noe Kindnes could charm or work upon their ill natures, nor that any protestant could be safe while there was any meanes left them of Effecting his Ruine.

62. A Controversy Over the Financial Settlement of the Revolution

A. A Letter from James Heath, Lord Baltimore's Agent, to the Revolutionary Government, June 2, 1690

[Browne, ed., *Archives of Maryland*, VIII, 182-83]

[Heath demanded] Imprimis: The delivery to him, the said Agent, of all the Bills and Bonds remaining in the Land Office or else where and belonging to his Lordship, being taken for Lands or otherwayes relateing to his private Estate.

Secondly: The delivery of Matapany House, Plantation, and Stock with an Account of the disposall of the latter, and his Lordships Mill with an Account of the proffitts thereof.

Thirdly: An Account of all shipping entred and cleared since the first of August last, and the Bills of Exchange or money received for the same.

Fourthly: The delivery of all other Papers, Matters and Things anywayes relateing or appertaining to his Lordships private Estate or concernes.

And the said James Heath desireth of such persons as at present execute publick Power in this Province that they will give their orders necessary for the delivery of the severall particulars as aforesaid and likewise withdraw their orders from all persons executing as Navall Officers or Collectors in this Province soe far forth as relates to the Revenue ariseing here, and that the same may be left to the management of the said Heath and his Deputies.

B. THE ANSWER OF JOHN COODE'S COMMITTEE, JUNE 18, 1690

[Browne, ed., *Archives of Maryland*, VIII, 183-84]

1. That all Bills and Bonds passed and made payable to his lordship remaining in the Land Office or elsewhere for Lands or otherwise relateing to his Lordships private Estate, be delivered to his Lordships Agent, excepting only for such Lands whereof no Certificates have been returned and recorded, the Collection whereof are to be suspended untill such time as the consideration of the said Bill and Bonds be complyed with by making a good and firm title to the same.

2. Mattapony House and Plantation being a Garrison inforted and by the late Government under his Lordship surrendered upon Articles to his Majestyes use, it is not thought fit or convenient to alter the property thereof untill such time as his Majestyes pleasure therein be known and his directions accordingly given, but as for the Stock (as it hath not been denyed soe) it is not the design of the present executive power to obstruct his Lordships Agent to make the best advantage thereof. Noe part thereof having been otherwayes employed or made use of by any of this present power or by their order more than what was necessaryly expended for their Majestyes service in the reduceing of the said late Government and is all there in being for anything known to the present authority save what Madam Darnall and Madam Sewall may have taken and applyed to uses best known to themselves.

That the said Agent have the use of the Plantation for the Benefit of his Lordships Stock thereon, the Cropp of Corn etc. thereon growing to be and enure to the use of person there resideing who planted the same.

3. This Article included and answered in the last conclusive part.

4. All papers, matters, and things any wayes relateing to his Lordships private estate (in whose hands soever) to be delivered up to his Lordships Agent.

His Lordships said Agent from henceforth to collect and receive by such wayes and meanes as he shall think fit the moyety of the 2 shillings per hogshead for every shipp or vessell hereafter to arrive and enter within this Province and that for the rest of the dutyes upon shipping here accrueing, according to the Law and usuall custome of this Province, they be collected by the Navall Officers appointed by the Representative Body of this Province in the late Generall Convention to such uses and by such wayes and meanes as therein is provided.

C. JAMES HEATH'S LETTER OF PROTEST AGAINST JOHN COODE'S COMMITTEE, JUNE 19, 1690

[Browne, ed., *Archives of Maryland*, VIII, 188-90]

It might have reasonably been expected from John Coode and others his Associates, who out of a pretence of a more than ordinary Zeale for their Majesties' service and the security of the Rights and properties of the people of this Province, have overturned this the late most peaceable and quiet Government, (of the which they assumed to themselves) their most ready complyance with the least intimation they should know of his Majesty's pleasure in any case whatsoever and that they would have behaved themselves towards the good people of this province as pretended. But as the Letter hath been maintained in the rifleing and pillageing of severall of the most emenent protestants Houses, the imprisoning of the persons of some, and sending armed men in persute of others, from place to place with warrants to Fetch them Dead or alive, thereby driving them from their Habitations, soe they have nott been less wanting in their obedience to his Majestie's pleasure, signified by his Letter bearing date the 1st day of February 1689 (and superscribed to such as For the time being take care For preserving the peace and administring the lawes in our province of Maryland in America) in severall causes thereof, butt perticurly whatt this Declaration and Protest of the Agent of the Right Honourable the Lord Proprietary of this province, James Heath will make manifest, which said Agent doth hereby signify unto all Persons concerned, that his Majesty in a particular clause in his said letter, directs the said persons to suffer the Proprietor or his Agents to Collect the Revenues arising here, and to apply only such part thereof For the support of the Government as was usually allowed and applyed by the Proprietor to that purpose. The said Agent hath applyed himselfe to such persons as assumed to themselves to be those to whome his Majestie's said letter was directed, who are the said John Coode and his associates, and of them hath de[s]ired to give theire orders as well to such persons as have collected any thing of the said Revenue, to render the same Agent an accompt thereof as to withdraw theire orders From all persons att present collecting

the same, butt that the same might be left to the management of the said Agent and his Deputies, Butt the said John Coode and his associates contemning and not regarding to comply with his Majestie's directions aforesaid, have denied and refused either to permitt any one to give the said Agent any accompts of what has allready bin collected on the accompt of Shipping, which is the principall Revenue of this province, or to suffer him to collect any thing From the Shipps now in the province (which will be the Shipping revenue of this yeare) contrary to the Lawes of this province, which enjoin the same to be paid to his Lordshipp (who otherwise must receive his rents from the Inhabitants of this province in moneyes). His Majestie's intention being as aforesaid, likewise whereby as by divers others circumstances is sufficiently obvious that notwithstanding the specious pretences of the said John Coode and his Associates as aforesaid, they have abused the King's Majestie by their Falce declaration and addresses, thereby to colour their designes in Tyrannizing over all such as will not joyne with them in their wicked practices, who appeare to be the best and chiefest of the protestant Inhabitants of this province. As alsoe they have already some, soe it is apparent their designes are to embezell and apply to their own private uses the aforesaid Revenue, nott only by taking Bills of exchange for the same into their owne names butt for other reasons justly suspitious, and as all due methods will be taken to Free the inhabitants of this province From the said John Coode and his Associates, their oppression and tiranny, soe to forwarne all persons From making undue and illegall payments of any part of the Revenue ariseing here, he the said Agent on the part and behalfe of the said Lord Proprietor, and touching the revenue ariseing here wherein the said Agent is concerned, holdeth himselfe obliged to declare and protest . . . against the aforesaid John

Coode and his Associates who hath denyed to render an accompt or permitted
him to collect as aforesaid, as against all
other person and persons whatsoever
that have already or that shall make
payment of any of the Revenues ariseing
in this province and payable to his Lordshipp to the aforesaid John Coode or
his Associates or to any person appointed by them or to any other person
whatsoever then to the said Agent or
his deputyes dureing his residence in
this province, and in his absence to Mr
Michaell Taney and Mr Richard Smith,

Jr., both of Calverts County who in the
said James Heath's absence are constituted his Lordship's Agents, hereby
holding For null, voyd and illegall all
payments that is or shall be otherwise
made of the Revenues aforesaid then
to him, the said Agent, or to his deputies or in his absence to the said
Michaell and Richard or their deputyes
or by their directions declaring the same
to be att the perill of the persons soe
paying or repaying the same again as
by law they may be compelled.

Maryland Becomes a Royal Province

63. The Royal Instructions of Governor Lionel Copley, August 26, 1691

[Browne, ed., *Archives of Maryland*, VIII, 272-
80]

And that we may be alwaies informed
of the Names and characters of Persons
fit to supply the vacancies of our said
Councill, You are to transmitt unto Us,
by one of our principall Secretarys of
State and to the Lords of our Privy
Councill, appointed a Committee of
Trade and Plantations with all convenient speed, the names and characters of
Twelve Persons, inhabitants of our said
Province, whom you shall esteem the
best qualified to succeed in that Trust
and so from time to time when any of
them shall dye, depart out of our said
Province or become otherwise unfit, you
are to nominate so many other Persons
to Us in their stead. And in the choice
and nomination of the members of our
said Councill, as also of the principall
Officers, Judges, Assistants, Justices and
Sheriffs, you are always to take care that
they be men of Estate and Ability and
not necessitous people or much in Debt
and that they be persons well affected to
our Government. . . .

And that it may be better understood
what Acts and Laws are in Force in

our Province of Maryland, You are with
the assistance of our Councill to take
Care that all Laws now in force be revised and considered, and if there be
any thing either in the matter or stile
of them which may be fit to be re-
trenched or altered, You are to represent the same unto Us with your Opinion touching the said Laws now in force
(whereof you are to send a compleat
Body to us) with such alterations as you
shall think requisite to the end our
approbation or disallowance may be
signifyd thereupon.

You shall take care that the Members
of the Assembly be elected only by Freeholders, as being most agreeable to the
Custome of England to which you are
as near as may be to conform yourself.

And you shall reduce the Salary of
the members of the Assembly to such
a moderate Proportion as may be no
grievance to the Country, wherein nevertheless you are to use your discretion
so as no inconveniency may arise
thereby.

You are to take care that no man's

life, Member, Freehold or goods be taken away or harmed in our said Province, but by Established and known Laws not repugnant to, but as much as may be agreeable to the Laws of Our kingdome of England.

You shall administer or cause to be administered the Oaths appointed by Act of Parliament, to be taken instead of the Oaths of Allegiance and supremacy and the Test, unto the Members and Officers of Our Councill and Assembly, all Judges and Justices and all other Persons that hold any Office in Our said Province, by vertue of any Patent under Our Great Seal of England or the Publick seal of Maryland. And you are to permitt a Liberty of Conscience to all Persons so they be contented with a quiet and peaceable Enjoyment of it, not giving offence or scandall to the Government.

You are not to pass any Act or Order within that our Province in any Case, for Levying money and inflicting Fines and Penalties whereby the same shall not . be reserved to Us for the publick Uses as by the said Act or Order shall be directed. . . .

Our will and Pleasure is, that all publick monies raised or to be raised within our said Province and Territory of Maryland for the use and support of the Government there be issued out by Warrant from you by and with the advice and consent of the Councill and not otherwise.

And whereas by an Act passed in the Assembly in Maryland the thirtieth day of Aprill 1679, an impost of two shillings per Hogshead is laid upon all Tobacco exported out of our said Province, one moiety of which impost, is by the said Act appropriated for the use and support of the Government, Our will and Pleasure is, that towards the maintenance in the Government of our said Province, you take to your own use, three fourth parts of the said moiety of the impost of two shillings per Hogshead of Tobacco, appropriated as aforemen-tioned by the said Act, And you are to take especiall Care, that according to the intention of the said Act, the remaining fourth part of the Moiety of the said impost be duly applied towards the maintaining a constant Magazine with Arms and Amunition for the defence of our said Province. . . .

You are to permit the Lord Baltemore, by his Agents or Officers appointed by him, to collect and receive the other moiety of the said impost of two shillings per Hogshead together with the Duty of 14d per Tun upon shipping trading to Maryland for his own use as Proprietary of our said Province. And you are not in any wise yourself or any other by your Order to intermedle with the said Moiety of the said impost of two shillings per Hogshead or the said duty of fourteen pence per Tun. But to permit the same to be collected and received by the Lord Baltimore or his Agents as aforesaid without any hindrance or molestation whatsoever.

You are from time to time to permit the Assembly to view and examine the Accompt of mony or value of mony disposed of, by vertue of such Laws as are now in force or shall be passed by them which you [are] to signify unto them as occasion shall serve. Our express will and Pleasure is, that all Laws whatsoever for the good Government and support of your said Province, be made indefinite and without Limitation of time except the same be for a temporary end and which shall expire and have its full effect within a certain time. . . .

You shall not remit any Fines or Forfeitures whatsoever above the summe of Ten pounds before or after sentence given, nor dispose of any Escheats Fines or Forfeitures untill you upon signifying unto our Committee of Trade and Plantations And to the Commissioners of our Treasury for the time being the nature of the offence or occasion of such Fines, Forfeitures or Escheats with the particular summes you shall have received our directions therein. But you may in the mean time suspend the Payment of the said Fines and Forfeitures.

You shall not permit any Act or Order to pass within our said Province whereby the Price or value of currant mony within your Government may be altered without our particular leave or Direction therein. And you are particularly not to pass any Law or do any Act by grant, settlement, or otherwise, whereby Our Revenue may be lessened or impaired without our especiall leave or commands therein. . . .

You shall not erect any Court or Office of Judicature not before erected and established without our especiall Order and you are to transmit unto Us with all convenient speed a particular accompt of all establishments of Jurisdictions, Courts, Offices and Officers, Powers, Authorities, Fees and Privileges Granted or settled within our said Province to the end you may receive our especiall direction therein. . . .

And that God Almighty may be more inclined to bestow his blessing upon us and you in the welfare and improvement of that our Province you shall take especiall care, that he be devoutly and duly served within your Government, the Book of Common Prayer as it is now established Read each Sunday and holiday and the blessed Sacrament administered according to the Rites of the Church of England. . . .

You are not to permit or Allow of any Appeals whatsoever to be made from the Governor and Councill unto the Assembly but whereas we judge it absolutely necessary that all our subjects may have liberty to Appeal unto Us, in cases that may deserve the same, Our will and Pleasure is, that if either party shall not rest satisfied with the Judgement or sentence of our Governor or the Commander in Chief and Councill they may then appeal unto us in our Privy Councill Provided the matter in difference exceed the reall value or summe of three hundred pounds sterling and that such appeal be made within one Fortnight after sentence and security first given by the Appelant to Answer such charges as shall be awarded in case the sentence of our Governor or Commander in chief and Councill in Maryland be confirmed. . . .

And forasmuch as great inconveniences may arise by the Liberty of Printing within our Province of Maryland, you are to provide by all necessary Orders that no person use any Press for printing upon any occasion whatsoever, without your speciall Licence first obtained.

CHAPTER NINE

THE CONSEQUENCES OF REBELLION

O N April 6, 1692, Governor Copley met for the first time with his
Council, which included Jowles and Blakiston. (It is interesting
that the same men who considered a salaried Council a grievance in
1682 were pleased to have such remuneration when *they* became councilors after the rebellion!) Four days later the first assembly under the
new regime convened, choosing Cheseldyne Speaker. On May 12 Copley
and his Council indicated their willingness to join the lower house in
inspecting the "Body of the Laws" after disposing of certain formal and
procedural affairs and confirming "all matters Judicial and otherwise
Since the Late Revolution." Three weeks later, after some slight con-
tention, the consensus was that "it is thought more proper to appeale,
Annul, abrogate and make void all Laws in General heretofore made
in this Province except what upon Review of the body of those Laws
this present sessions have deemed fit and Convenient for the good government of this Province." Thus the books were cleared for a fresh set
of statutes reflecting the changes desired and wrought by the revolu-
tionaries. An examination of the titles of this legislation provides an
insight into the sort of housecleaning the burgesses thought they were
accomplishing (No. 64).

This work was perhaps the most important but not the only effort
of the new assembly. Harmonious relations had to be established with
the Indians. On the first day of the new session the little town was filled
with resplendent chiefs, and four days following, three nearly identical
treaties were made with as many tribes. Although Indian-white animosities did not entirely abate—defense measures were required in
1693—the years after the revolution were generally characterized by
quiet on the frontier.

A third issue of importance at this assembly was the initiation of action against the Proprietor for alleged financial irregularities. A fourth was the adoption by the lower house of a system of self-regulating procedures. And still other objects of consideration were the various appeals by members of the ousted party for indemnification or restoration of lost property.

Friction arose at this time between the new regime and Henry Darnall, now acting as Lord Baltimore's agent, who demanded that he be rendered all of his master's dues and revenues, picking up where James Heath left off. (This dispute was finally quieted in 1695 when the Council ordered the "strict collection of the . . . dues belonging to Lord Baltimore.") The controversy over the collection of the Proprietor's income was exacerbated by the fact that while the Protestant Association reigned supreme illicit trade was extensively effected, so that many fees and bonds had not accumulated. Lord Baltimore and his agents were not alone antagonized by this. The arrant Edward Randolph, Surveyor General of His Majesty's customs, arrived in Maryland in May, midway through the first legislative session. He quickly communicated to his superiors in London the conditions of commerce and politics in the new royal province. In the process he alienated Lionel Copley, causing a feud which helped keep the colony in turmoil (No. 65).

Lord Baltimore, his agents, the itinerant Randolph, and Copley were joined in the race for revenue and fees by Sir Thomas Lawrence. He was appointed Secretary of Maryland when Copley became Governor, vied with his colleague for perquisites and patronage, and their conflict compounded the Copley-Randolph tension. But whereas Randolph soon departed, Lawrence remained to complicate provincial politics (No. 66).

Thus Maryland's new status as a royal colony brought an injection of invidious officials external to her indigenous society. The presence of these placemen with their petty intrigues tended to displace or divert attention from the revolutionary issues. Hence the reorientation of political controversy was conditioned to a significant degree in the province by the presence of a hierarchy detached from the tumultuous events recently passed. In this respect the newcomers were a mixed political blessing.

While alterations in the structure of provincial politics were manifest in the spats between the adherents of the proprietary party, the querulous new officials from England, and the erstwhile Associators, the reorganization of political society was intimately related to the positions men had taken at the time of the rebellion. This restructuring is reflected on the one hand by men who lost provincial and county offices after 1689, and on the other by the meteoric careers of many of the rebel leaders and their accomplices. (John Coode was a notable exception:

when the Crown assumed the government from the convention and its committee, power seems to have passed from Coode's hands. After his return from England he played a minor political role, ultimately disgracing himself.) The creation of parishes and vestrymen proved nearly a social duplication of this reconstruction.

The attempt to establish the Church of England, however, was marked by many vicissitudes in the 1690's, at Whitehall as well as in Maryland, where the dissenters protested bitterly. But by 1702 an Anglican victory was assured and their rapid growth attested that fact, as did the plight of Quakers and Catholics alike (No. 68). Some historians have claimed that the shift of the capital from (Catholic) St. Mary's to (Protestant) Annapolis in 1695 was an indication of the new locus of religious strength. But it is equally likely that commercial and political factors necessitated the move. It is noteworthy that many of those who joined in protesting the shift in 1694 had been political enemies in 1689 (No. 67).

Counterbalancing the various changes which followed the revolution were a variety of conditions which were unaffected by the proprietary demise. Frontier rangers seem to have remained a nuisance in the 1690's, as they had been in 1688. Nor were the new authorities any more permissive about the Indian trade than their predecessors. Those who lost land grants made just prior to the revolution were naturally upset, as were colonists who felt the land office functioned no more fairly after the insurgency than before. A few of the Associators continued to protest multiple officeholding, particularly in the judiciary. But many of the greatest offenders in the 1690's had complained the loudest before the Calverts were ejected. The revolutionary bias against pluralism seems to have been less a matter of principle than of personal exclusion.

The death of Governor Copley in 1693 led to considerable albeit temporary confusion, and it seemed for a moment as though the events of 1689 would be re-enacted with Lawrence and Blakiston as protagonists (No. 69). Blakiston had worked closely with Copley against Lawrence, and after Copley's death it became necessary to suspend Blakiston from the Council to preserve quiet and avoid disputes. Sir Edmund Andros took possession of the Maryland government in September until Francis Nicholson was installed as governor. Nicholson's administration (1694-98) was uneventful in many respects, but the reappearance of John Coode's star falling across his path hindered his efforts to restore calm (No. 70). Once Nicholson actually caned Coode for drunken brawling at divine service!

EPILOGUE: In 1715 Charles Calvert, third Lord Baltimore, died, followed in seven weeks by his apostate son. Sixteen-year-old Charles—

raised a Protestant—became the fourth proprietary and the fifth Lord Baltimore. His guardian immediately petitioned for a political restoration of the government. This was granted. But the apostasy is doubly ironic. Not long after Benedict Leonard Calvert deserted Catholicism for politically preferable Protestantism, the heirs of Coode and Cheseldyne abandoned the faith of their fathers for the Roman Catholic Church.

Politics and Personalities After the Revolution

64. Old Statutes Give Way to New, May-June 1692

[Titles of Some Acts Passed by the First Assembly to Meet with the Royal Governor, May 10-June 9, 1692, Browne, ed., *Archives of Maryland*, XIII, 421-24]

An Act for the Service of Almighty God, and the Establishment of the Protestant Religion within this Province.

An Act concerning what shall be allowed to the Grand Juryes that are summoned out of the body of this Province to attend Provinciall Courts.

An Act for limitation of certain actions for avoideing Suites att Law.

An Act for quieting Possessions.

An Act prohibiting Commissioners, Sheriffs, Clerks, and Deputy Clerks to plead as Attorneys in their respective Courts.

An Act for the more speedy bringing to tryall and suppressing Criminalls and Limiting their punishments for Certaine Offences when prosecuted in the County Courts.

An Act declareing what shall be Done by the Sherriff Ex Officio.

An Act for secureing Merchants and others Tobacco after they have Received it.

An Act Impowering Commissioners of the County Courts to Leavy and raise Moneyes to defray the Necessary Charges of their Countyes.

An Act for publication of all Lawes with in this Province.

An Act for the Election of Sherriffs.

An Act for Limitation of Officers Fees.

An Act for Limitting the County Clerks Fees within this Province.

An Act Relateing to the Seizure of Tobacco by the Sherriffe.

An Act for the better administration of Justice in probate of Wills granting Administrations, Recovering of Legacies, and secureing Filliall portions.

An Act for the Enrollement of Conveyances and securing the Estates of Purchasers.

An Act for ascertaining the Expences of the Commissioners of the Provincial and County Courts.

An Act for the due recording of all the Laws in this Province in the Secretary's Office.

An Act for the Ordering and regulating the Militia of this Province for the better defence and security thereof.

An Act for Takeing away all errors in Proceedings at Law and equity and in the Court for probate of Wills occasioned by the late Revolution.

An Act for appointing Court days in each respective County within this Province.

An Act for the Easement of the inhabitants of this Province in suites of Law for Small Debts.

An Act for preventing vexatious and unnecessary suites at Law.

An Act for Encouragement of Tillage and Raiseing Provisions for Advancement of Trade with in this Province.

An Act for the Secureing Creditors.

An Act Limiting the Extent of Attachments and provideing what shall be Leavyed on Attachements and Executions.

An Act imposing a penalty on all such who shall dispose of Tobacco Seized and Received by the Sherriffs and others.

An Act for the better administration of Justice in the County Courts of this Province.

An Act for Amerciements in the Provinciall and County Courts.

An Act for Punishment of persons Suborning of Wittnesses or Comitting wilfull and Corrupt perjury.

An Act for the preservation of orphans real Estates.

An Act directing the manner of electing and Summoning Delegates and Representatives to serve in succeeding Assemblyes.

An Act prohibiting Trade with the Indians.

An Act of Repeale of all Lawes here to fore made in this Province and Confirmeing all Lawes made this Generall Assembly.

65. Crown Officials Feud

A. EDWARD RANDOLPH'S LETTER TO WILLIAM BLATHWAYT, JUNE 28, 1692

[Toppan and Goodrick, eds., *Randolph Letters*, VII, 373-85]

I have made a cursory visite as farr as Phyladelphia, and hearing the Generall Assembly of Maryland was to sitt at St. Maryes, the 10th of May, I made my visite to Colonel Copley. He gave me a faint reception. He allowed my deputation from the Custome house, but speaks very coldly of yours. He entertaind me with grave discourse, but nothing to the purpose, but advised me to write to you that he would serve you. Once in his drink he said you were a Jacobite and a great enemy to their present Majesties. That your Commission of Auditor ought to be renewed upon their Majesties coming to the Crown. I told him my deputation was allowed of and signd by the Lords of the Treasury, and pressed him that it might be registred, but [he] refused saying it was not a proper tyme. I discoursd him about the Treasurers and receivers of the publick money of the Province, whether he found any of itt at the tyme of his arrivall. He told me he was especially commanded to take care of it and give their Majesties an Account and was very unwilling to do anything about the Deputation till he had done his busines with the Assembly.

The Cheife Tooles he works with are Blackstone, now Colonell, who before he gott to be Collector of Customs was a poor Atturney not worth a Hogshead of tobacco. Nor now if he be forcd to pay the great arreares due from him to their Majesties upon the duty of 1 penny per pound. He is a starchd, formall fellow, as great a knave but not so cunning as Mr Dudley. He is next in Councill to the Governor and carryes a great stroak amongst those silly animalls, the Councill. With their advise he has permitted 22 ships to sayle without convoy. Most of them from the Out ports came out without Licence from the Lords of the Committee. They did not passe without a decent acknowledgment to his Excellency.

His second Jac[k]all is Mr Plater, the Collector of Patuxent River. His busines has been to plye for wine, Brandee for the Governor amongst the ships. He has presented the Governor with a horse and has a young wife at his Excellency's service. The next is a dull Welch Lawyer, the Attourney Generall, made a freeman of St. Maryes, then chosen one of the Burgesses of that Corporation. He takes Entrys of retaining fees of one Hogshead of Tobacco to be paid yearely by the contentious Client, to appeare for him in all Courts *Contra omnes;* for so I saw it entred in his Alminach. He, like the Master of Ceremonyes, directs the Councill and Assembly how they are to behave themselves towards their Governor. . . .

The Governor slaves and toiles for Blackstone and Plater. Whenever I would enter upon busines with them, or examine their books and accounts, so that I could do nothing whilst the Assembly sat. . . . The Revennue of that Government is to be managed by him [Copley] and to be at his dispose. In their New Laws No person appointed to be Receiver Generall or Treasurer but himselfe and all money to be paid by his Order.

The Good methode to obtain this was managed by the great care and industry of Mr Chiselden, the Speaker, with the Attourney Generall and some others of their Caball who purged the house of all members not for their turn, tho' chosen by the far greater part of the Electors as being enemyes to their present Governors. The Merchants of London gave their Correspondents in Maryland an Account of the ill circumstances of their Governor and advised them to be good husbands of their Countryes money, thus (and for no other reason) sending home men (not papists) of good estates, ordring new writts for electing others to serve in their Rooms. During

their absence and before New ones could come the house proceeded to make their Laws which were all compleated before the New Burgesses arrived. As to the Members of the Councill you may guesse at their qualifications by the Agents they sent to England, of whom Colonel Georg Robotham (a halfe faced Quaker), Mr Tench, an Irish Merchant, and Colonel Jolls, a Surgeon are tolerable. The Rest are such a contemptable crew. . . . Butt those silly Animalls, charmd with the tedious, impertinent Haranges the Governor made them, in praise of his own meritt, parts, and interest at court, were all his humble servants (Jolls excepted, who would do nothing till often mellowed with wine and a present of 40,000 lbs. of tobacco), and now Elevated with their New Honor and 30 lbs. a yeare a peece to support it. . . . I saw better men sent back by the house of Burgesses then most of the Councill.

Now matters sett thus in tune; upon the 10th of May his Excellence, attended by the Councill, went from his appartment (a nasty, stinking Ordinary, formerly the house of Mr Calvert, the Chancellor); and the Burgesses, having notice of his being at the other house, he did bespeake them. . . . The 14 pence per Tunn upon all vessells trading in Maryland is given to their Majesties but at their dispose, out of which 350 lbs. yearely to the Councill to keep them firm to the Governors interest. The 40 shillings to be paid by the Masters for all ships trading there is given to the Governor and he is to pay his Navall Officers out of it. . . .

Besides the 240,000 lbs. of tobacco Given to the Governor, Mr Chiselden and Colonel Jolls, there is (as I am informd) an old fragment of 1,300,000 lbs. yet behind and unpaid. Captain Code is Now arrived. He must be presented with 100,000 lbs. and Major King, who attended the Agents as farr as Plymouth, is to be considered. These are the New Methods to encrease their Majesties

Revennue upon tobacco, the Inhabitants murmur. Some talke of leaving off planting. The Scotch Irish have sett up a linnen Manufacture in Summersett County, the cheife in Authority being of that nation.

Lieutenant Governor Nicholson, hearing of disturbance at the heads of Rapahannack and Patomeck Rivers, went thither, and in his Toure made Colonel Copley a visite. He was received with Complement and a larg apology for want of better accomodation. The Members of the Councill and the house of Burgesses waited upon him at his lodgings and gave him their hearty thanks for his care of them now and in the tyme of their Revolution. The next day he entertaind the Governor, Councill, and Burgesses with a very plentifull breakfast (and all well pleased but the Governor and Mr Blackstone) at my house in St Maryes. And now that I mention my house, it was thus. At my first arrivall at St Maryes I had a lodging at the Governors, but after I visited Mr Blackstone and entertaind him with melancholy discourse of Scotchmen and New England men being permitted by him to load tobacco upon slender security, and what was more affrighting to him, to enquire what money was remaining in his hands due to their Majesties upon the duty of the penny per pound, he told me he could not then give an account. The Governor, to oblige him and many of the Councill and Burgesses (who could not be satisfied to see me entertaind by the Governor) left me to lodge where I could. Blackstone having taken possession of my Chamber, I went to an old, uninhabited house which once had Glasse windows, without bed pillow or any sort of necessaryes, save onely 2 bedsteds with sacking bottoms not worth carriing away. There I lodgd, till the house of Burgesses would lett me go away. The Governor ordred a Constable to presse me a Boat to go to the Eastern shoare. They hearing I was intended to seize a Scotch ship at Delaware, would not lett him do it, so I was delayed, till upon notice sent beforehand of my coming, our Scotchman sayld away from thence loaden with tobacco 4 dayes before I could gett to the Howkill. . . .

Sir, Since there are now 3 vacancyes in the Councill of Virginia, I desire I may be appointed One there, and of Maryland also. Robotham is now going to England; Sir Thomas Laurence is not arrived. If I be made One of the Councill there [Maryland] I shall be in a condition to inform of all things. Besides, if the salary of £30 a yeare be confirmd to them of Maryland it will add to support me in my extraordinary charg of travelling. . . .

Amongst the 22 ships which sayld without convoy by Governor Copleys order were many who had not leave at home. The suing some of their Bonds will make others more carefull to observe orders. I have bespoak some ceder and will make it my business to gett what I can to adorn your House at Durham. . . .

I expect you shall receive Articles against me from Maryland because I was diligent in prosecuting my seizures. Mather and the New England agents misrepresented me to those of Maryland and some of them have been so weak as to give them creditt. So soon as the fleet is sayld I will call at St Maryes and see in what humour I shall find the Governor. I have done nothing to disoblige him nor will, but he aimes to be the sole Manager of the Countrey and Revennue, and till he be better instructed from the Lords of the Treasury it will not be otherwise.

B. Governor Copley's Letter to the Lords of Trade, July 29, 1692

[Browne, ed., *Archives of Maryland*, VIII, 335-37]

Having already rendered your Lordships an account of occurrences, and my transactions since my arrivall here, I should now forbear to give your Lordships any further trouble at this time, did not the apprehension of some malitious misrepresentation of me by Mr Rand[olph], their Majesties Surveyor in these parts, incite me thereunto, not soe much to sett forth (in its pure, natural, naked colour) the exorbitant and malignant temper of the Informer, as to vindicate and defend myselfe from his base and ignominious aspersions, he hath been pleased to caste upon me and indeed the whole Government here, which the rancour and heate of his spirit cannot prevent him from discovering even to the most mean and inconsiderate capacities notwithstanding (for the character he bears). I have proved myself more than ordinarily kind and obliging to him, to the admiration of all persons here, that ever have had the misfortune of his company or acquaintance. He is one (I must be bold to inform your Lordships) that scornes to be particular, but generall altogether in his base reflections and scurrilous haughty behaviour and deportment under the specious pretence of his zeale for their Majesties service, though at the same time the greatest impediment imaginable in the effect, and pleases himselfe more with satiateing his revengeful humour and private animosities against their Majesties subjects then effecting anything for their Majesties interest as he hath sufficiently demonstrated in the late seizure and bringing two or three shipps here, barely upon the account (as himselfe hath and doth frequently declare against all of the place and Nation in generall) of being New England rogues and doggs and pitifull damned Scotch Pedlars, and at last when he had had all the favour and countenance, aid and assistance possible shewn him, he has not stuck to vilifie and abuse the Jurors onely (persons of the best fame and repute these parts afford) by calling them base, perjured and foresworne rogues, threatening them with the pillory and loss of their ears etc., but also in publick aspersed, bespattered and affronted the Justices themselves, persons appointed by their Majesties to assist me in the Government with their Councill and advice (although basely by him said to be picked and packed by me, as were the Assembly of this Province to make such Laws as my inclinations or own private interest should dictate to them, which how farr their Majesties Honour and the interest of the Crown have had the preeminence and almost only prospect, the Laws themselves will declare in contradiction to his damnable suggestions). By such meanes their Majesties interest extremely suffers, and matters of the greatest weight, candour and truth under his management are become of little credit and repute and he himselfe so remarkable and notoriously turbulent (even to the Inhabitants here of both publick and private capacities) by pressing, seizing, and violently takeing away and makeing use of their horses, boates, goods and servants without paying or making any satisfaction for the same, otherwise than in the returne of ill language, that indeed should he bring a cause never soe plausible before any jury, though of the best principles and inclinations, his insolent and too well known behaviour would soe dimm and obscure their eyes that they could not make a right inspection thereinto but look upon the same as the effects of his hot and inveterate braine

. . . he hath indeed effected here what he hath done in all other parts of the world . . . made the whole Country weary of him. . . . I humbly beg pardon for this progression, assureing your Lordshipps that the vindication of myself and those Gentlemen of their Majesties Councill assigned me here (whom I find to be persons of loyalty, candour and integrity) from the vile calumnies and aspersions of soe ungrateful and turbulent a man as he is, that they may have noe effect or influence upon your Lordshipps to our prejudice without better proofe then his base allegations.

66. A Scramble for Perquisites and Patronage

A. A Letter from the Governor and Council of Maryland to the Lords of Trade, October 14, 1692

[Browne, ed., *Archives of Maryland*, VIII, 414-17]

Since the Departure of the grand Fleet from hence we have not had an oppertunity of giving your Lordships any Account of Affairs in these parts. Neither indeed hath any thing of moment offered worthy your considerations till of Late since the arrivall of Sir Thomas Lawrence, their Majestys Secretary for this Province, who hath given us occasion to render your Lordships the following Account particularly of himself and his proceedings here. How far they are pursuant or consonant to his Commission and Instructions we humbly refer to your Lordships better Judgment and Determination. Soon after his arrivall here he applyed himself to us, their Majestys Governor and Councill of this Province, and produced his Commission and Instructions relating to his Office. To which we readily yielded all due respect and he was accordingly admitted and sworn Secretary, one of the Councill, and Justice of the Provinciall Court, since which without having given any Security for the due and true Performance and Execution of his Office of so great trust and moment according to the custom and usage of this and others their Majestys Collonys and Plantations as was required of him fully to Capaciate himself for that Office, he hath presumed of himself to exercise his Authority in manner following. . .

In the first Place, having made diligent scrutiny and Inquest and by that means throughly informed himself of the annual perquisits of the ten respective Clerks places of this Province, he hath taken and seized into his hands three of the best and most Principal places managed by the most expert, able, and choice Clerks, men who had faithfully and diligently served their Majestys, been obedient to the Government and well Behaved themselves in their places to the generall Satisfaction of the Country, whom he hath discarded upon no other reason or pretence whatsoever (that himself can or doth alledge) then his own power and perogative to make a vacancy and supply the same when and as he pleases. One of the said Places he has conferred upon his Son, under Age, to be managed for him by a deputy whom he brought with him for that purpose. Another of them he hath conferred upon another of his creatures he brought in with him to be also managed by a Deputy as not at present capable of Officiating himself. And on the third he hath laid a reserve, for whom it is not yet Certainly known, but as is generally reported and given out to be executed by some mercenary person for his own private use and Benefitt, altho himself at his arrivall was pleased to declare that no Person was to be employed in any of the said Places that cou'd not officiate himself in Person, for deputys were in no wise (according to his Instructions) to be allowed of, and under that Pretence with his own Authority aforesaid displaced the three aforesaid most Considerable Clerks. Others of the old Clerks he has treated with and of all demands an account of their perquisits since the date of his Commission, for which he pretends they are to be accountable to him and not only so but must pay him also considerably for their Commissions which he hath extorted. . . . By the express words of his Commission he is no Longer nor no otherwise Secretary then during the Kings pleasure and his Residence in this Province notwithstanding also, his said Commission possitively forbids the making Sale of any the said places or any other profitt thereby then the reservation of the tenth part of the annual Incomes to be estimated by the Governor and Councill upon a vacancy and no more. These Contrary Proceedings of Sir Thomas are resented by the People in generall as very grievous and burdensome and call for our Representation thereof to your Lordships for redress. We are told of and expect daily Complaints from the Commissioners of the County Courts touching the Insufficiency of their new imposed Clerks and the turning out of those of whose abilitys and integretys they have had so good Proof and Experience: Nor indeed can we much admire at these irregular and unwarrantable proceedings of Sir Thomas since we find him associating, caballing, and advising and indeed conversing with none

but the Kings open professed Enemies and Malignants to the present Government who insinuate nothing into him but Lyes and Fallacies relating to his Office and the prequisits thereof; how the same have been managed under the late Popish, Arbitrary Government and put him upon these exorbitant measures to satisfy his avaritious and greedy appetite. With such society and advice he is so far taken up and possessed that he hath in a manner deserted and alienated himself from any of our Consultations and stands as it were at a distance from, and in defiance of the Government, seeking all oppertunitys of Complaints against the same tho never so unjust and Fictious; Insomuch that having calmly and candidly debated in Councill the Fees and perquisits properly belonging and incident to his Office, whereby to ascertain and Distinguish the same from those appropriated to others Offices, we at last proposed to refer the same to the consideration and Decision of the Assembly who were the best Interpreters of the Laws themselves made. From this he violently flew of[f] and threatned to protest against the same as well as against the Laws themselves because they Corresponded not with his Ravenous Expectation and Inclinations aforesaid, having Valued himself at least a Thousand Pounds Sterling at Sight upon the Bare disposition of the Clerks Places, as (is said) himself hath reported and upon the least occasion though never so trivial, speakes of nothing less than appealing to the King and Councill, and this so publickly that he gives occasion to other malignants as well as himself to set at nought and have in Contempt the Authority of this their Majestys Government.

B. THE PETITION OF SIR THOMAS LAWRENCE, SECRETARY OF MARYLAND, TO THE CROWN, 1692

[Browne, ed., *Archives of Maryland*, VIII, 450-52]

Your Majesty having been graciously pleased by your Letters Patents bearing date the 5th day of September 1691, to grant unto your Petitioner the Office and place of Secretary of Mariland in America with all rights, Priviledges, Profits, Perquisites and advantages to the said Office belonging, incident or in any wise appertaining, Your Petitioner prepared himself with all diligence for his voyage thither, but was not able by reason of severall disappointments and a long continuance on board the Wolf from the 12th of April to the 30th of August, to come into Mariland from New York untill the 16th day of September last 1962.

At his arrivall your Petitioner was much surprised to find all advantages taken against him and his Office in his absence, for by one Act of the Generall Assembly of this Province held the 10th of May last at St Mary's, entituled an Act for settling of the Naval Officers Fees within this Province, the yearly income of clearing of ships, which in that very Act is called Secretary's Fees, and which were payable by a Law to the Secretary from the year 1662 to the year 1676, are now made payable by a Fee of forty shillings for every vessell to His Excellency the Governour. And also by another Act of the same late Assembly called an Act for regulating Ordinaries, all the benefitt of licencing them through this Province which had for 14 or 15 years last past to the beginning of the late Revolution, been collected by the Sheriffs and paid for the Ordinary Keepers to the Secretarys proper use, is now also vested in the Governor, to his [the Secretary's] yearly loss of at least one hundred and fifty pounds sterling. Both which Lawes were in June last sent over for your Majesty's confirmation.

And whereas by one other Law passed in the same Generall Assembly termed An Act for limitation of Officers Fees, the Fees and chief profits of the Secretary are enacted and confirmed in the very same words and manner as they have stood for many years past, His Excellency notwithstanding by a single Order of Council dated the 17th of August 1692 hath thought fitt, contrary to that Law to appoint that all the Writts called Chancery Writts, always issuable, and now going out of the Secretary's Office should thenceforth issue out of Chancery, and the Fees thereunto belonging to be paid to the present Chancelor (now Colonel Jeremiah Blakiston), who of a bare ministerial Officer and Keeper of the Seal, as by his Fees in the late Law sett down appears, is now made sole Judge in Chancery, though at the same time, he sits next Commissioner to the Governor in the Provinciall Court, Supreme Court of Common Law, which said Order though not yet put in execution, is by another late Order affirmed to be fitt and just, but referred to the next Sessions in April following, though within the three years to be enacted and confirmed. And your Petitioner is also ordered to abide by their determination, and also to refer himself to the said Assembly touching two thousand pounds security, which His Excellency and the Councill have already judged fitt he should enter into, for the true performance of his Office; a precedent wholy new and never practised in this Province, nor possible for him a stranger to comply with.

Your Majesty's Petitioner therefore, his Protestation not being admitted in Councill, doth humbly cast himself at Your Majesty's feet and doth protest and appeal to Your Majesty against these hardships and unusual practises, which he cannot but think illegal, and doth humbly pray that he may quietly enjoy what the former Secretarys always had, and what Your Majesty by your Letters Patents hath been graciously pleased to grant him, and that Your Majesty would please to confirm to him the benefitt of either of the two Laws of Naval Officer or Licencer of the Ordinarys, one of which or other was always belonging to his Office. That Your Majesty would please to command the said Order of the 17th of August to be recalled and vacuated and to order your Petitioner to give such security for the true discharge of his Office as former Secretarys of this Province have given, or as he reasonably may or ought to give.

67. The Shift of the Capital from St. Mary's to Annapolis

A. THE ADDRESS OF THE MAYOR, OFFICIALS, AND FREEMEN OF ST. MARY'S TO GOVERNOR NICHOLSON, OCTOBER 1694

[Browne, ed., *Archives of Maryland*, XIX, 71-74]

They proceed humbly to Supplicate your Excellencies grace and Favour in granting and Continuing to them their antient Franchises, rights, and priviledges granted them by their Charter, with such other benefitts and advantages as hath been accustomed and usually allowed and from time to time confirmed to them by your predecessors, Governors and Rulors of this province, humbly Offering and proposeing to your Excellencyes these following reasons. . . .

Imprimis: As that it was the prime and originall Settlement of this Province and from the first Seateing thereof for above Sixty yeares hath been the Antient and Chiefe Seate of Government.

2. In consideration whereof the Lord Baltemore by his Letters pattents did incorporate and constitute the same a City with Severall immunityes, rights, benefitts, and priviledges thereunto belonging, above and beyond all other parts and places of the province.

3. The Scituation in it Selfe is most pleasant and healthfull and naturally commodious in all Respects for the purpose, being plentifully and well watered with good and wholesome Springs, almost encompassed round with Harbour for Shipping where Five hundred Saile of Shipps at Least may securely ride at Anchor before the City, haveing alsoe most sutable and convenient points of Land and proper places for Erecting and building of Forts, block houses, and Other Fortifications and Edifices for the Security and Defence of such Shipping, the keeping and preserveing the publick Magazine and the Records of the Province.

4. And as such and for divers other reasons then appeareing, in the yeare 1662 a convenient part or portion of the said Land was by the representative body of the province bought and purchased for the building of a State house and prison, and twelve yeare after, to wit Anno 1674, his Lordshipp, by and with the advice and consent of the representative body of this province, passed An Act for the building of a State house and prison in the said place which cost the Countrey at that time three hundred and thirty thousand pounds of tobacco. . . .

12. It hath hardly been knowne and indeed Scarce any president can be produced of soe Sudden a change as the removeall of the antient and Chiefe Seate of Government upon the bare sug-

gestion and Allegations of some particular persons for their owne private Interest and Advantage. Neither is it in the power wee humbly conceive of the Subject, but the prerogative Royal invested in your Excellencie as their Majesties Lieutenant, at whose feete we humbly cast our selves for Releife and Support against the Calamitys and ruin wherewith wee are threatened, wholly relying upon your Excellencies grace and favour therein, with whome wee alsoe conceive should be good manners in all persons first to treate and interceed before they presume to make any peremptory result in a case of soe high a Nature as this may be.

13. Wee cannot omitt to represent to your Excellencie that the very last Assembly held in the time of the late deceased Governor, Anno 1692: It was then put to the Vote of a full house whether the holding of Courts and Assemblyes at St Maries were a greviance or not and carried in the Negative.

14. At which time Wee humbly conceive that house did well consider all difficulties as well as the vast charge and Expence they already had been at (to noe purpose if the Courts etc should be removed) as alsoe what must Necessarily follow (and it may be to as little purpose) in building of New Courts and Offices in other places and makeing provisions for the holding and keeping the same, besides the hazard and casualties of removeing and transporting the Records from one place to another of which already some Experience hath been had. . . .

16. That [as for] the Scituation of the place [St. Mary's] being not in the Center of the province and consequently not soe convenient for some persons to apply to. . . . Wee humbly represent Even the place of our Nativity the Kingdom of England and the Imperiall Court their held in the City of London, as far from the center of England, as St Maries in this Province . . . and almost all other their Majesties American plantations where are still kept and continued in their first, antient Stations and places the Chiefe Seat of Government and Courts of Judicature.

B. THE ANSWER OF THE ASSEMBLY, OCTOBER 11, 1694

[Browne, ed., *Archives of Maryland*, XIX, 76-77]

This House have read and considered of the petitions and Reasons of the Mayor, Aldermen, and others calling themselves Common Councill and Freemen of the City of St Maries against removeing the Courts and Assemblyes from this Corner and poorest place of the province to the Center and best abilitated places thereof. Although wee conceive the motives there laid downe are hardly deserveing any Answer at all, many of them being against the plaine matter of Fact, some against reason, and all against the Generall good and well faire of the province, Yet, because your Excellency has been pleased to lay them before us, wee humbly returne this our sence of the same. That as to the . . . [first eight] Reasons relateing to what his Lordship has thought fitt to doe to the Citty of St Maries, it is noe rule nor Guide to their Majesties, your Excellencie, nor this house. Itt seemes in some parts to reflect on his Lordship more then this house beleives is true or deserved by his Lordship. . . .

To the 12: 13: and 14: they say that they doe not hold themselves accountable to the Mayor and his Bretheren for what they doe for their Countreys Service, nor by what Measures they doe the same, nor what time they shall take to doe it in, nor for what Reasons, and are and will be as carefull of the Records and properties of the people as the petitioners. . . .

To the 16: this house conceive that the Citty of St Maries is very Unequally Rankt with London, Boston, Port Royall etc.

The Religious Settlement

68. The Church of England Established

A. A Quaker Dissent, 1695

[A Petition from the Quakers of Maryland to the Governor and Assembly, 1695, W. S. Perry, ed., *Papers Relating to the History of the Church in Maryland, 1694-1775* (n.p., 1878), 4-8]

It hath been sufficiently known that we have been a suffering people, both in our persons and estates, ever since the Lord was pleased to raise us up to be a people, and particularly in discharge of their consciences to God, in refusing of all Oaths whatsoever, which command of Christ we dare not disobey. . . .

For, first: If any of us be called to answer to any Bill framed against us in Chancery, allthough in obedience to the Summons we do appear, and are ready to give our testimony according to the truth of the Case and best of our knowledge, yet because we cannot take the formal Oath, and Attachment is granted forth against such of us concerned; and because we cannot yet answer according to form, a Writ of Rebellion comes forth against such, whereby both persons, estate, wife, and children may be brought to ruin.

Secondly: When any of us do die intestate, as sometimes it happens, our wives, who, for conscience sake, can not swear, are therefore put by the Administration of their deceased Husband's estate, and a stranger perhaps suffered to administer, to the great injury of the Widow and Orphans.

Thirdly: If any of us . . . be nominated executors in trust or by right of law and equity ought to have administered as being greatest Creditor, yet forasmuch as we cannot swear, we are therefore put by and made incapable either to serve our deceased friend, or to get our just debt, which have been of very evil consequences to many.

Fourthly: We are made answerable to our neighbours in divers respects, for if we are called to bear witness to the truth of controversys, which often happens amongst Neighbours, and because we cannot take an Oath, our neighbours' just Case suffers.

Fifthly: If any of us are inclined to use the way of merchandize, either for ourselves or as factors for others, yet divers of us, seeing the great inconveniences that may fall because we cannot swear, have therefore in great part forborn that way of trading, which might not only have been beneficial to themselves, but advantageous to the province, for if a person die in either of our debts, his executors or administrators perhaps put us to prove the debt, which, if it is per account, we cannot do, and if it be per Bill or Bond, perhaps we are put to swear that we never received any part or parcel, which we can not do, although we know in our consciences we have not, and although the honest judge may be persuaded that we are wronged, yet knows not how to right us.

Sixthly: We are in many cases answerable to the King and the Government, for although we are a considerable Member of this province, and in many respects might be serviceable both to the King and Inhabitants, according as our capacities might be thought fit, yet because we cannot swear, we are therefore made almost as a useless member, and not capable to be helpful and an use to our neighbours, nor pay our services due to the King. And if any of us should happen to hear any seditious words, or know of any private intention to Rebellion against the King or Government, or for any felonious Act committed, yet may we not, without great danger to ourselves, discover these things, because we cannot give such formal testimony, as the law requires; the partys perhaps may by law be cleared of the fact only for want of such formal testimonys, and then bring their Action against us as Slanderers.

These things we do in humble manner lay before you, desiring that our suffering Case may be taken into your most serious consideration, and that a law may be made in this province, whereby we may be eased of the mischiefs which we suffer upon the Account of Oaths, and that our solemn attestation or denial may be taken instead of an Oath, and that in case any pretending tenderness of conscience in the case of Oaths, shall be found to falsify their solemn attestation, that then they suffer the pains and penalties of perjury.

The next thing we have at this time to lay before you, is the suffering we are under by reason of a late Act which enjoyns [us] to pay a certain tax towards the building of Churches . . . and maintaining of those called Ministers, which for pure confidence to God we can not do, but must forever bear our testimony against all such as preach for hire, knowing that the Ministers of Christ never preached any such thing: by reason of which we suffer and our goods are seized and taken from us.

B. A LETTER FROM THE ANGLICAN CLERGY IN MARYLAND TO THE BISHOP OF LONDON, MAY 18, 1696

[Perry, ed., *Papers Relating to the History of the Church in Maryland, 1694-1775,* 8-13]

We, your Lordship's most dutiful inferior Clergy of the Church of England, living in His Majesty's Province of Maryland, being removed at so great a distance from your Lordship's personal inspection and care over us, that we are debarred the privilege of making our frequent applications to your Lordship for advice and instructions in the managing ourselves in our Cures where Providence hath placed us, do humbly presume to trouble your Lordship with an account of our present state. . . .

When His Excellency, Governor Nicholson, came into the Country in the year 1694, there were but 3 Clergymen in Episcopal Orders, besides 5 or 6 popish priests, who had perverted divers idle people from the Protestant Religion. There was also a sort of wandering pretenders to preaching that came from New England and other places; which deluded not only the Protestant Dissenters from our Church but many of the Churchmen themselves, by their extemporary prayers and preachments, for which they were admitted by the people and got money of them. . . .

His Excellency, upon his arrival with several of us that waited on him to his Government in Maryland, continued those 3 Clergymen in their places where he found them. And he having (as we are bound in confidence to God, and must in honour to his Excellency's name confess), with all possible care and expedition erected Churches in most parishes proportionable to the quantity of those sums of Tobacco that were in arrears in the Sheriffs' or Vestrymen's hands ever since the Act for 40 lbs. Tobacco per poll made in Governor Copley's days, placed us in the best vacancies (as he hath since done by others coming with your Lordship's permit) that were most convenient for the more general serving of the Country. . . .

Tobacco being the one and only staple commodity of the Country, is that out of which our small incomes are paid, the manner of which is thus: Every planter, for himself and his male children and White Servant-Man, as also for his Negro Slaves (both male and female), after their age of 16 years, is assessed 40 lbs. Tobacco per poll, demandable in the Winter Quarter upon execution by the Sheriff; 5 lb. in the hundred being deducted for his trouble in collecting it, and 1,000 lbs., by a late Act of Assembly, being also deducted towards the maintenance of a Parish and Vestry Clerk, which was not provided for in the Act made for the support of a regular Clergy, in Governor Copley's time. But some of us are forced to give 2,000 lbs. to the Clerks by reason of their going so far to do their Dutys on the Lords's Day.

The tobacco which is raised by the Public levy of the 40 lbs. per poll for secular offices and other charges of the Country, is generally freighted by the English merchants, being not reckoned (when received) to be worth above one fourth part of that (quantity for quantity) which the Planters cure (as they term it) or manage for their own freight and Sale; the reason for which the Public Tobacco is generally freighted is that the Planters cull the best of their Crop for their own freighting, or selling it for Goods or Bills of Exchange; and kept the refuse and discoloured Tobacco to pay the Sheriffs for their taxes and Duty.

The Merchants are not for meddling with this Tobacco, not only because it is much worse than the other, but because it is generally very troublesome for them to get it paid in any reasonable time, and that often they cannot get it at all, wholly losing their time and labour in going from place to place to demand it of those Planters to whom the Sheriffs send them.

That it is a great and inevitable damage, and forebodes a total disappointment of such as have their dependence on the public pay of the Country.

The extent of our Parish is generally very large, some of them being about 20 from 30 miles in length; by reason of the Inhabitants of this Country having (many of them) vast tracts of land, live at least a mile asunder from their next neighbours. This large extent of Parishes obligeth us to keep one, or sometimes two horses to ride on. The charges of our Board and keeping our horses take up one fourth of our greatest Incomes, and the remaining 3 parts (considering the rate we pay for English Goods in the stores, and that the Merchants will allow us in goods at prime cost, very rarely a penny and sometimes but an halfpenny or a farthing a Pound for our Tobacco in bartering with them) will hardly find us with Clothes and other necessaries. If we have any overplus when our necessaries and conveniences are served, it's hazardous for us to freight it, lest it should prove a drug in the English or Holland Markets, and by paying from 10 sometimes to £16 Sterling per Ton for freight, besides the King's Custom, etc., it should bring us in debt.

So that should some of us that have wives in England send for them, and go to house keeping, we could not tell how to maintain them here, not yet being provided any Minister's House and Glebe, except at St. Mary's. . . .

But notwithstanding that small provision which is made for your Lordship's Clergy, and the precariousness and great uncertainty of the tenure of what we have, the Papists and Quakers (of both which there are some of the richest men in the province) are much dissatisfied.

And we have lately received very certain advice from London that those of our Quakers that went for England in the last Maryland and Virginia fleet have petitioned the Lords of the Committee of Trade and Foreign Plantations to have the 40 lbs. per Poll taken off as a burden upon their estates and (as we suppose they might pretend) upon their consciences too.

Should they obtain their petitions only for themselves, the incomes of some of the best Parishes, in respect of the Tobacco raised by the 40 lbs. per poll, would be so impaired that there would not be left a tolerable subsistence for a single Clergyman and his horse. . . .

Could the Quakers clear themselves of the 40 lbs. per poll, the Papists might all pretend to do so too, because they have Priests of their own to provide for; and could both these parties effect their designs, the Clergy and Church of England would be left in a very naked and poor condition here, besides that we might expect many that have their religion still to choose, would turn either Papist or Quakers, and refuse to pay too, for many of them look upon the Sacraments as needless impositions, and go neither to the Papists' Mass nor the Quakers' meetings, and seldom or ever to Church.

Now we become most humble petitioners to your Lordship, that if there should be occasion (as we have reason to fear there is) your Lordship would be pleased to espouse our Cause, and intercede with His Most Gracious Majesty that we may not be wholly discouraged from staying in these parts of the English Empire, and preaching the Gospel here, as well as the Papists and Presbyterians and Quakers do after their manner, and our just hopes, and that we shall not be thought much worse by great good and wise persons, for the Quakers' insinuations against us behind our backs, which

we doubt not have been as maliciously as cunningly contrived.

We hope your Lordship will be likewise pleased upon occasion to make such further intercession for us with His Majesty as that we may not be prejudged before we have each to answer for ourselves, both against Papists and Quakers, either by writing or by proxies, when we shall know the particulars of their pretended advances, and what may be falsely said against us by those two inveterate enemies to the Church of England.

May it please your Lordship, as far removed as the Quakers and Papists seem to be in their different sentiments about religion, they are jointly bent against our Church, and daily endeavour to draw people to their parties, by suggesting to them that Lord Baltimore will govern here again; than which nothing can be more pleasing news to libertines and loose persons, who can seldom or never be gotten to come to Church at all. And should my Lord rule as formerly, the insolence of the Romish priests (who are somewhat curbed by his Excellency's great care and vigilance) would soon be intolerable in these parts, that are so remote from England.

Besides there being great numbers of Irish Papists brought continually into this province, and many Irish Priests being suspected to be coming incognito among us (as having no better place of refuge in the King's Dominions) upon their being banished from Ireland, there is great reason to fear there will be as much discouragement and danger coming upon all his Majesty's good Protestant subjects here as upon the English Clergy.

This expectation of the Lord Baltimore's being restored to the Government of Maryland animates the Priests and Jesuits to begin already to inveigle several ignorant people to turn to their religion. To which end they do (contrary to the Act of Parliament to deter them from perverting any of His Majesty's Protestant subjects to popery) introduce themselves into the Company of the sick, when they have no Ministers, that his Excellency hath been lately forced to issue out his proclamation against their so doing, to restrain them.

The Revolutionary Settlement: Fragility and Stability

69. Factionalism Renewed, 1693

[H. R. McIlwaine and W. L. Hall, eds., *Executive Journals of the Council of Colonial Virginia, 1680-1754*, 5 vols. (Richmond, 1925-45), I, 298]

Upon Reading a Letter from Richard Lee, Esqr., bearing date the 18th of Sept 1693, Acquainting His Excellency that he had Just received advice from Maryland, that Colonel Copley the Governor of that Province, departed this life that day seavennight, that Colonel Blackston imediately came down to St Maries, upon itt, and sent for two of the Councill, Mr Tench and Colonel Greenbury. Butt before their Coming he declared, that the Assembley was dissolved by the Death of the Governor and all Commissions, Civill and military, fallen, that Sir Thomas Lawrence was suffered to Escape by the Sheriff, leaving the doore open, and biding him go att his perill, that he made hast to St Maries, haveing Captain Coode and others in his Company, that he was there Attacked by order of Colonel Blackston but delivered next day; that both Blackston and Sir Thomas Claim the Government,

Sir Thomas by being President of the Councill, Colonel Blackston by the last Will and Testament of Governor Copley. Not knowing how far the destractions amongst them, might Concerne soe near Neighbours as this Countrey is to them, he thought itt his Duty to Acquaint His Excellency with what he had heard. Upon which His Excellency caused to be read in Councill, Their Majesties Commission to His Excellency bearing date at Kensinton the third day of March 1691-2 Constituting and Appointing, His Excellency, Sir Edmond Andros, upon the Death of Captain Francis Nicholson, or in the Absence of Colonel Lyonell Copley, to be Comander in Cheife, in and Over the said Province and Teritory of Maryland, during their Majesties pleasure, with all the Rights, profitts and advantages, to the same belonging, and apperteining.

70. Governor Nicholson Summarizes the Situation in Maryland, 1697

[Governor Nicholson to the Council of Trade and Plantations, Mar. 27, 1697, W. Noel Sainsbury *et al.*, eds., *Calendar of State Papers, Colonial Series, America and West Indies, 1696-97*, No. 862]

First I give a brief account of this province before the Revolution. While Lord Baltimore resided here all things were pretty quiet, but on his departure he left the Government in the hands of the Council, the principal of which were

papists. They had generally the places of profit and trust; and there were Quakers in the Assembly and other places of Government. The Church government was in the hands of Jesuits and priests, and their chief residence was within two miles of St. Maries, where they had a good brick chapel, and five or six wooden ones in other parts of the country. Of priests and Jesuits there are commonly six or seven in the country, and they have several good plantations to live upon; but I suppose they have allowances from England and other places and from the people of their persuasion in the Colony. The Quakers are also dispersed all over the country, but are more numerous and have more places of worship. There were seldom above three or four clergymen of the Church of England resident in the country, and they were maintained only by voluntary contributions, by which also their places of worship were built. Sabbath-breaking, cursing, swearing and profane talking, whoring and drinking (especially the last) were much practised; some of the men having two wives and some of the women two husbands; and such sins were seldom punished. Five schools there were, and those very mean ones either for master or house; but the Jesuits had some, especially one brick one at St. Maries. After Lord Baltimore's departure the Courts of Justice were very dilatory, and though people were fined by law and became sureties for one another, as also for strangers in Navigation bonds and other matters, yet the fines were seldom collected or the bonds seldom put in suit. I suppose the Jesuits and priests were willing to have a very loose Government both in Church and State, that they might bring the people to be Atheists in order to make them Papists; wherein they would have met with no great opposition, for the country was first seated by but an indifferent set of people.

Between the time of Lord Baltimore's Government and Governor Copley's arrival, things were very unsettled and the Government very loose. The public debts grew great and others also, especially those to Lord Baltimore on account of quit-rents. While Governor Copley lived the debts were not paid, nor during Sir Edmund Andros's Government, though there is an annual charge for the support of the Council, Burgesses, Rangers, Justices and County Courts, paid in tobacco and levied *per* poll; hence when I arrived I found the country much in debt and illsettled alike in church, civil and military government. But I have endeavoured to model them, as my letters and the public records will shew. . . . In Governor Copley's time a law was passed for establishing the Church of England, which was disallowed by the King. Another is now sent, and the Journals of Assembly will show how great were my difficulties with it. When I came I found few of the churches built according to the former Act of Assembly, but I hope that they will be finished this year, and then we shall want clergymen and a commissary, for whose maintenance an Act is now sent to you. . . . There is often, and now especially, great want of good clergymen and schoolmasters in these parts, and I will not venture to answer for some of their abilities, lives and conversations. . . .

I enclose a list of the Council. Several of the inhabitants are not qualified to serve the King in any employment, which makes it difficult to supply it with good men, but I have given the names of some. . . .

The reason why the inhabitants leave this province is, I think, the encouragement which they receive from the Carolinas, the Jerseys and above all from Pennsylvania, which is so nigh that it is easy to remove thither. There handicraft tradesmen have encouragement where they endeavour to set up woollen manufactures, and there is great encouragement for illegal traders and privateers, or rather pirates, which causes many men to run from the King's ships, especially from the Virginia and Maryland convoys and also from the merchant ships. This is one reason why they are long in loading, especially this year, for I have accounts that over one hundred seamen have left this fleet. . . .

But unless there be some naval force to secure this whole bay, it is morally impossible to secure it otherwise. Every river and creek are harbours, and most people have landing-places at their plantations. To make tenable forts would cost a great deal of money—I reckon that one good one would cost £4,000—and it would secure only one river, if that, while to keep it in repair would be more chargeable than in England, for all buildings decay sooner here. To make wooden platforms or batteries (as they here call them) would be so much money thrown away, for I have seen some of this foolish sort of fortifications spoiled before they were finished. Again, such fortifications may be a danger as encouraging not only an enemy, who can easily seize them, but also rebellion, when they can be mastered at little hazard. But a naval force, if it include a fire-ship, or at any rate materials for making fire-ships, will I think hinder illegal traders, keep the country in awe, and protect us from pirates.

I have endeavoured to hinder illegal trade, but have met with great difficulties, especially in the Courts and the Assembly. I enclose a copy of an address to the King about the navigation bonds and a paper from the Committee of Grievances, with two others. They complain of the security required, because I had ordered the Collectors not to accept such poor securities as formerly. The oath is that masters and others who take an account of ships shall give an account on oath of the number of hogsheads and great quantity of bulk tobacco, paying no duty for them, which I think is a fair step to their running tobacco when in England. A great means to check illegal trading and secure the King's Customs would be the appointing of a few certain places for all ships to load and unload at. . . . I believe that it will be found, if examination be made, that the Acts of Trade and Navigation are oftener broken than kept there. . . .

The bounds between Maryland and Pennsylvania are very uncertain, especially in the three lower counties in the territory of Newcastle [Delaware]. In King James's time there was a dispute between Lord Baltimore and Mr. Penn, and I have seen copy of an Order in Council to divide the provinces, but I do not find that the line was ever run. Several of Pennsylvania have tried to encroach upon Maryland, but I shall not be wanting to defend the King's right. I believe it would be for the welfare not only of the King's interest but of both provinces if the boundaries were settled, but I propose that they should not be adjusted until enquiry has been made in these parts, for then the upper part of the bay might be well-seated, and be a check to the Pennsylvanians. . . . Some persons have taken up great quantities of land both in Virginia and Maryland, of whom few or none are able to improve it all, and this is one great reason why young English Colonists and freed servants leave these Colonies and go either Southward or Northward; for they are naturally ambitious to be landlords, not tenants. Unless I am much mistaken there is little land to be taken up either in Virginia or Maryland except it be several miles beyond any of the inhabitants. Those distant and straggling plantations, where there is often not above one or two men, sometimes tempt the Indians to murder and plunder, while they are on their hunting expeditions or going to or returning from them. . . .

I would humbly propose that the King should grant an Act of pardon to this province. It has only lately been taken under his immediate Government. The former Government was very loose, and may have been guilty of crimes which they generally pretend were not from disobedience to the laws but from not being used to them. They therefore hope that the King will forgive them.

THE REVOLUTIONARY
SETTLEMENT IN AMERICA

THE American revolutions of 1689 had major consequences for the English colonies and the British Empire in the eighteenth century. The Dominion concept of colonial unification was reluctantly discarded, and recognition of colonies as separate units became the settled policy of the English government. Although Massachusetts failed in its quest for the restoration of its original charter, it received a new charter as a royal colony in 1691. At the same time that it lost its status as an independent republican commonwealth, however, it won a privilege which no other royal colony enjoyed—a council elected by the lower house. New York, also rid of the Dominion, returned to its individual existence as a royal colony and was granted an assembly in Governor Sloughter's instructions, although the Crown continued to muster the military authority of the northern colonies by giving the governor of New York additional authority over neighboring colonies. In Maryland, where the revolutionary program coincided with William and Mary's animosity for proprietary governments, the insurrectionaries gained complete approbation. Royal government replaced political control by the Calverts for a generation, although the proprietor retained title to the soil.

The orientation of political factions within Maryland, New York, and Massachusetts was determined for many years by the events of 1689. The history of the lower house in Massachusetts swirled about the figure of Elisha Cooke, who stood at the head of that faction which in 1689 and afterwards sought complete independence from English control. In New York the enmities engendered by Jacob Leisler's rule during 1689-91 determined local political alliances and even swept up successive royal governors as partisans of one side or the other. In Maryland, although the proprietor was restored in 1715, the impetus given to self-government in 1689 continued as the main line of political development down to the War for Independence.

In English colonial policy the Glorious Revolution also altered the relations of the colonies to the mother country and the course of political development in the different colonies. The diverse experiments with the structure of colonial governments which characterized the seventeenth century were replaced in the recently rebellious colonies by a set of standard governmental agencies: a royal governor, an appointive council—except in Massachusetts where it was elective—and an elective assembly. The principle of representative government, re-established by the rebels in Massachusetts, New York, and Maryland, gave an underlying similarity to colonial political institutions; for the first time, such disparate colonies as proprietary Maryland, royal New York, and independent Massachusetts turned in the same direction at the same time.

The familiar balance between governor, council, and representative assembly which became the normal pattern was a compromise between demands in each of the colonies for representative self-government on the one hand and the desire of the royal government in London for an efficient and centralized colonial administration under the authority of the King on the other. Paradoxically, the Glorious Revolution, which overthrew the theory of divine right monarchy in England, was followed by an expansion of royal prerogative in the colonies. William and Mary, like Charles II and James II, tried repeatedly to systematize colonial administration under the direct control of the Crown. That British imperial policy had not changed was most clearly demonstrated by Parliament's passage of the Navigation Act of 1696, which greatly increased the King's prerogative power in America, and by the creation of the Board of Trade and Plantations by royal edict in the same year.

In 1689 the great majority of colonists allied themselves with the principles and fortunes of Parliament. The history of the growth of power in the lower houses in the American colonies is an analogue of the expansion of Parliamentary power in England. Had Massachusetts, New York, and Maryland not rebelled when they did, there is every reason to believe that the aggressive centralizing forces of the executive bureaucracy in London would have dominated the constitution of the empire in America. Then uniformity, administrative efficiency, and subordination to the Crown and its agencies would have characterized eighteenth-century American politics. But the revolutions of 1689 made this unlikely. Instead particularism, local representative government, and an ever-growing strength of the legislative power were the characteristic features of the years after 1689.

By shaping a set of imperial relationships and by defining the rights, liberties, and privileges of American subjects, the revolutionary movements of 1689 made possible the formation of the First British Empire. Only when Parliament made an effort after 1763 to alter the pattern created in the 1690's—to reorganize the relationships and rights —did the old empire begin to disintegrate. When that occurred, the colonists fell back on a heritage of rights and privileges of Englishmen, rights and privileges which had been developed by the Americans continuously since 1689. But that involved another—and for the Americans, a greater—Revolution.

SUGGESTED READINGS

A. GENERAL:

Charles M. Andrews, *The Colonial Period of American History*, 4 vols. (New Haven, 1934-38)

Charles M. Andrews, ed., *Narratives of the Insurrections, 1675-1690* (New York, 1915)

Herbert L. Osgood, *The American Colonies in the Eighteenth Century*, 4 vols. (New York, 1924)

A. P. Thornton, *West-Indian Policy under the Restoration* (Oxford, Eng., 1956)

B. NEW ENGLAND:

Bernard Bailyn, *The New England Merchants in the Seventeenth Century* (Cambridge, Mass., 1955)

Viola F. Barnes, *The Dominion of New England: A Study in British Colonial Policy* (New Haven, 1923)

Michael G. Hall, *Edward Randolph and the American Colonies, 1676-1703* (Chapel Hill, 1960)

Thomas Hutchinson, *The History of the Colony and Province of Massachusetts Bay*, ed. Lawrence S. Mayo, 3 vols. (Cambridge, Mass., 1936)

Everett Kimball, *The Public Life of Joseph Dudley: A Study of the Colonial Policy of the Stuarts in New England, 1660-1715* (New York, 1911)

Kenneth B. Murdock, *Increase Mather, The Foremost American Puritan* (Cambridge, Mass., 1925)

C. NEW YORK:

John R. Brodhead, *History of the State of New York*, 2 vols. (New York, 1871)

Lawrence H. Leder, ed., "Records of the Trials of Jacob Leisler and His Associates," New-York Historical Society, *Quarterly*, 36 (1952), 431-57

Lawrence H. Leder, *Robert Livingston, 1654-1728, and the Politics of Colonial New York* (Chapel Hill, 1961)

Bernard Mason, "Aspects of the New York Revolt of 1689," *New York History*, 30 (1949), 165-80

Jerome R. Reich, *Leisler's Rebellion: A Study of Democracy in New York, 1664-1720* (Chicago, 1953)

Mariana (Mrs. Schuyler) Van Rensselaer, *History of the City of New York in the Seventeenth Century*, 2 vols. (New York, 1909)

D. MARYLAND:

Wesley Frank Craven, *The Southern Colonies in the Seventeenth Century* (Baton Rouge, 1949)

Michael G. Kammen, "The Causes of the Maryland Revolution of 1689," *Maryland Historical Magazine,* 55 (1960), 293-333

Beverly McAnear, ed., "Mariland's Grevances Wiy The[y] Have Taken Op Arms," *Journal of Southern History,* 8 (1942), 392-409

F. E. Sparks, *Causes of the Maryland Revolution of 1689* (Baltimore, 1896)

B. C. Steiner, "The Protestant Revolution in Maryland," American Historical Association, *Annual Report for 1897* (Washington, 1898), 281-353

B. C. Steiner, "The Royal Province of Maryland in 1692," *Maryland Historical Magazine,* 15 (1920), 123-68

A. W. Werline, *Problems of Church and State in Maryland During the 17th and 18th Centuries* (South Lancaster, Mass., 1948)

E. ENGLAND:

G. H. Guttridge, *The Colonial Policy of William III in America and the West Indies* (Cambridge, Eng., 1922)

Philip Haffenden, "The Crown and the Colonial Charter, 1675-88," *William and Mary Quarterly,* 3rd Ser., 15 (1958), 297-311, 452-66

David Ogg, *England in the Reigns of James II and William III* (Oxford, Eng., 1955)

Lucile Pinkham, *William III and the Respectable Revolution* (Cambridge, Mass., 1954)

F. FICTION:

John Barth, *The Sot-Weed Factor* (New York, 1960)

J. P. Kennedy, *Rob of the Bowl* (Philadelphia, 1860)